C1
ADVANCED

FORMULA

FOR EXAM SUCCESS

EXAM TRAINER and eBook

with key

CONTENTS

READING AND USE OF ENGLISH

WRITING

LISTENING

SPEAKING

C1 ADVANCED PRACTICE EXAM

The first page of each exam part begins with a section entitled ABOUT THE TASK. This provides key information about this exam task and its key testing aims.

The first TEST section starts with a mini exam PRACTICE TASK, which is a reduced version of what you will find in the actual Cambridge C1 Advanced exam.

The TEACH section provides detailed practice of the strategies and skills required to perform well in the exam part. You are guided through in a systematic, step-by-step way, building on each skill as you progress.

LISTENING - Part 1 Multiple choice

ABOUT THE TASK

- In Listening Part 1 you listen to three short dialogues, each with a different topic focus.
- There are two multiple-choice questions on each of the dialogues.
- Each question has three options, and you must choose the correct one based on what you hear.

- The questions can be about the purpose or function of the conversation, the main idea of what the speakers are talking about, or what they agree or disagree about.
- The questions can also be about one or both of the speakers' opinions, attitudes or feelings.
- You will have time to read the questions before you hear the recording, and you will hear each dialogue twice.

Practice task

1 🎧 L01 You will hear a conversation between two teachers who are discussing the idea of using rap music in teaching. For each question, choose the best answer (A–C).

1 How does the woman feel about using rap music in her own lessons?
   A convinced of its educational value
   B cautious about over-using it in class
   C concerned about students' reaction to it

2 The man mentions an activity he did with students about rap music in order to
   A make a point about rap music's ability to engage learners.
   B suggest some learners may benefit more than others.
   C question the validity of a teaching method.

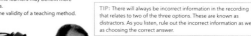

How did you do?

2 Check your answers.

3 Read the audioscript for Ex 1 question 1. Match each highlighted part with the topic of one of the options (A–C) in question 1.

... [1]but they're generally far more up for new methods of learning than teachers, in my experience. So, there was little chance they'd find it a waste of time, but [2]it's too early to tell whether it's as good as other ways of developing their understanding, but [3]I want to avoid a mistake I always make, which is to include a new technique I've learnt in every class. The novelty soon wears off and students get as fed up with it as the old ones.

> TIP: There will always be incorrect information in the recording that relates to two of the three options. These are known as distractors. As you listen, rule out the incorrect information as well as choosing the correct answer.

4a Read the audioscript for Ex 1 question 2. Match each highlighted part with the topic of one of the options (A–C) in question 2. One option has two sections connected to it.

I had a class discussion about rap a few weeks ago. [1]What took me aback was the passion it generated throughout the group. [2]I half expected it not to work as a whole-class activity, as [3]I thought the minority who have no interest in it would withdraw from the debate. They had just as much to say as its greatest advocates, though, [4]which suggests it's a powerful vehicle for getting across the things we want to teach.

4b Which highlighted part of the audioscript gives you the answer to Ex 1 question 2? Why are the other options wrong? Answer the questions to help you.
1 Does the man think that his activity was unsuccessful?
2 Does he think that some students were left out of the discussion?

The practice task is followed by a series of 'How did you do?' questions that encourage you to reflect on how you performed.

LISTENING - Part 1 Multiple choice

Strategies and skills
Understanding attitude and opinion

Speakers will rarely state that they are going to offer an opinion. You must therefore listen carefully to identify when the opinion is given. In addition, the language used in the options will always be paraphrased in the recording.

> TIP: In the exam, you have some time before each conversation to look at the options for each question. Use this time to familiarise yourself with the options and prepare yourself for what you are likely to hear.

1 🎧 L02 Listen to some speakers (1–3). What is their attitude or opinion? Choose the correct option (A–C). Highlight the section of the audioscript where the correct option is paraphrased.

1 The glossy leaflet describing how great it would be was some distance from the reality, I'm afraid. I was seriously hoping that a course with as many sessions as this one would be able to explore the issue in the kind of detail I enjoy. However, the opposite was the case.

What did the man think of the course?
A It was too long.
B It lacked depth.
C It met his expectations.

2 In my day, school seemed to reward those who were good at academic theory and didn't address the needs of those who were good at practical applications. I was in the latter group, of course, and although I suppose some staff tried to make the lessons as interesting as they could, I still left with very little to show for it, despite many years of consistent effort.

When talking about her schooldays, the speaker reveals
A her respect for the teachers.
B regret at not having worked harder.
C resentment with the education system.

3 In some ways, the majority of modern movies are extremely clever. They contain both visual and verbal in-jokes that appeal in different ways to different age groups. What's turned me away from going to the cinema so often, though, is the idea of 'good guy is threatened by a powerful bad guy but eventually wins' has become almost universal. I just really crave something that doesn't use that same tired formula.

What does the man think about most new movies?
A They share a common theme.
B They lack a moral message.
C They contain unconvincing dialogue.

2 🎧 L03 Listen to some speakers (1–3). What is their attitude or opinion? Choose the correct option (A–C). This time, you do not have the audioscript to help you.

> TIP: You will hear each speaker twice. Use the second time you listen to check your answers.

1 When talking about the new gym she uses, the woman is
   A impressed by the equipment.
   B critical of how it's managed.
   C surprised at the cost.

2 What does the man say about his new boss?
   A She has a lot of relevant experience.
   B She consults with staff effectively.
   C She organises her time well.

3 In the woman's opinion, travel companies are offering ecotourism
   A to improve their corporate image.
   B to broaden their product range.
   C to increase their profits.

SPEAKING BOOST

Discuss or answer.
1 What do you think 'critical thinking' is? How important is it?
2 What's the best way to tackle fake news?

In Reading and Use of English and Listening exam parts, you can find optional Speaking boost tasks. These provide questions to prompt speaking practice in class, or individually at home, to help develop your communicative skills.

71

72

There are TIP boxes which give targeted advice on how to approach the particular exam part.

Identifying purpose and function

3 Read what the speakers (1–8) say. What are they doing? Choose the correct option (A, B or C).

1 'They had every intention of paying but if the ticket office was closed and the machine was out of order, what else were they supposed to do?'
   A advising   B defending   C describing

2 'It might be an idea for you to think about what training you'll need in the next few months and come up with a list.'
   A suggesting   B requesting   C explaining

3 'If the management devoted as much energy to putting what we recommended into action as they do to writing reports about it, we wouldn't be facing this dilemma.'
   A emphasising   B recommending   C complaining

4 'Personally, I think that kind of music would be right up your street and, after all, the tickets are only £10.'
   A accepting   B persuading   C highlighting

5 'As soon as I'd told you I'd be able to finish the work on time, the director asked me to meet some clients and take them out for lunch, so it's going to be a little late, I'm afraid.'
   A justifying   B offering   C reassuring

6 'So the play's about a woman who was separated from her twin sister at birth. It explores all the ways it has affected her and her determination to find her twin.'
   A summarising   B identifying   C demanding

7 'I'd seriously think twice about taking the car out in this weather. Even where there isn't snow on the road, there's black ice, which you can't even see.'
   A emphasising   B warning   C agreeing

8 'That's incredibly kind of you – it's such a privilege to witness two people who are clearly in love getting married. I'm actually going to be away on holiday when that's all happening, though.'
   A refusing   B praising   C enquiring

Identifying feeling

4 🔊 L04 Listen to some speakers (1–8), and decide how they feel. Choose the correct option (A–C).

TIP: Remember that a word such as 'insecure' can have a slightly different meaning in a different context. As you listen, make sure that you think about the context and not just about the word itself.

1 A frustrated   B insecure   C protective
2 A respectful   B impatient   C astonished
3 A content   B bitter   C self-conscious
4 A determined   B desperate   C dissatisfied
5 A eager   B irritated   C realistic
6 A stubborn   B arrogant   C suspicious
7 A sympathetic   B unsure   C enthusiastic
8 A doubtful   B concerned   C impatient

SPEAKING BOOST

Discuss or answer.

1 Do you think we would be more productive if we studied or worked fewer but longer days?

2 What's your most productive time of day? Can you think why this might be?

73

Each strategy, skill or language focus is clearly labelled, and there is a variety of exercise types throughout.

Identifying agreement

5 Read six short conversations. Do the speakers agree or disagree?

1 A: The new system means anywhere that serves food is inspected every year and has to put a sticker in the window saying what their hygiene rating is. It's a great idea.
   B: I worry that establishments will make sure everything's perfect when the inspectors are there, though, then do exactly what they want for the rest of the year.

2 A: Gym membership's never what it seems. I thought I'd be able to go whenever I wanted, but there are apparently limitations on the times I can use it in the terms and conditions.
   B: Those documents are so long that no one ever bothers to read them, and then everyone gets caught out by some regulation at the bottom of page seven.

3 A: I didn't actually have very high expectations of the course, but have been thoroughly impressed by how it was run and by how much of the content will be useful for work.
   B: I've actually put some of the principles we discussed in several of the seminars into practice already and I'm keen to implement others when I have more time.

4 A: The book falls into the trap of many popular psychology titles in that it overgeneralises what people are like, so they end up being put into broad categories.
   B: That's a common approach, and one which many readers tend to like. I found that most of the chapters managed to steer clear of doing anything like that, though.

5 A: In my opinion, studying philosophy's as relevant today as it's always been. If anything, given the increasingly volatile world we live in, it could even be made a mandatory school subject.
   B: I can certainly see the benefit of getting students to think about things a little more deeply. Forcing it universally onto the curriculum is perhaps going a little too far.

6 A: City living's slowly become more intense, to my mind, but because the changes are relatively gradual, few people living there actually notice.
   B: I'm sure residents would say the cities they live in are pretty much the same as ten years ago, apart from a few cosmetic changes, which isn't the case to an objective observer.

74

EXAM TASK

🔊 L05 You will hear three different extracts. For questions 1–6, choose the answer (A, B or C) which fits best according to what you hear. There are two questions for each extract.

Extract One

You hear a scientist being interviewed about plastic pollution.

1 What is the man doing?
   A explaining how the problem can be solved
   B identifying who is primarily to blame for the problem
   C emphasising that the problem must be addressed

2 Why does the man use the examples of plastic bags and bottles?
   A to support the main point he's making
   B to highlight a popular misconception
   C to introduce a new argument

Extract Two

You hear two friends talking about a place where they spent a lot of time as children.

3 The woman is reluctant to return there because
   A she's worried it will ruin her memories of the area.
   B she'd rather not meet some of the people there.
   C she's convinced she won't like how it's changed.

4 How does the man respond to the woman's concerns?
   A He attempts to persuade her to go anyway.
   B He suggests they're unlikely to be valid.
   C He admits he feels the same way as her.

Extract Three

You hear two scientists talking about food hygiene in restaurants.

5 They both think that
   A current laws are insufficient.
   B more inspections are needed.
   C owners don't take the issue seriously.

6 How does the woman feel about advising the government on food hygiene issues?
   A uncomfortable at how critical she needs to be
   B frustrated by the response to her suggestions
   C cautious about appearing overenthusiastic

TEST

All the full exam tasks are clearly flagged like this in every exam paper and part.

The final TEST section is a full-length exam task. This provides an opportunity to put the strategies and skills you have studied into practice. You should apply the strategies and skills that you have practised when you do the task to perform well. Completing the full exam task also gives you valuable experience of the kind of task you can expect to find in the Cambridge C1 Advanced exam.

An Answer Key for all tasks is provided, either in the back of your book or via the Pearson English Portal.

All audioscripts are printed in the back of the book.

5

What is *Formula*?

Formula is a brand-new exam preparation course that provides teachers and learners with unrivalled flexibility in exam training. The course offers complete and extensive preparation for the Cambridge B1 Preliminary, B2 First and C1 Advanced exams. The core materials provide thorough, step-by-step targeted exam training, helping learners to develop a deeper understanding of the strategies and skills needed to succeed. Comprehensive practice of these skills and strategies for each exam task type is systematically provided through engaging, contemporary topics.

The course comprises two core print components: the **Coursebook** and the **Exam Trainer**. These can be used as stand-alone components, or together, depending on the learning environment.

What is the *Formula* C1 Advanced Exam Trainer?

The *Formula* **C1 Advanced Exam Trainer** is a book specially designed to maximise your chances of success in the Cambridge C1 Advanced examination.

It can work either as a standalone component or in combination with the *Formula* **C1 Advanced Coursebook**. Its structure follows the Cambridge C1 Advanced exam, working systematically through each Paper and Part, from Reading and Use of English Part 1 to Speaking Part 4. Each Paper is introduced with a detailed overview of the exam task format, followed by a 'Test, Teach, Test' approach, to improve understanding and performance.

The Test, Teach, Test approach

TEST: A mini 'practice task' that reflects the Cambridge C1 Advanced exam task for that Part, with a 'How did you do?' reflection activity. This helps learners familiarise themselves with the task type and quickly highlights any obvious focus for improving performance.

TEACH: An extensive series of explanations, tips and targeted tasks to practise the strategies and skills for improving performance in the exam. The skills are organised in priority order, so students with little time know which sections to focus on to make the most progress.

TEST: A full-length, authentic-style exam task to put the exam training to the test, with a full, 'smart' answer key.

At the back of the Exam Trainer there is also a full, authentic-style Cambridge C1 Advanced exam, with accompanying audio. We advise that this exam is taken under exam conditions when the training phase is complete.

All audio for the Exam Trainer is available via the App on the Pearson English Portal. The audio is available for download so you can save it to your device to listen offline.

How can I use the *Formula* C1 Advanced Exam Trainer?

The *Formula* **C1 Advanced Exam Trainer** is a flexible component and can be used effectively in a number of different learning environments. Here are some typical situations:

You are studying for the Cambridge C1 Advanced exam with other students in a classroom scenario, probably over an academic year.

You are using the *Formula* **C1 Advanced Coursebook** in class. Sometimes you will also do the related exercises or even a whole exam part from the *Formula* **C1 Advanced Exam Trainer** in class, though your teacher will ask you to do exercises from it at home as well. You will use the entire **Exam Trainer** or you will use it selectively, depending on your needs and the time available.

You have already completed a Cambridge C1 Advanced exam course or a general C1-level English course. You are enrolled on an intensive exam preparation course with other students to do targeted exam practice.

You may have already worked though the *Formula* **C1 Advanced Coursebook** or perhaps another Cambridge C1 Advanced coursebook. You will use the *Formula* **C1 Advanced Exam Trainer** in class to give you a concentrated and highly focused short exam course. This will provide systematic, teacher-led exam training paper by paper, with Speaking boosts for communicative activities in class. You may focus on the exam sections in class, and the skills and strategies at home, or the reverse. There is also a full, authentic-style Practice Exam included in the title, which you can sit under exam conditions prior to taking the exam.

You only have a short time available to prepare for the Cambridge C1 Advanced exam and are not enrolled in an exam preparation course.

You have been attending general English classes and your level of English is already nearing Cambridge C1 Advanced exam standard. You now need targeted exam skills practice. You will use the *Formula* **C1 Advanced Exam Trainer** independently to work through each of the exam papers in order, so that you are familiar with the exam tasks and equipped with key strategies for improving your performance. The Speaking boost sections provide valuable speaking practice and the full, authentic-style Practice Exam can be sat under exam conditions prior to taking the exam.

You only have a short time available and are preparing for the exam on your own.

Maybe you are not attending English classes at present but wish to take the Cambridge C1 Advanced exam and prepare for it independently. You will use the *Formula* **C1 Advanced Exam Trainer** independently to work through each of the exam papers in order, so that you are familiar with the exam tasks and equipped with key strategies for improving your performance. The Speaking boost sections provide valuable speaking practice and the full, authentic-style Practice Exam can be sat under exam conditions prior to taking the exam.

TEST

- In Reading and Use of English Part 1, you read a short text with eight gaps.
- There are four multiple-choice options for each gap.
- You choose the word or phrase that best fits each gap.
- The gaps can test your knowledge of differences in precise meaning between similar words, of collocations, or of words that occur in fixed phrases.

- They may also test your understanding of verb patterns, for example whether a verb is followed by an infinitive or a clause.
- The gaps may also test your understanding of complementation, for example which preposition certain words are followed by.
- Some gaps may test your knowledge of phrasal verbs and linking words.
- Each question is worth one mark.

Practice task

1 Read the first paragraph of a text about an animal called an octopus. Choose the correct answer (A, B, C or D). There is an example at the beginning (0).

THE OCTOPUS:
an extraordinarily talented animal

Octopuses are far from the one-hit wonders of the animal kingdom, having **(0)** _____C_____ the world's oceans for the past 300 million years. They are especially well known for their astonishing intelligence and ability to change colour in order to blend in with their surroundings. The **(1)** _____ majority of species live in surface waters but a small number are found in the ocean depths. They have an amazing ability to squeeze into and through the smallest of holes and spaces, and live a largely **(2)** _____ existence, only meeting up with others of their species to breed. Octopuses are, for the most **(3)** _____ , predatory animals. Their diet is largely **(4)** _____ up of small fish, crabs, shellfish and worms.

0	**A** existed	**B** resided	**C** inhabited	**D** dwelt
1	**A** vast	**B** enormous	**C** immense	**D** gigantic
2	**A** lone	**B** solitary	**C** lonely	**D** unsociable
3	**A** measure	**B** amount	**C** share	**D** part
4	**A** made	**B** taken	**C** built	**D** put

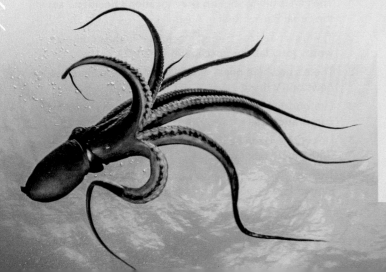

How did you do?

2 Check your answers.

3 Read the five answers for Ex 1 again, including the example.

1 Which answer tests your knowledge of a phrasal verb?
2 Which answer tests your knowledge of the patterns of words that typically follow a vocabulary item?
3 Which answer tests your knowledge of a fixed phrase?
4 Which answer tests your knowledge of collocation?
5 Which answer tests your knowledge of precise meaning?

4 Look at the four sets of words in context. What do you notice about how each one is used? Then look at the gaps in the text in Ex 1 again. Can you see why the answers are correct?

1 The **vast majority** of the population agreed with the government's policy.
An **enormous number** of people came out to watch the fireworks.
The announcement attracted an **immense amount** of publicity.
A **gigantic statue** appeared in the empty square overnight.

2 A **lone** figure appeared on the horizon, slowly moving nearer.
James liked the **solitary** life that living on the island necessitated.
Leanne felt **lonely** once the children had gone.
Fiona felt **unsociable** that evening so decided to stay in.

3 The reviews **serve as a measure of** how good this film is.
No amount of persuasion could convince Martin to change his mind.
We've had our **fair share** of bad weather lately.
Good luck **had a part to play** in the team's success.

4 The team is **made up of** both men and women.
No one has **taken up** my offer of a lift to work.
The new teacher really helped to **build up** her confidence.
A shopping centre is being **put up** where the old factory used to be.

TEACH

Strategies and skills

Fixed phrases

Gaps in Reading and Use of English Part 1 texts are often filled by words that are found in fixed phrases.

1 Use the nouns in the box to complete the fixed phrases in the sentences below.

> balance   desire   hesitation   horizons
> notice   power   room   things

1   All _____ considered, third place in the competition was perhaps a fitting result.

2   I don't know why the concert was cancelled at such short _____ .

3   As an actor, it's not always possible to strike a _____ between work and home life.

4   Max had a burning _____ to be famous from a young age.

5   Kelly did everything in her _____ to get a deal with a publisher.

6   There was definite _____ for improvement in Danny's performance.

7   The judges had no _____ in awarding the prize to Olivia Hanrahan.

8   Reece decided to expand her _____ by applying for work in other countries.

2 Choose the correct option to complete each sentence.

1   It was sometimes difficult to **hold / grab / seize / grasp** the complexities of the plot.

2   Seven shows in one week really **had / took / put / made** their toll on Gina's health.

3   The singer even **broke / smashed / cracked / split** a few jokes between songs.

4   What **drove / sent / pressed / steered** her to give up acting remains a mystery.

5   I had no idea he **believed / maintained / held / felt** such strong opinions on the issue.

6   The newspaper headline really **activated / caught / motivated / encouraged** her attention.

7   The test didn't really **present / award / donate / raise** any great difficulties to Diana.

8   These technical flaws **create / cause / offer / pose** very real threats to the film's success.

Discuss or answer.

1   If there's one goal you'd want to achieve, what would it be? What would you do to achieve it?

2   What do you think the phrase '15 minutes of fame' means? What's your opinion of celebrity culture?

Collocations

Gaps often test knowledge of collocations: words that naturally go together. Many of the collocations are formed with verbs. It is important to learn as many of these as you can.

3 Choose the verb which best completes each sentence.

1   She told her daughter to close her eyes and _____ a wish.
    A get   **B** make   **C** do   **D** have

2   The teacher asked the students to _____ note of the new lesson times.
    A take   **B** use   **C** put   **D** write

3   Fiona _____ Max making the dinner and went swimming.
    A left   **B** allowed   **C** let   **D** sent

4   Playing the piano really _____ naturally to some people.
    A appears   **B** develops   **C** arrives   **D** comes

5   I can't always _____ the difference between a true masterpiece and a fake.
    A state   **B** reveal   **C** tell   **D** say

6   Appearing on TV allowed Nathan to _____ a lifelong ambition.
    A fulfil   **B** complete   **C** conclude   **D** finalise

4 Choose the correct word to complete the collocations in the sentences.

1   The film is being shot on **site / location / position / set** at the Great Barrier Reef in Australia.

2   There's a need for trained mechanics in the country's **work / job / labour / occupation** market.

3   There's nowhere **near / close / like / approaching** enough news on TV these days.

4   Ecotourism is a real growth **trade / business / industry / corporation** these days.

5   He promised me he'd come, so I hope he keeps his **truth / fact / talk / word**.

6   The receptionist spoke only **broken / damaged / spoiled / injured** English so I couldn't understand him.

Phrasal verbs

Some questions test your knowledge of phrasal verbs. Sometimes the whole phrasal verb is missing, or sometimes just the verb or the particle.

> **TIP:** Make sure you learn as many phrasal verbs as you can.

5 Choose the option which best completes each sentence.

1 Madeleine _____ into an old school friend while she was visiting the city.
   A bounced B knocked C bumped D collided

2 After reading the article, Rick decided to _____ red meat from his diet.
   A cut out B take away C give up D keep off

3 Ruth found it hard to work out what the writer was _____ at in the poem.
   A intending B trying C pushing D getting

4 It took a while before the effects of the medication started to _____ in.
   A shoot B kick C jump D hit

5 The management put _____ several proposals for staff to discuss and vote on.
   A forward B out C through D over

6 Andy's uncertainty about what to do _____ from a lack of experience.
   A appeared B approached C created D stemmed

Easily confused words

Sometimes you need to choose between words with similar meanings.

> **TIP:** Think carefully about the particular meaning each word has, and also think about the prepositions, collocations and patterns each word is used with.

6 Choose the correct word to complete the sentences.

1 The president condemned the shocking response as an act of **violence / force / aggression / fighting**.

2 The **acclaimed / commended / admired / applauded** violinist played some of her most popular pieces.

3 Despite being favourites, the team were **systematically / comprehensively / broadly / exhaustively** beaten in the final.

4 He was alarmed to discover that $4,000 had been **subtracted / detached / extracted / withdrawn** from his account without his consent.

5 There was a lot of **assumption / speculation / deduction / supposition** about who would be the next party leader.

6 Temperatures at the research station **plunged / dived / crashed / collapsed** as soon as night fell.

Prepositions

The correct choice for a gap sometimes depends on correctly matching the option with the preposition after the gap.

7 Choose the correct option to complete the sentences, paying attention to the preposition in bold that follows. What prepositions are the other words followed by? Which words are not usually followed by a preposition?

1 The prices were _____ **to** those on the internet.
   A consistent B matching C comparable D alike

2 _____ **to** popular belief, bread is not the best food for birds.
   A Contrary B Opposing C Contrasting D Distinctive

3 The company was fined because its actions were not in _____ **with** the law.
   A contract B accordance C duty D assurance

4 He decided to write to the manager in _____ **of** the staff member's behaviour.
   A concern B regard C connection D respect

5 The videos are _____ **for** anyone who wants to learn to play the guitar.
   A aimed B intended C directed D focused

6 There's no need for you to be _____ **with** the arrangements for the meeting.
   A disturbed B troubled C worried D concerned

8 Complete the sentences with the prepositions in the box.

> about in of on to with

1 I realised I was completely dependent _____ Alice to translate everything for me.

2 Professor Atkins had dedicated her life _____ the study of these fascinating creatures.

3 Please leave the building by the nearest exit in the event _____ a fire.

4 There's certainly no harm _____ applying for the talent show.

5 I'm in two minds _____ learning to dive.

6 I couldn't keep pace _____ the fastest runner, so ended up coming second.

SPEAKING BOOST

Discuss or answer.

1 What is the greatest challenge sport has faced recently in your opinion?

2 Apart from physical fitness, what do you think the benefits of exercise are?

Verb patterns

Sometimes you need to think about what kind of pattern follows a verb, e.g. an infinitive, a noun, an *-ing* form or a *that* clause.

9 Choose the correct verb pattern to complete each sentence.

1 It's anticipated **that prices will rise / prices rising** as a result of the decision.

2 Consumers should beware **to spend / of spending** beyond what they earn.

3 The bank's policy just seems to complicate **matters further / further matters**.

4 He couldn't envision **to make / making** so much money in a single deal.

5 Staff were instructed **to avoid / avoiding** talking to the media about the issue.

6 The director was invited **to give / for giving** a presentation at the event.

Linking words

Some questions test your knowledge of linking words and phrases.

10 Complete the sentences with the linking words in the box.

> consequently   interestingly   nonetheless
> or   owing to   whereas

1 Healthcare has improved dramatically although, _____ , life expectancy has remained about the same.

2 The outward journey took three hours _____ the return was more than double this.

3 He must have enjoyed the performance _____ he wouldn't have stayed for the whole thing.

4 He'd spent all his money by the end of the first week and _____ had nothing left for the rest of the holiday.

5 Four extra concert dates have been announced _____ high demand for tickets.

6 The water temperature was only 6°C, but she went swimming _____ .

EXAM TASK

For questions 1–8, read the text below and decide which answer (A, B, C or D) best fits each gap. There is an example at the beginning (0).

IS THE 10,000 HOUR RULE A MYTH?

For a number of years, there has been a widely-**(0)** _____D_____ belief that practising a particular skill for 10,000 hours will turn anyone into a world-class expert. Perhaps unsurprisingly, few have been sufficiently **(1)** _____ to put this theory to the test. The **(2)** _____ originally appeared in a popular psychology title, *Outliers*, by Malcolm Gladwell. A key stipulation of the concept was that the practice in **(3)** _____ had to be 'deliberate' practice. A casual half hour a day strumming a guitar would not **(4)** _____ this requirement.

However, recent research into deliberate practice has **(5)** _____ to some intriguing conclusions. The study **(6)** _____ that even in something as traditionally practice-based as learning a musical instrument, deliberate practice **(7)** _____ for just 21 percent of the observed improvement. When it comes to professions such as business, in which the skills are **(8)** _____ less tangible and more difficult to define, the figure falls to a tiny one percent. So, if practice is responsible for such a small proportion of the improvement, what is causing the rest?

0	A kept	B said	C thought	D held
1	A disciplined	B controlled	C restricted	D ordered
2	A deduction	B principle	C value	D regulation
3	A request	B demand	C subject	D question
4	A complete	B succeed	C meet	D reach
5	A pointed	B finished	C decided	D achieved
6	A uncovers	B reveals	C exposes	D releases
7	A amounts	B accounts	C generates	D justifies
8	A cautiously	B uncertainly	C doubtfully	D arguably

ABOUT THE TASK

- In Reading and Use of English Part 2, you read a short text which has eight gaps in it. You have to think of the word that best fits each gap.
- There are no options to choose from.
- You have to think about the structure of the language in the text and the meaning of the text.
- The word you write must be spelled correctly, and must fit the gap grammatically.
- You cannot write contractions such as *don't* or *won't*.

- The gaps test your understanding of different kinds of grammar, e.g. auxiliary and modal verbs, dependent prepositions, relative pronouns, articles, etc.
- They also test your knowledge of phrasal verbs, linking words and expressions and fixed phrases.
- The answer is always a single word.
- Occasionally, there is more than one possible correct answer.
- Each question is worth one mark.

Practice task

1 Read the first paragraph of a text about a project monitoring animals called humpback whales. Think of the word which best fits each gap. Use only one word in each gap. There is an example at the beginning (0).

THE **WHALE TAIL** DATABASE

Each human face is unique, making it easy for us to differentiate **(0)** ___BETWEEN___ people we know and those we have never previously met. When **(1)** _____ comes to attempting to identify a humpback whale, however, we have to turn **(2)** _____ an alternative means of recognition.

Research teams worldwide have long used the whales' tails to identify whether individuals they encounter are new to the area or are whales that they are already familiar **(3)** _____ . An increasing number of teams are now contributing to an international database, in **(4)** _____ the main resource is photos of humpback whales' tails. This is done so **(5)** _____ to monitor population size, migratory routes and the distribution of individuals in resting, calving and feeding areas around the world.

How did you do?

2 Check your answers.

3 Read the answers to the five questions in Ex 1 again. Which answer

a   is a dependent preposition that's used with an adjective?

b   is a relative pronoun?

c   is a pronoun in a fixed phrase?

d   is a phrasal verb particle?

e   is an adverb used in a fixed expression?

4 Match the sections of the text with their paraphrases a–e.

Section of text

When **(1)** _____ comes to

to turn **(2)** _____

familiar **(3)** _____

in **(4)** _____ the

so **(5)** _____ to

Paraphrase

a   look for help from

b   in order to

c   on the subject of

d   know about

e   that contains

Strategies and skills

Perfect and continuous tenses

The gaps sometimes test your knowledge of present verb tenses. The gapped word is often an auxiliary verb, for example a form of the verbs *be*, *do* or *have*. The verb may use the perfect aspect and/or be in the active or passive form.

1 Complete the sentences with one word in each gap.

1 The team has _____ monitoring the group of whales for several years.

2 The waters there _____ believed to be where female whales give birth to their young.

3 The extent to which the whales' habits _____ been altered by human activity is unclear.

4 So what reason _____ researchers give for the whales returning to the area each year?

5 After _____ photographed, the whale's tail is uploaded to the database.

6 The database _____ been added to by research teams from all around the world.

Conjunctions

Some gaps test your knowledge of linking words.

> **TIP:** Think about what the linking word is doing in the sentence: is it adding similar information or ideas, giving a reason, contrasting ideas, etc.?

2 Look at the gaps in the sentences (1–7) and think about what is missing. Answer the questions (a–d).

1 _____ many residents are happy with the standard of maintenance in the complex, others feel it is poor, given the high service charges.

2 _____ from allowing the experience to put him off kite surfing, it actually made him more determined to succeed.

3 Expanding on answers at an interview demonstrates good subject knowledge in _____ to giving the speaker confidence.

4 The participants in the experiment actually put on weight, _____ the fact that they were doing more exercise.

5 The new electric car is expected to go into production soon, _____ that any design faults are rectified quickly.

6 Being able to hold down a demanding full-time job _____ also studying is a combination that few achieve without some difficulty.

7 She did extremely well in her first professional game, especially _____ how nervous she had been beforehand.

a Which ones need a word to express contrast?

b Which one needs a word to introduce a similar idea or information?

c Which ones introduce a reason or explanation?

d Which one needs a time expression?

3 Choose the correct words in the box to complete the sentences (1–7) in Ex 2. Add capital letters where necessary.

> addition   although   considering
> despite   far   provided   whilst

Discuss or answer.

1 Does art imitate life, or life imitate art?

2 'Writing is the most important human invention of all time.' To what extent do you agree with this argument?

Conditional forms

The gaps sometimes test your knowledge of conditionals. Make sure you know the more complex conditional forms, and learn the difference between *if* and *unless*. The gaps may also test your knowledge of structures with *wish*.

4 Choose the correct words (A–C) to complete the sentences.

1 If I hadn't gone back to sleep, I _____ be really tired now.
A could   B will   C would

2 You _____ have avoided all the traffic if you'd set off an hour earlier.
A will   B should   C could

3 I might have passed my driving test _____ I not made one silly mistake.
A had   B would   C if

4 I wonder where I would _____ ended up if I'd continued driving along that little road.
A had   B have   C be

5 You'll lose your job _____ you stop browsing the internet at work.
A if   B because   C unless

6 If I _____ the lottery, I would probably give a lot of the money to charity.
A won   B win   C winning

7 You really should set off now _____ you want to be home before 11 p.m.
A unless   B although   C if

8 I would have chosen to go by train if I had _____ the choice.
A got   B had   C have

Future tenses

The gaps sometimes test your knowledge of future forms, such as the future continuous, future perfect and future perfect continuous. The gapped word is usually an auxiliary verb, for example a form of the verbs *be* or *have*. They may also test your knowledge of future forms of *be able to* and *have to*.

5 Choose the correct phrase to complete the future forms in the sentences.

1 This time next week, they **will be sailing / will have been going to sail** across the Atlantic Ocean.

2 The traffic will be really bad then, so I **have to / will have to** leave plenty of time to get there.

3 By midnight tonight, I **will have been travelling / will be travelling** for 48 hours.

4 The car has been repaired so I **would be able / will be able** to pick you up from the station.

5 The solar eclipse **will witness / will be witnessed** by millions of people all over the world.

6 If we don't leave soon, the film **will have started / will have been starting** by the time we get to the cinema.

6 Complete the sentences with one word in each gap.

1 Thankfully, the rocket will _____ repaired in time for the launch.

2 The damaged car will be repaired before _____ returned to its owner.

3 The match on TV will _____ already finished by the time we get home.

4 It's funny to think that in just 24 hours, I will _____ taking part in my first marathon.

5 She won't _____ to stay late if she gets all her work done before 5 p.m.

6 By the time the birds arrive at the breeding grounds, they will have _____ travelling for several weeks.

SPEAKING BOOST

Discuss or answer.

1 How important will sustainability be in 2050?

2 What do you think 'There is no planet B' means?

Relative clauses

Some gaps test your knowledge of relative pronouns in relative clauses.

> **TIP:** Think about what the relative pronoun refers to: is it a person, location or thing?

7 Look at the words before and after the gaps in these sentences. How do you know that a relative pronoun is missing from each gap?

1 The city in _____ I grew up has changed a lot since I left.

2 The captain _____ boat we were sailing in was obviously highly experienced.

3 There were ten people on the course, five of _____ had already tried surfing.

4 It was the instructor _____ first saw that one of the young climbers had got into difficulties.

5 I couldn't find my glasses, without _____ it was impossible for me to read the instructions.

6 I've just heard that the school _____ we met has closed down.

8 Complete the sentences in Ex 7 with one word in each gap.

Comparative forms

Gaps sometimes test your knowledge of comparative forms. At this level, these are unlikely to be basic comparatives and superlatives, but other more complex structures.

9 Match the sentence halves. Think about the sentence structures and make sure you understand the meanings. In each case, it's the highlighted word that would be gapped in a Part 2 task.

1 At the very least,

2 There was comparatively little

3 They still need a great deal

4 I didn't expect it to take such

5 He was nowhere near

6 She is surely one of the world's most

a interest in the book when it first came out.

b a long time to get here.

c highly respected politicians.

d more money to be able to buy the business.

e you should say sorry to him.

f as tall as he expected.

10 Complete the sentences with the words in the box.

> except   far   more   neither   no   rather   so   to

1 The project is _____ likely to succeed if there is international cooperation.
2 Most drivers prefer to stay within the speed limit _____ than risk getting a fine.
3 It was by _____ the largest number of birds that had ever been seen at the lake.
4 She couldn't come up with any new ideas and _____ could he.
5 No one went out in the freezing cold _____ for the film crew.
6 Wrestling is particularly popular in Iran, and _____ is football.
7 There's _____ question that it's the biggest celebration of the year in this country.
8 The prices were comparable _____ those found on the internet.

Reference words and impersonal structures

Gaps sometimes test the use of words such as *this*, *that*, *these*, *those*, *it*, *what* and *there*.

11 Choose the correct word to complete the sentences.

TIP: For this kind of gap, you need to read the whole sentence or context so you can understand the meaning.

1 Whilst **that / what / there** they witnessed was interesting, it wasn't enough to convince them to become involved.
2 **There / It / This** was an unusual sound coming from the adjacent room, somewhere between music and speech.
3 **There / It / This** is close to impossible to know for sure how many people would attend the event.
4 The conclusions drawn in the article are clear: **what / that / there** human activities are responsible for much of the decline in animal populations.
5 From the look on the director's face, **it / there / that** was clear that the announcement was not going to be good news.
6 The research paper made clear that **those / there / what** were several potential solutions to the problems it was investigating.

Phrasal verbs, prepositions and fixed phrases

Gaps in Part 2 texts are often related to phrasal verbs, dependent prepositions and fixed phrases.

12 Complete the sentences with the phrasal verb particles in the box.

TIP: Try to learn as many phrasal verbs as you can, especially ones with common verbs like **come**, **get**, **take**, etc.

> against   back   into   of   off   on   out   together

1 Jimmy had the idea for the business after unexpectedly **bumping** _____ an old friend.
2 It's always a good idea to **check** _____ the competition when launching a new product.
3 Sarah **came up** _____ a lot of opposition to her plan to modernise the company.
4 Tom was careful to investigate environmentally-friendly ways of **disposing** _____ waste products.
5 The suppliers said that they would **get** _____ **to** Abigail as soon as they could with delivery dates.
6 Rohan **insisted** _____ being involved with all of the company's major business decisions.
7 Unfortunately the enterprise had to **lay** _____ several members of staff due to the recession.
8 Asha **put** _____ an impressive business proposal as part of the application for the bank loan.

13 Match each phrasal verb or fixed phrase from Ex 12 with its meaning (a–h).

a to have to deal with a problem or difficulty
b to prepare a plan or document
c to contact a person at some point in the future
d to examine carefully to get more information
e to sack a person so they lose their job
f to meet by accident
g to make sure that something happens
h to throw an item or material away

14 Complete the fixed expressions in the sentences with one word in each gap.

1 Their success was all down _____ good planning and excellent teamwork.

2 They decided to deal with the problem _____ and for all.

3 _____ all, it was only her first lesson so she couldn't expect to be perfect.

4 Danny knew he would go ahead with his plan _____ or not his parents supported him.

5 If you _____ yourself in their shoes, you can see why they might not like the idea.

6 It was _____ a doubt the best song she'd ever written.

7 For those who had worked closely with Elliot, it came as _____ surprise that he won the competition.

8 The headteacher had no other choice _____ to suspend the students for what they'd done.

EXAM TASK

For questions 1–8, read the text below and think of the word which best fits each gap. Use only one word in each gap. There is an example at the beginning (0).

The world's remotest hotel?

Winterlake Lodge lies in excess **(0)** _____OF_____ 300 km north west of Anchorage, the largest city in the USA's most sparsely populated state, Alaska.

Getting to the hotel is **(1)** _____ easy task. Guests are obliged to take a picturesque one-hour light-aircraft ride from Anchorage. The aircraft is equipped **(2)** _____ floats in summer, allowing it to land on the adjacent lake, and skis in the winter for landing on snow. As **(3)** _____ rule, the first thing that guests notice after being dropped off at the hotel is the sense of isolation. There aren't any other properties **(4)** _____ sight and there is zero noise pollution thanks to the absence of traffic, industry and neighbours.

As guests settle **(5)** _____ they can choose from the many activities **(6)** _____ offer, such as hiking, fishing, dogsledding or yoga. Co-owner Kirsten Dixon is a Cordon Bleu trained chef. Guests can enjoy her high-quality meals made from the finest ingredients, many of **(7)** _____ come from the hotel's gardens. Others have **(8)** _____ flown in from high-class speciality stores in New York.

Staying at Winterlake Lodge is undoubtedly a unique experience.

TEST

- In Reading and Use of English Part 3, you read a short text with eight gaps.
- At the end of each line with a gap, you will see the base form of the missing word.
- You have to change the form of the word so that it fits correctly into each gap.
- You can change the form by adding a prefix, a suffix, or both, e.g. by changing **consider** to **considerable**, by changing **satisfied** to **dissatisfied** or by changing **intend** to **unintentional**.

- Sometimes you need to make more significant internal changes to the word, e.g. by changing **long** to **length** or by changing **receive** to **reception**.
- Occasionally you need to make a compound word, for example by changing **rain** to **rainfall**.
- Sometimes you need to make a noun plural after you have changed it.
- Each question is worth one mark.

Practice task

1 For questions 1–4, read the text below. Use the word given in capitals at the end of some of the lines to form a word that fits in the gap in the same line. There is an example at the beginning (0).

THE SCIENCE OF MEMORY

There's no **(0)** <u>STRAIGHTFORWARD</u> answer to the question: 'in which part of the brain are memories stored?' However, scientists have identified the areas which play a **(1)** _____ role in allowing us to make, store and retrieve things from our past experience.

FORWARD

SIGN

Our long-term memories have an **(2)** _____ capacity to store information. But in order for this to become memories we can access for years, or throughout our whole lives, it first passes through short-term memory. Research **(3)** _____ have shown that this processing takes place in the highly-developed part of the brain called the pre-frontal cortex.

ORDINARY

FIND

The **(4)** _____ from short- to long-term memory takes place in another part of the brain called the hippocampus.

CONVERT

How did you do?

2 Check your answers.

3 Look at the five answers again, including the example.

In which answer or answers do you need to

a add a prefix to change a meaning? _____

b form an adjective from an adverb? _____

c form an adjective from a noun? _____

d form a noun from a verb? _____

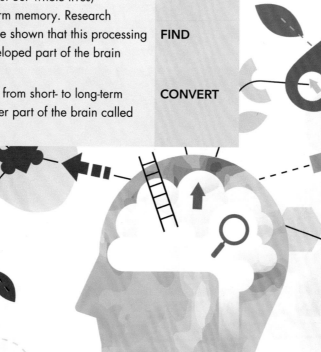

Strategies and skills

Prefixes

At least one item in each Part 3 task usually requires a prefix to be added. This does not always change the meaning from positive to negative, although it may.

> **TIP:** Before you start trying to work out the answers to the task, read the text carefully so that you have a good understanding of it as a whole.

1 Complete the gaps in the table. Do any of the words also have a verb form?

noun	adjective	negative adjective
1 _____	normal	2 _____
logic	3 _____	4 _____
5 _____	satisfied	6 _____
7 _____	mature	8 _____
9 _____	relevant	10 _____

2 Add prefixes to the words to give them a similar meaning to the definitions in brackets.

1 _____ sequence (result)
2 _____ behave (to behave badly)
3 _____ confident (having too much confidence)
4 _____ biographical (written by the person who it's about)
5 _____ active (designed to involve the user in the exchange of information)
6 _____ consider (to think about something again)

> **SPEAKING BOOST**

Discuss or answer.

1 What's your most vivid memory?
2 What do you want the most memorable thing about you to be?

Suffixes

Suffixes are often used to form nouns from verbs and adjectives.

3 Complete the table with nouns formed from the words in the box. Can you add any more nouns for each suffix?

> **TIP:** Remember, sometimes other spelling changes may be necessary.

> allow annoy assign cancel capable competent
> consume deficient disapprove innocent jealous
> leader nervous receive rude selfish sensitive willing

suffix	nouns	suffix	nouns
1 -ity	_____	6 -ness	_____
2 -ship	_____	7 -tion	_____
3 -ce	_____	8 -ance	_____
4 -y	_____	9 -ment	_____
5 -al	_____	10 -cy	_____

4 The word you need to use in a gap could be a noun to describe people. Write the nouns for people formed from these words.

1 archaeology _____
2 advice _____
3 profession _____
4 technical _____
5 embassy _____
6 consult _____
7 fishing _____
8 novel _____
9 civil service _____
10 surgery _____

In Part 3, you will often be asked to use suffixes to form adjectives from nouns and verbs.

5 Complete the sentences using adjectives formed from the words in the box.

> **TIP:** Think about the spelling very carefully. In the exam, your answer is only correct if you have spelled the word correctly.

> administration change diplomat eat
> exhaust ideal persuade reputation

1 Maxine applied for the job immediately because she'd heard it was a highly _____ company.

2 The receptionist explained that his account had accidentally been closed because of an _____ error.

3 The weather in the region is very _____ , and sometimes snow, sun, rain and thunder occur on the same day.

4 The president of the company, who was not known for being _____ , managed to insult several of the guests.

5 Although the fruit didn't look at all appetising, the guide assured us that it was perfectly _____ .

6 At 128 pages long, the report on the incident was certainly _____ as it went into great detail about every stage of what happened.

7 Often, the party leader's _____ aims were dismissed as having very little connection to reality.

8 Sally could be extremely _____ , which is probably why she was the top sales representative at the company.

17

Adjectives can be formed from many different suffixes.

6 Use the words in the box to create adjectives, then put them in the correct column. There should be two words in each column.

> aggression compare confidence construct
> convince courage news occasion refresh
> respond space statistic substance terror
> trust vary

-ive	-ous	-ing	-tial

-worthy	-able	-al	-ible

7 Can you think of any other adjectives with these suffixes? Add them to the table. What are their root words?

Some gaps require an adverb. You may have to form an adverb from an adjective, or you may have to form it from a noun or verb.

> **TIP:** When you have to form an adverb from a noun or a verb, it can help to think about the adjective first, then make it into an adverb.

8 Complete the sentences with an adjective or adverb from the word in capitals.

1 He couldn't _____ explain where he had been all night. **SATISFY**

2 A horribly long and _____ silence followed Jack's reading of his poem. **COMFORT**

3 Henry finally admitted that he had obtained the computers _____ . **HONEST**

4 The two peace campaigners were _____ awarded the prize. **JOIN**

5 The models were so _____ that it was hard to see they were plastic. **REALISE**

6 The crowd were _____ quieter after the star player was sent off. **NOTICE**

7 The sports centre was _____ opened by the prime minister. **OFFICE**

8 The country is far more _____ advanced than any of its neighbours. **TECHNOLOGY**

Most gaps in Part 3 tasks are nouns, adjectives or adverbs, but sometimes the missing word is a verb.

9 Complete the sentences with verbs formed from the words in capitals.

> **TIP:** When the gap is a verb, remember to think about the correct form and tense.

1 He received a letter _____ the receipt of his application. **KNOWLEDGE**

2 The twins were so alike that it was extremely hard to _____ between them. **DIFFERENCE**

3 Participants are always asked to _____ the effectiveness of the course. **VALUE**

4 The criminals were _____ for a period of at least seven years. **PRISON**

5 As spring arrived, the days slowly started _____ . **LONG**

6 The students couldn't understand the text so the teacher _____ it. **SIMPLE**

Discuss or answer.

1 Who is the luckiest person you know?

2 What's the difference between luck and privilege?

Internal word changes

You may need to make internal changes to the spelling of the root word, as well as adding a prefix and/or suffix.

10 Read these sentences. Which part of speech is needed in each gap (adjective, verb, adverb, noun, etc.)?

1 It is not _____ to eat a great deal of food with a high salt content. **ADVICE**

2 Without the atmosphere, the sun's rays would be even more _____ . **DESTROY**

3 The speaker was asked to _____ her position on global warming. **CLEAR**

4 Martin wasn't very _____ so couldn't choose which option to take. **DECIDE**

5 Her theories regularly challenged conventional _____ on the subject. **WISE**

6 Thankfully, _____ changes were required from the original design. **MINIMUM**

11 Complete the sentences in Ex 10 with the correct words formed from the word in capitals.

Some words change internally when a suffix is added.

12 Write the correct answer for each language 'sum'.

1 His idea wasn't very (**believe** + **able** =)
_____ .

2 He was quite a (**control** + **ing** =)
_____ person.

3 The hotel room was incredibly
(**luxury** + **ous** =) _____ .

4 The whole day was such a (**pleasure** + **able** =)
_____ experience.

5 The decision turned out to be a
(**disaster** + **ous** =) _____ one.

6 The music was terribly (**repeat** + **itive** =)
_____ .

> **TIP:** Learn new vocabulary in word groups
> (verbs, nouns, adjectives, adverbs and
> opposites) from the same root word, e.g. **suit**:
> **suitability, suitable, suitably, unsuitable**.

Compounding

13 Match words from each list to create new compound words.

1	eye	a	side
2	back	b	spread
3	along	c	ground
4	water	d	natural
5	wide	e	catching
6	super	f	proof

14 Complete the sentences using the compound words in Ex 13.

1 There was _____ support for the president's approach to the crisis.

2 Although the car has an _____ design, it proved to be highly unreliable.

3 Travis made the mistake of failing to pack a single item of _____ clothing.

4 The manager provided Helen with a detailed _____ to the case.

5 Steven didn't believe in _____ powers so he knew there was a rational explanation.

6 The company director stood _____ her deputy when making the announcement.

15 Complete the text with nouns formed from the words given in capitals at the end of some of the lines.

An American tech company held a news conference today to demonstrate a **(1)** _____ new delivery drone it has developed. — **GROUND**

Despite numerous **(2)** _____ , the team have finally come up with a design that works exactly as required. In tests, this **(3)** _____ device delivered a 5 kg package to an address across the city much more quickly than a traditional delivery driver. — **BACK** / **SAVE**

The delivery drone needs to **(4)** _____ many more checks before it can be rolled out. In the **(5)** _____ , many delivery drivers will be worried about what the future holds for them. No mention **(6)** _____ was made during the news conference of the device's potential impact on jobs. — **GO** / **TIME** / **WHAT**

EXAM TASK

For questions 1–8, read the text below. Use the word given in capitals at the end of some of the lines to form a word that fits in the gap in the same line. There is an example at the beginning (0).

The importance of **krill**

Krill are small, shrimp-like animals that only grow to around 5 cm in **(0)** ____LENGTH____ , yet are one of the most important species on the planet. They may appear to be a relatively **(1)** _____ sea creature. However, their position at the bottom of the food chain of hundreds of larger **(2)** _____ has led to them being described as the 'fuel' that runs the engine of marine ecosystems **(3)** _____ . — **LONG** / **SIGNIFY** / **ORGAN** / **WORLD**

There are 85 known species of krill, amongst the most important of which are Antarctic krill. **(4)** _____ , they congregate in such large numbers at certain times of year that they are clearly **(5)** _____ from space. — **INTRIGUE** / **VISION**

Krill form a **(6)** _____ part of the diets of many birds, fish and whales, but are themselves mainly herbivorous. They feed on microscopic plants called algae that float near the surface of the ocean. — **CRITICISE**

Recent scientific studies suggest that krill numbers have fallen **(7)** _____ since the 1970s, perhaps by as much as 80 percent. Should krill populations fall further, then all the animals that are **(8)** _____ on them would also be in serious trouble. — **DRAMA** / **DEPEND**

TEST

TEST

- In Reading and Use of English Part 4, you read six pairs of sentences. The sentences in each pair have a similar meaning, but they are expressed in different ways.

- There is a gap in the second sentence which you have to complete, using between three and six words. Contractions count as two words.

- You need to show that you can express a sentence in a different way, without changing its meaning.

- You are given one of the words (called the key word) which you must use, and you can't change this word in any way.

- This part tests your knowledge of both grammar and vocabulary, by testing your ability to express the same ideas using different grammatical forms and different words.

- There are two parts that you will need to change in each sentence, and there is one mark for each part.

Practice task

1 For questions 1–4, complete the second sentence so that it has a similar meaning to the first sentence, using the word given. Do not change the word given. You must use between three and six words, including the word given.

1 It took several weeks for Emily to persuade Huang to join her on the bike trip.

TALKED

Huang _____ Emily on her bike trip after several weeks.

2 'I must warn you that cycling on ice can be very risky,' Lisa told Peter.

RISKS

Peter was given a _____ on ice by Lisa.

3 Carol said that the instructor explained how to repair the bike clearly.

GAVE

'The instructor _____ how to repair the bike,' said Carol.

4 Without the help that Hannah gave me, I think my bike would still be broken.

BEEN

If it _____ help, I think my bike would still be broken.

How did you do?

2 Check your answers.

3 Look at the four answers again.

In which answer or answers did you need to

a transform indirect speech to direct speech? _____

b transform an active verb form into a passive? _____

c use an idiomatic phrase? _____
_____

d transform direct speech to indirect speech? _____

e transform a present verb into a past participle? _____

f transform a verb into a noun? _____
_____

g transform an infinitive into an -ing form? _____

h transform an adjective into a plural noun? _____

Strategies and skills

Passive forms

In Part 4, the second sentence often uses the passive form of a verb. Make sure you know the passive forms for all verb tenses. Remember, we use *by* + agent to say who does the action in a passive verb form.

> **TIP:** Learn how to use common passive impersonal structures like **He is thought to be …** , **It is believed to have been …**

1 Complete each second sentence with the correct passive form of the verb.

1 Council workers are repairing the road at the moment.

IS

The road _____ at the moment.

2 The party guests had finished all of the food before Madeleine even arrived.

BEEN

The food _____ by the time Madeleine arrived at the party.

3 Ellen and Greg have cleaned the house because guests are coming to see them.

HAS

The house _____ because Ellen and Greg have guests coming to see them.

4 I remember my dad teaching me how to ride a bike.

TAUGHT

I remember _____ how to ride a bike by my dad.

5 Firefighters had to rescue a cat which had become stuck up a tree.

BE

A cat which had become stuck up a tree _____ by firefighters.

6 The government may lower the age at which people can vote quite soon.

LOWERED

The age at which people can vote _____ quite soon.

7 Frank would have fed the dog if he had known it was hungry.

BEEN

The dog _____ if Frank had known it was hungry.

8 Oliver felt that some people at his new workplace were ignoring him.

WAS

Oliver felt that _____ by some people at his new workplace.

Discuss or answer.

1 Are you a team player or do you prefer working independently?

2 What does 'Two's company, three's a crowd' mean? In which situations would you agree with this phrase?

Reported speech

You may need to transform sentences between direct and reported speech. Make sure that you know the patterns with different reporting verbs, and that you know how to report questions.

2 Complete the second sentence in each pair using between three and six words, including the key word.

1 'I was having my lunch when the electricity went off,' said Pascal.

BEEN

Pascal told me that he _____ when the electricity went off.

2 'I really didn't mean to offend anyone,' said Kerry.

TO

Kerry said that she really _____ offensive.

3 'When are you going to write the rest of your conclusion?' asked Adam.

FINISH

Adam asked me when _____ my conclusion.

4 'Putting the apparatus together will be easier than you imagine,' said Saskia.

STRAIGHTFORWARD

Saskia reassured us that putting the apparatus together _____ imagined.

5 'When can we have a meeting to discuss the content of the presentation?' asked Niall.

POSSIBLE

Niall wondered _____ meet to discuss the content of our presentation.

6 'You should have included more examples in your report,' said Hilary.

BETTER

Hilary said that it would _____ included more examples in my report.

Comparative forms

There are often questions about different comparative structures and clause patterns in Part 4.

3 **Choose the correct option (A–C) to complete the sentences.**

1   The school was _____ any of the others he had attended.
    A at least twice as big as
    B more than twice bigger
    C twice as big than

2   Rain was now falling _____ before.
    A increasingly heavily than
    B just more heavily than
    C a great deal more heavily than

3   Your essay is _____ mine.
    A just as well-written than
    B very much as long as
    C so much more interesting than

4   The more you claim to be innocent, _____ you seem.
    A the guiltier
    B more guiltier
    C guiltier than

4 **Choose the correct option to complete the second sentence so that it has a similar meaning to the first.**

1   I expected the play to last for far longer than it actually did.
    The play **wasn't anywhere near as long / didn't last quite as long** as I was expecting.

2   It seems ridiculous that this tiny amount of gold costs so much.
    I can't believe that **such a small amount of / so small amount as** gold costs so much.

3   People always seem to think that the past was better than it actually was.
    In reality, the past was never **much better than / as good as** people generally believe it to be.

4   I had never seen Jeremy clean the workshop as fast.
    Jeremy cleaned the workshop **more speedily than / as speedily as** I had ever seen before.

Verb and noun phrases

Some items in Part 4 test knowledge of synonymous phrases.

> **TIP:** Try to learn all the possible forms of words: verb, noun, adjective and adverb.

5 **Complete the phrases with the words in the box so that they have a similar meaning to the first phrase.**

> a hand   faith in   get in   go into
> hang of   quite   raise   take a

1	help me	give me _____
2	to contact	to _____ touch with
3	to shout	to _____ your voice
4	slightly smaller	not _____ as big as
5	truly believe	have great _____
6	to learn how to do	to get the _____
7	to explain fully	to _____ great detail
8	to travel	to _____ trip

6 **Complete the phrases by using the key words in capitals and different forms of the words in bold.**

1   She didn't **describe** the house very clearly.
    CLEAR
    She didn't _____ of the house.

2   I really didn't **consider** what impact the bad weather would have.
    INTO
    I didn't _____ the impact the bad weather might have.

3   People generally **assume** that advertisements basically tell the truth.
    COMMON
    It's _____ that advertisements basically tell the truth.

4   Very few people actually **accept** alternative medicine.
    LITTLE
    There's _____ of alternative medicine.

5   An almost complete lack of cheap housing means most young adults can't **afford** a house.
    VIRTUALLY
    There is _____ housing so young adults can't buy a house.

6   Stella was always known for having a very active **imagination**.
    HIGHLY
    Stella's friends knew her to be _____ .

SPEAKING BOOST

Discuss or answer.

1   What are some of the most famous symbols you can think of?

2   Why do you think symbols are so important?

Clause patterns

You may have to transform one kind of clause to another.

> if + past participle   imperative + future tense
> should there + infinitive without to
> the best + pronoun + can or could

7 **Complete the sentences with one word in each gap.**

1   Volunteers did the best they _____ to clean up the oil, but it wasn't enough to save some birds.

2   _____ disturbed, the birds give a loud call and fly off as quickly as they can.

3   _____ there be a particularly warm spring and summer, the birds may breed twice rather than just once.

4   _____ attention to the different calls of a bird and you will soon gain a basic understanding of what they mean.

8 Rewrite the sentences using the clause types in the box on page 22 and the words given.

1   Sometimes it's only possible to see four or five different species on a winter's day.

    HOPE

    Sometimes seeing four or five species is _____ for on a winter's day.

2   If the bird emits a loud, repetitive call, it's certain that it's seen a potential threat in the area.

    BE

    The bird will emit a loud, repetitive call _____ a potential threat in the area.

3   Listening carefully to the call of a bird will usually allow you to identify the species.

    TO

    The call of a bird will enable you to identify the species _____ carefully.

4   You can tell if the bird is male or female by looking at the colour of its feathers.

    AND

    Look at the colour of the bird's feathers _____ whether it's male or female.

Collocations and fixed phrases

Some Part 4 tasks test your knowledge of collocations and fixed phrases.

9 Complete the second sentence in each pair with the phrases in the box so that it has a similar meaning to the first.

> accustomed to   any difference   behind the times
> dedicated himself   dependent upon   felt compelled
> in two minds   no harm in

1   I really don't mind if she comes to the party.

    It honestly doesn't make _____ to me if she comes to the party.

2   I've got out of the habit of waking up early.

    I've become _____ waking up late.

3   Some of his ideas are a bit old-fashioned.

    He's a bit _____ with some of his thinking.

4   She was so upset that I just had to do something to help her.

    I _____ to do something to help her because she was so upset.

5   He spent the whole of his life fighting for equality for the poor.

    Throughout his life, he _____ to fighting for equality for the poor.

6   The amount of tax you pay is directly related to how much you earn.

    The amount of tax you pay is _____ how much you earn.

7   You have nothing to lose by applying for the job.

    There's _____ applying for the job.

8   Alicia couldn't decide whether to tell her boss or not.

    Alicia was _____ about telling her boss.

For questions 1-6, complete the second sentence so that it has a similar meaning to the first sentence, using the word given. <u>Do not change the word given</u>. You must use between <u>three</u> and <u>six</u> words, including the word given.

Here is an example (0).

0   New evidence has appeared, which means the police are reopening the case.

    LIGHT

    The case HAS BEEN REOPENED IN THE LIGHT of new evidence.

1   The company decided to build the new factory despite local people objecting to it.

    REGARDLESS

    The company decided to build the new factory _____ of local people.

2   I can't understand how Phil managed to move the wardrobe on his own.

    CLUE

    I _____ Phil managed to move the wardrobe on his own.

3   Winning the award was a complete surprise to Hannah.

    BLUE

    Winning the award _____ for Hannah.

4   'I think there will be a general election soon,' said Billy.

    INCLINED

    Billy said he was _____ be a general election soon.

5   Fiona booked a holiday before she'd asked for time off from work.

    LIBERTY

    Fiona _____ a holiday before she'd asked for time off from work.

6   I phoned my mum as soon as I arrived, so that she wouldn't worry about me.

    REST

    I put my mum's _____ as soon as I arrived.

ABOUT THE TASK

- In Reading and Use of English Part 5, you read a long text.
- There are six multiple-choice questions with four options.
- You have to choose the correct options based on information in the text.
- The questions can be about the general meaning of the whole text, or paragraphs within it.
- Questions can also be about details and ideas in the text, or the writer's attitude, opinion or purpose.
- Some questions test implied meaning, your understanding of unfamiliar words and expressions in context and the use of examples, comparisons and reference words in the text.
- Each question is worth two marks.

Practice task

1 Read the first two paragraphs of an article about noise pollution. Ignore the highlighting. For questions 1 and 2, choose the answer (A, B, C or D) which you think fits best according to the text.

1 The writer mentions both humans and wildlife in the first paragraph in order to
   A suggest one is more seriously affected by noise pollution than the other.
   B contrast the specific effects of noise pollution on each group.
   C illustrate the scope and scale of the issue of noise pollution.
   D outline the historical growth and development of noise pollution.

2 What point does the writer make about noise pollution in the second paragraph?
   A People feel powerless to start tackling the problem.
   B Public awareness of the issue is beginning to rise.
   C It's easy to identify the organisations which cause it.
   D There's a lot of denial about the scale of the problem.

How did you do?

2 Check your answers.

3 Read the options for question 1 in Ex 1 again and answer the questions.

1 For A, the writer mentions ways in which animals and humans are affected by noise pollution, but do they suggest which group is affected more seriously?

2 For B, does the writer contrast the different ways in which animals and humans are affected by noise pollution or list them?

3 For C, does the writer refer to both animals and humans to compare them or to show that noise pollution affects all living things?

4 For D, does the writer mention both animals and humans to make a point about how noise pollution has worsened and spread?

4 Look at the four highlighted sections in paragraph 2 of the article.

a Match each highlighted section (1–4) with the option it relates to (A–D) in Ex 1 question 2.

b Which of the options matches the meaning of the highlighted text exactly?

c Why don't the others match?

ONE SPECIES, A LOT OF NOISE

The world is a far noisier place than it once was. It'd take a solo voyage an awfully long way from civilisation to find the kind of peace that once existed almost everywhere. Inevitably, humans are responsible for this turning up of global volume, which is causing chaos in the natural world. Stressed insect pollinators, seed dispersers such as birds, and the predators that feed on both have been forced to flee to avoid chronic noise levels, thus altering not just the distribution of wildlife in many areas, but the shifting of entire ecosystems. Although people may seem to have become remarkably adept at consciously filtering out excess noise, there's a well-documented public health crisis looming for us too. Stress, disrupted sleep patterns and high blood pressure are just a few of the symptoms.

While other environmental issues such as climate change are increasingly in the public eye, noise pollution is seldom discussed. Why? Although ¹it's undoubtedly easier for everyone from government level down to individuals to pretend that it doesn't exist, this seems an unlikely reason. ²A few conveniently blame business and industry, but the truth of the matter is that we're all contributing to it. This raises a dilemma for each of us, which also serves as an explanation as to why we're so reluctant to talk about the issue: ³how do we as individuals even begin to deal with something that everyone on the planet is responsible for? Yet ⁴facing up to this and arriving at a solution is the only way to improve the situation.

Strategies and skills

Understanding inference and implication

Some questions rely on working out implied meanings in the text: meaning which is not directly stated, but is still clear to the reader.

1 Read the short texts and choose the correct answers (A–D). How do you know?

1   It was often difficult to stop Phil going on about how important his team's contribution to the project was. When the issue of overspending on the budget came up at the meeting, however, he remained unusually quiet.

The writer is suggesting that
A   Phil is an especially difficult person to work with.
B   Phil does an excellent job of managing his team.
C   Phil is responsible for the overspending on the budget.
D   Phil takes all the credit while his team do all of the work.

2   Many fans of Heywood's writing remain hopeful that a sequel to her ground-breaking 2008 novel *The First Kick* will hit the shelves one day. I suspect that there's more chance of me going for a picnic on the sun than this happening.

The writer is suggesting that
A   there will never be a sequel to *The First Kick*.
B   the sequel to *The First Kick* isn't as good as the original book.
C   the sequel to *The First Kick* will be published quite soon.
D   Heywood's fans talk too much about a sequel to *The First Kick*.

3   While the tour guide was friendly enough, he seemed to have certain favourites within the group to whom all of the most interesting information was directed. Altogether, not the kind of person I could ever imagine going out for a coffee with.

The writer is suggesting that
A   the tour guide didn't take them to enough cafés or restaurants.
B   it's unlikely that she and the tour guide will ever be friends.
C   some members of the tour group disliked the tour guide.
D   a few group members shared an interest with the tour guide.

4   Despite the company president's repeated insistence that equality amongst his staff is paramount, he has singularly failed to put anything into place that would actually help to bring it about. Action, or in this case a lack of action, speaks louder than words.

The writer is suggesting that the company president
A   doesn't have time to do all aspects of his job.
B   gets very little help and support from his staff.
C   claims he's better at his job than he actually is.
D   doesn't genuinely believe in equality for his staff.

Discuss or answer.

1   Would you ever eat in a restaurant by yourself? Why? / Why not?

2   If a solo traveller visited your country or region, what would you recommend they do?

Understanding purpose and attitude

Questions often ask about the attitude of the writer. This is not usually stated directly in the text, but is expressed using different words to the questions.

2 Read the extracts from reading texts and answer the questions.

1   While Madison's book is hardly short of fascinating anecdotes about the more unusual applications of virtual reality, it's surprisingly thin on the ground when it comes to diagnosing the technology's potential drawbacks.

Was the reviewer more impressed by Madison's anecdotes or the analysis of any drawbacks? How do you know?

2   I suspect that my fellow travellers' enthusiasm for being at the ruins had more to do with the number of likes they might get online from friends back home than any genuine interest in the history of this fascinating ancient settlement.

Did the writer visit the ruins for the same reason as his fellow travellers? How do you know?

3   The developers claim that there are many psychological benefits to be gained by using their particular methodology. I have no issue with their assertions, but would argue that the same can be said about every apparently revolutionary technique that came before this one, and probably all of those yet to come.

Does the writer use the word 'revolutionary' in a positive or dismissive way? How do you know?

4   When the music emerges from the speakers, contrary to the composer's claims, it's just about possible to discern that every sound on the recording is, in fact, a human voice. What I could never have been prepared for is the richness that this gives the composition.

What is the writer surprised by? How do you know?

3 Read the extracts and choose the word (A–C) that best expresses the writer's opinion or attitude. Which words or expressions in each extract confirm this?

1   It goes without saying that the author's conversational style will appeal to many. For others, myself included, dealing with a subject as serious as this in such a way became somewhat exasperating after fewer than two pages.

   A satisfied   **B** impressed **C** irritated

2   Our team leader was a woman of few words. In some people, this characteristic generates a feeling of being judged in those around them. In her case, however, it created the unspoken impression that we could follow her anywhere without a single problem coming to pass.

   A trusting   **B** suspicious **C** confused

3   The organisation is perhaps unique in politely refusing affiliation of any sort with outside agencies, be they businesses, charities or governmental bodies. This hyper-vigilance might appear outdated to many. It has, however, not only ensured its survival in an increasingly dog-eat-dog world, but brought about unprecedented growth.

   A cautious   **B** critical   **C** admiring

4   When asked about having failed to create a successful lightbulb after 10,000 attempts, American inventor Thomas Edison replied, 'I have not failed. I've just found 10,000 ways that won't work.' I imagine the research team must have taken great comfort from Edison's words after the initial set of experiments proved inconclusive.

   A sympathetic **B** proud   **C** discouraged

SPEAKING BOOST

Discuss or answer.

1   Describe your ideal city. What five facilities would you prioritise?

2   Which would you prefer to visit or live in: a traditional or smart city?

Matching meaning

It is important to read the relevant part of the text very carefully to match the exact meaning in the text with the meaning in the correct answer.

4 Read the extracts carefully and decide if the sentences (A–D) are true or false. How do you know?

> **TIP:** If something isn't mentioned in the text, it cannot be the correct answer.

1   The moment I emerged from sleep, I became instantly aware of the cold biting at my face, the only part of my body that was exposed. The fire had long gone out in the small cabin. How on earth, I thought, can such tiny creatures as hummingbirds survive in these conditions?

   A The writer has failed in an attempt to find hummingbirds.
   B The writer is astonished that hummingbirds live in such a cold place.
   C The writer is impressed by the landscape where hummingbirds live.
   D The writer suggests that hummingbirds are more resilient than humans.

2   The first person I met on entering the family reunion was Great-Aunt Caroline. Her whole manner radiated authority to such an extent that, without her having to utter a word, I found myself transported back to the headteacher's office at school, providing unconvincing excuses for my behaviour.

   A Caroline was rather rude to the writer at their first meeting.
   B The writer is surprised at being taken immediately to Caroline's office.
   C Caroline's presence conveys more meaning than what she says.
   D The writer is reminded of a childhood experience on meeting Caroline.

3   Once the main hub of steel production in the country, the city never recovered after cheaper foreign imports flooded the market. Had a strategy been devised for replacing traditional industry with high-tech alternatives, it might have been a very different story.

   A A lot of high-tech industry has been established in the city.
   B The city's difficulties are part of a country-wide problem.
   C Insufficient planning was carried out for the city's future.
   D There is no more steel production happening in the city.

4   The concept of living underground is developing quite a following these days. Some architects have clearly taken inspiration from the earliest known human dwellings in creating their subterranean homes. Others, meanwhile, apply a thoroughly modern dynamic to their work.

   A An increasing number of people are interested in underground homes.
   B There is a lot of disagreement about the best type of underground home.
   C Many underground homes contain a wide range of modern facilities.
   D There are many different reasons why people want to live in underground homes.

5 Read the first paragraph of an article about whale watching. Answer the questions.

1 What do we learn about the International Whaling Commission?
2 What is the subject matter of the International Whaling Commission data?
3 What kind of vessel was involved in the majority of collisions?
4 Why do you think the writer finds the information about whale-watching boats ironic?

The organisation charged with collecting data about collisions between whales and boats, the International Whaling Commission, has recently released data showing a breakdown of the types of vessels most often involved in a collision. In the majority of cases, the offending craft is never actually identified. However, in instances where positive recognition was possible, whale-watching vessels were, ironically, the worst offenders, with motor yachts, naval vessels and ferries not far behind. One interpretation of the data holds that certain types of vessel are far more likely to report hitting a whale, thus distorting the true picture. Whether or not this explanation comes from within the whale-watching industry has yet to be determined.

TIP: Words or ideas in the options often occur in the text, but this does not mean that that particular option is correct. They may be distractors. Read the relevant part of the text very carefully to see if the meaning matches.

6 Now read the exam question about the paragraph in Ex 5 and choose the correct answer.

What does the writer suggest about the International Whaling Commission statistics?

A The accuracy of the numbers of collisions is open to question.
B They may have been analysed in a self-interested way.
C The breakdown of figures is roughly what would be expected.
D Numbers of reported collisions are likely to rise in the future.

Using context to guess the meanings of unknown words

Some questions rely on working out the meanings of unfamiliar words and phrases in the text. To answer these, you need to use the context to guess the meaning.

7 Read the sentences and answer the questions.

1 Although the illness had left him feeling **frail** and **washed out**, he regained his strength within a matter of days.

Do the words 'frail' and 'washed out' mean that he felt weak or strong? How do you know?

2 The **blunt** manner in which the guards asked to see Alicia's passport left her in no doubt that she was in serious trouble.

Is being dealt with in a 'blunt' way a pleasant or unpleasant experience? How do you know?

3 Max was determined to appear calm, despite the bad weather throwing the plane casually around in the air. However, the way in which he was anxiously flicking through the magazine he'd bought at the airport suggested he was anything but.

Does Max look through the magazine slowly or quickly? How do you know?

4 Never before had I seen such energy put into celebrating a festival. And unlike the short-lived festivities at similar events in my own country, they seemed to be continuing **indefinitely.**

Does 'indefinitely' mean for a long time or a short time? How do you know?

5 The coach could see that his new training regime had left the players far more exhausted than he'd anticipated. He decided to **cut them some slack** over the following few days.

Does the phrase 'cut them some slack' mean the players will do less or more training? How do you know?

6 The hotel looked reasonable from the outside so we booked a room for three nights. On the first night, however, the noise from the nightclub opposite made sleep impossible and, furthermore, there was no hot water. The plate of supermarket biscuits offered as breakfast the following morning was **the last straw** and we checked out immediately.

Does the phrase 'the last straw' mean something positive or negative? How do you know?

Understanding text organisation features

Some questions ask about text organisation features such as the use of referencing, examples and comparisons. To answer these, you need to read the text very carefully to find out what a reference refers back to, why an example has been used and what comparisons have been made.

8 Read the texts and the questions that follow them, which focus on referencing. Choose the correct answer (A–D).

1
I doubt many would argue with the observation that the teenage years bring with them periods of moodiness and the need to isolate from parents and siblings. In soap operas and dramas, teenagers are often portrayed as exhibiting these negative behaviours almost constantly, with only fleeting glimpses of the loving person beneath. Their parents complain constantly about their selfishness, drawing sympathy from neighbours who have witnessed the young person's conduct first-hand. In the case of my own children, however, **this image** has thankfully turned out to be far from the truth.

What does '**this image**' refer to?
A   teenagers who are more loving than most
B   teenagers who show stereotypical behaviour
C   parents who complain about their teenage children
D   neighbours who are affected by teenagers living nearby

2
Phoning the company's customer service helpline was an experience in itself. At the start of the call, the person I spoke to insisted that when the laptop had been dispatched three days ago, the correct model was in the box. During the call, I actually emailed the advisor photos of the box itself and of the incorrect laptop that I had received within it. **Even then**, there was still no admission that I'd actually been sent the wrong one.

The words '**Even then**' refer to
A   when the writer received the laptop.
B   the start of the call to customer services.
C   after the advisor had seen the photos.
D   the whole period of time of the call.

9 Read the texts and the questions that follow them, which focus on using examples. Answer the questions (a–e).

a   Read Text 1 and try to answer the question.
b   Match each of the options in question 1 with the highlighted part of the text that they relate to.
c   Which of the options in question 1 matches the meaning of the highlighted text exactly?
d   Why don't the other options match exactly?
e   Read Text 2 and answer the question.

1
Take the recent TV drama, *Amelia*. On the surface, [1]it looks different to anything in recent memory due to the unusual context in which it's set. [2]The production standards are faultless and [3]the cast are all seasoned TV actors, capable of producing compelling drama in their sleep. Yet the story is worryingly familiar and the dialogue incredibly superficial. [4]Everyone, it appears, prefers style over substance these days, and producers are only too happy to oblige with dramas such as this.

The writer mentions *Amelia* as an example of a programme which
A   is part of a current trend.
B   shows poor production quality.
C   demonstrates a great deal of originality.
D   nurtures lesser-known talent.

2
Several of the songs of my youth were branded as 'unlistenable' by my parents, and there was debate on TV about what effect they might be having on the tender ears and sensibilities of the young. And yet twenty years later, as I was browsing the crisps and snacks section of my local supermarket, what should come over the store loudspeakers but one of the offending pieces of music in all its glory. No one in the store even seemed to notice.

What point is exemplified by the reference to the supermarket?
A   Retailers often make poor choices of music in their stores.
B   Music has less influence on people's state of mind than it used to.
C   The public acceptance of certain songs broadens with time.
D   Songs sound better to us as adults than they do as children.

TIP: If you are unsure of an answer, make a note next to the question and revisit it later in the exam.

10 Read Texts 1 and 2 and the questions that follow them, which focus on using comparisons.
Answer the questions (a–c).

a   Read Text 1 and try to answer the question.

b   Why don't the others match?

c   Read Text 2 and answer the question.

1   What's striking is how deeply entrenched attitudes are. Classical music sits alone atop the hierarchy of worthiness and is, of course, what all teenagers should listen to, even though very few actually like it. Add typical teenage leisure activities to this hierarchy and computer games are probably bottom of the heap, closely followed by social media. Yet both are social, intellectually engaging and develop imagination. Reading teenage novels, however, a highly solitary, even antisocial activity, is seen as the thing every parent wants their children to do.

In the paragraph, the writer draws a comparison between classical music and

A   typical teenage activities.

B   playing computer games.

C   using social media.

D   reading books.

2   Climate researcher Chlöe Villeneuve's projections are serious, but not as serious as those of some scientists. 'I've yet to be convinced that Earth is in danger of following Venus down the 'runaway greenhouse effect' route, which sees surface temperatures there regularly reaching 450°C. What it does serve as, though, is a reminder that the greenhouse effect and global warming are not theoretical. Even the most ardent climate change sceptic can hardly disagree that a planet that was once very similar to how Earth is today has changed considerably.'

Chlöe Villeneuve compares Earth to Venus in order to

A   issue a worst-case scenario warning about global warming.

B   convince those who are in denial about global warming.

C   illustrate some common characteristics of global warming.

D   show gratitude for being able to prevent global warming.

The beauty of pauses

Machines work well at a constant speed – and the faster the better. They are designed and built for it. Whether they are spinning cotton or crunching numbers, regular, repetitive actions are what they excel at. Increasingly, our world is designed *by* machines, *for* machines. Digital technology brings them ever more intimately into our lives. We hold our phones in the palm of our hand, but it is they that have us in their grasp. We adapt to machines and hold ourselves to their standards: people are judged by the speed with which they respond, not the quality of their response. We find ourselves in a state of 'continuous partial attention' – rarely stopping, never fully present. Such ideas are being woven into our culture.

Most of us are busy most of the time these days, if not with work then with family, domestic tasks or our social networks – real and virtual. When I ask people how they are, they almost always answer 'busy' or some variation of it. 'Always on' has become something to aspire to. The moral high ground belongs to those who get on with things, not those who delay. We feel we are being 'sensible', 'logical', 'responsible', 'practical'. Ticking things off the 'to-do' list becomes a means of defining, or escaping ourselves. Faced with this, we try to keep calm by carrying on, but what are we missing out on?

A few years ago I became very interested in what it means to pause. I realised that this isn't as simple as it might seem. A pause could be a moment of silence or a year's sabbatical. I sought out people who pay attention to pauses: from actors and artists to musicians and film-makers. I asked them about the value of gaps and spaces, about how they create them and what they get as a result. I realised that a pause is not nothing. It acts as a kind of switch or opening. As Helene Simonsen, a classical musician, says, 'Whatever you are doing, if you want something else to happen, you need to pause.' A film director spoke of how he used a tiny delay to grab the crew's attention on set: 'Pause for the space of a breath or two, before

you say "Action!" and it changes everything.' It became clear to me that a pause is not so much an absence of thought or action, but an integral part of it.

I started to notice where pauses show up. For example, I realised that when writing, a short walk was a more effective way to break a creative block than concentrating harder. When people came to visit me at my rural Spanish home, I saw how powerful brief periods of disconnection could be. As one friend commented, 'After a day here, I found myself solving problems I didn't know I had.' **Time can have a profound effect, when it's allowed to.**

Some people were distinctly unsettled when I told them I was working on a book about pauses. There was one who immediately and indignantly declared, 'But there is always a cost to pausing.' The very idea created a kind of panic for her. There was an awkward silence. A pause, in fact. After a minute or so her husband added, 'Perhaps … but there is always a cost to not pausing as well.' This illustrates the dilemma we are caught in. If time is money, then pausing will cost you. But what about the cost of not pausing? What about the opportunities you miss, the perspective you lose, the connections you don't make, the enjoyment you forsake? It's clear which option we've become conditioned to choose.

There is more to life than getting things done. Time isn't a commodity, scarce or otherwise. Our experience of it varies wildly. A minute eating ice cream doesn't feel the same as a minute doing press-ups. Even time itself isn't a uniform raw material, as the physics of Einstein shows. Letting go of the idea that time is linear, regular and objective, and thinking of it in the same way we experience it – as elastic, variable and layered – can only be a good thing. Instead of setting work and life against each other, pauses can be used to lighten our experience. They are like the yeast that makes bread rise: you don't need much, but it is a vital ingredient.

You are going to read an article about the importance of pauses. For questions 1-6, choose the answer (A, B, C or D) which you think fits best according to the text.

1   In the first paragraph, the writer refers to mobile phones in order to

    A   make an observation about the efficiency of machines.
    B   point out an irony in people's use and appreciation of machines.
    C   show how machines have negatively impacted on human relationships.
    D   draw a comparison between machine and human behaviour.

2   In the second paragraph, the writer suggests that people's motivation for staying busy is driven by

    A   a deep sense of commitment.
    B   an increased need to be organised.
    C   a response to technological change.
    D   a desire to feel superior to others.

3   In the third paragraph, the writer is

    A   outlining how he benefits from pausing in daily life.
    B   summarising others' definitions of what pauses are.
    C   describing how his understanding of pauses has shifted.
    D   illustrating contrasting views on the importance of pausing.

4   In the fourth paragraph, what is the writer emphasising in the sentence '**Time can have a profound effect, when it's allowed to**'?

    A   Certain contexts offer more opportunities to pause.
    B   Different activities appear to pass at different rates.
    C   Travelling can alter people's perception of time.
    D   The effects of pausing are stronger when with other people.

5   What does the writer suggest in the fifth paragraph?

    A   There are several unexpected drawbacks to pausing.
    B   The need to pause is generally misunderstood.
    C   Certain people gain more from pausing than others.
    D   The majority of people value the material over the spiritual.

6   In the final paragraph, the writer puts forward the view that people should

    A   attempt to alter their attitude towards time.
    B   spend more time engaging in agreeable activities.
    C   resist the temptation to overanalyse how we experience time.
    D   endeavour to plan their time more carefully.

ABOUT THE TASK

- In Reading Part 6, you read four texts.
- Each text contains a writer's opinions about a central topic.
- Within each text, the writer gives their opinion about three or four issues related to the central topic.
- There are four questions, one about each of the four issues that the writers comment on.
- The texts can also be four different reviews about the same book, film, etc.

- You have to identify shared or contrasting opinions on each of the issues.
- You need to skim and scan each text to find what each writer says about an issue.
- You must then decide if the writers' or reviewers' opinions are the same or different.
- Each question is worth two marks.

Practice task

1 Read extracts from four reviews of a book about global politics. Answer the questions.

Which reviewer

1 shares an opinion with reviewer D about the depth of analysis in the book?

2 has a different opinion to the other reviewers about the regions the author has chosen to focus on?

How did you do?

2 Check your answers.

3 Read the first question in Ex 1 again.

1 Highlight the sections of text in each review that comment on Campbell's depth of analysis.

2 Read the opinion expressed by reviewer D. Is the reviewer positive or negative about the level of Campbell's analysis?

3 Read the opinions expressed by reviewers A, B and C. Which one is closest in meaning to that of Reviewer D? Why?

4 Read the second question in Ex 1 again.

1 Highlight the sections of text that relate to the choice of regions included in Campbell's book.

2 Make notes in the table below about what each reviewer (A-D) says about the choice of regions included in Campbell's book.

A	B	C	D

3 Which three reviewers have very similar opinions?

4 What is the answer?

THE GLOBAL GAME

Four reviewers comment on Sheila Campbell's book

A

The Global Game is an ambitious book about decision-making on a global scale. Each of its twelve chapters covers one of the world's geopolitical hotspots, identifying and analysing the decisions that have led to their instability and suggesting likely scenarios as to how events there will unfold. There's everywhere you'd expect to be included in such a book and plenty of surprises too. However, the treatment of the current situation in each region, and the influence that global superpowers have or are seeking to have there, borders on the superficial at times.

B

What I found unusual about Campbell's impressively researched book is how often I found myself agreeing with the conclusions she draws at the end of each chapter. Not only that, I discovered revelation after revelation in her detailed exploration of each of the regions, and the decisions that led up to their current state of unrest. Had I been asked to name the twelve most significant areas of political tension around the globe, my list would have included perhaps six of those selected by Campbell. I would never have predicted the others she's included.

C

The blurb on the back of Campbell's book makes the rather extravagant promise that never before has a book of this type examined global geopolitics so comprehensively. The majority of books that make such claims often then spectacularly fail to live up to them, but this is definitely not the case with *The Global Game*. However, I can't help wondering whether Campbell was adventurous enough when making the decisions about where to write about. It would have upped the interest levels considerably had I come across at least a few chapters on somewhere I wasn't expecting to read about.

D

As one would expect, the longest chapters in Campbell's book deal with the places that we see in the news most often. What I was pleasantly taken aback by, however, was the inclusion of sections dealing with the situations in parts of the world where I didn't even know tensions existed. That said, it wasn't always possible to come away from many, if any, of the chapters with a good understanding of the actual circumstances there. Campbell appears to have avoided tackling much of the complexity that one needs to fully comprehend any region.

Strategies and skills

Identifying contrasting opinions

Texts in Part 6 often contain opinions which appear to contradict what the writer actually believes. The speaker puts forward one opinion, but also indicates that she or he actually holds a contrasting view.

1 Read the short extracts from Part 6 texts and choose the correct answer (A–C).

1 Whilst the majority of commentators on the subject of economic progress believe there should be a reduction in regulation for businesses to almost zero, I'm of the opposite opinion entirely.

The writer believes that there should be
A no regulation for business.
B less regulation for business.
C more regulation for business.

2 I came to this book having heard from many different quarters that Kinsella was a truly original writer. I'm not sure how many other authors those who told me this had read, but it can't have been many.

The writer believes that Kinsella
A writes in an original way.
B isn't a particularly original author.
C writes some original and some unoriginal material.

3 I've never gone along with the opinion which many educational policy-makers hold that having art lessons in schools should be universal.

The writer believes that
A not all students should have to go to art lessons.
B art lessons should be compulsory for all students.
C decisions about art lessons should be left to the government.

4 Imposing an immediate ban on single-use plastics seems attractive but may ultimately end up being counterproductive, as the processes used in creating replacement materials are equally polluting.

The writer believes that a ban on single-use plastics
A must be implemented straight away.
B is impossible as there are no replacement materials.
C should be thought about carefully before imposing it.

5 There's a general consensus that student behaviour in schools is on the decline, yet the majority of evidence that's presented to support this viewpoint is subjective.

The writer believes that standards of behaviour in schools
A are open to question.
B are falling.
C are the same as before.

6 We're already seeing several effects of the new transport policy, which are perhaps not what what the government had in mind when it promised that the policy would lead to cleaner air in the city.

The writer believes that the government's new transport policy
A was full of empty promises.
B has had unexpected consequences.
C is creating cleaner air in the city.

2 Highlight the sections of text in each extract that allowed you to work out your answer.

SPEAKING BOOST

Discuss or answer.

1 Do you think modern life makes decision-making easier or more challenging? Why?

2 How would you approach making a life-changing decision?

Identifying similar opinions

3 Read the pairs of sentences. Do they have a similar meaning or different meanings?

1 A The false assumption that many would-be authors make is that writing is a natural talent.

   B Those who see themselves as future authors often mistakenly believe they were born into the role.

2 A Archaeology is of as much use to us as a species as learning how to cook plastic.

   B I think the view of archaeology as an outdated field of study has thankfully gone out of fashion.

3 A Climate change must be at the front of every organisation's mind when making any business decision.

   B No plans should be made in companies without considering the implications for climate change.

4 A The billions it costs to stage huge sporting events would be far better spent on directly funding new amenities for residents.

   B I've yet to see a city that's hosted a big sporting event that doesn't have a huge legacy of publicly accessible facilities that wouldn't otherwise have been built.

5 A Thorough inspections in the country's schools are of equal importance today as they ever were.

   B Calls for a relaxation of the strictness of the school inspection framework are misguided and should be resisted.

> **TIP:** Once you have found the information in each text that the question relates to, read it very carefully to work out exactly what each person's opinion is.

4 Read the two extracts from Part 6 texts. Decide whether the statements (1–10) that follow are true or false.

EXTREME SPORTS

Anna Calcedo

There's a highly vocal minority who continually call for the abolition of extreme sports. While I can comprehend the motivation behind their arguments, that they cost lives and taxpayers' money to treat them when things go wrong, I have a more fundamental issue with their approach: how to define an extreme sport. Far greater losses to life and the economy occur due to people sustaining injuries or serious health issues such as heart attacks while playing tennis than happen because of base jumping. One suggestion is to replace extreme sports with electronic equivalents, which of course carry little or no risk. I was distinctly sceptical about these at first but have greatly warmed to the idea after trying an early prototype of just such a system. There's far more regulation of dangerous sporting activities these days, thanks to governing bodies being set up to supervise these sports and ensure events are as safe as can be. People would revert to doing the sports illegally and in a far more hazardous way should a ban on extreme sports be implemented.

Stephen Tenby

I appreciate that the majority of extreme sports have had official organisations put into place overseeing them, which set standards that participants must follow. While this has been applauded by many, I find the idea of creating rules for something so inherently dangerous utterly pointless. It simply doesn't get away from the fact that a disproportionate number of people who partake in these sports end up dead or seriously hurt. The only solution to this is to prevent these sports from being practised anywhere. Given the correct incentives, I'm convinced that those who thrive on the kind of adrenaline rush extreme sports provide could be encouraged to become involved in safer versions of their chosen sport, which either already exist or are in the latter stages of development. Free-fall parachuting in a wind tunnel is an example of one that's already in place. Virtual reality simulations of sports such as base jumping must also be a possibility, given the computing power we have at our disposal these days.

1   Calcedo is part of a minority who oppose the abolition of extreme sports.

2   Calcedo has no sympathy with the reasons given for banning extreme sports.

3   Calcedo suggests that conventional sports cause more actual harm than extreme ones.

4   Calcedo thinks that virtual reality versions of extreme sports aren't worth considering.

5   Calcedo says banning extreme sports would cancel out the positive effects of sports governing bodies.

6   Tenby thinks having governing bodies overseeing extreme sports is a waste of time.

7   Tenby thinks it would be close to impossible to persuade people to stop practising extreme sports.

8   Tenby says alternative versions of extreme sports either are, or soon will be, available.

9   Tenby uses free-fall parachuting as an example of a safe, virtual extreme sport that's already available.

10 Tenby believes electronic versions of many different sports are possible.

5 Read the texts in Ex 4 again and decide whether Calcedo and Tenby are likely to agree or disagree with these statements.

1   Extreme sports should be subjected to a complete ban in all forms.

2   Regulatory bodies for extreme sports have had a positive effect.

3   Virtual versions of extreme sports are something that should be encouraged.

4   Certain people seen to be at risk should be prevented from playing conventional sports.

SPEAKING BOOST

Discuss or answer.

1   How do you think people feel when they do extreme sports?

2   Who's the most empathetic person you know? Why?

Identifying paraphrases and synonyms

Often, each writer uses vocabulary and expresses ideas related to the topics of the questions in different ways. It's important to be able to identify paraphrases and synonyms that will guide you to each writer's opinion on a particular topic.

6 Match vocabulary used by Anna Calcedo (1–8) with a synonym or paraphrase used by Stephen Tenby (a–h).

Anna Calcedo		Stephen Tenby	
1	abolition	a	version
2	regulation	b	oversee
3	prototype	c	end up hurt
4	governing body	d	put into place
5	sustain injuries	e	prevent from being practised
6	electronic equivalent	f	official organisation
7	supervise	g	virtual reality simulation
8	implement	h	standard

TIP: Words or ideas in the options often occur in the text, but this does not mean that the option is correct. They may be distractors, placed there to make the correct answer more challenging to find. Read the relevant part of the text very carefully to determine whether the meaning matches.

7 Write as many synonyms of the words and expressions in bold as you can.

1   the **business** was a success   _____

2   an **environmentally friendly** product   _____

3   the **implications** of the policy are unclear _____

4   **reducing** employees' hours   _____

5   her writing has improved **vastly**   _____

6   it had **minimal** impact on the economy   _____

7   these are **challenging** times   _____

8   **progress** has been good   _____

You are going to read four reviews of a book about the media. For questions 1-4, choose from the reviews A-D. The reviews may be chosen more than once.

Which reviewer

has a different opinion from the other reviewers about how confidently Grahame discusses the media?

| 1 | |

shares reviewer B's opinion about how original Grahame's ideas are?

| 2 | |

shares a view with reviewer D regarding Grahame's concerns about the political influence of newspapers?

| 3 | |

has a similar view to reviewer B about Grahame's predictions regarding online media?

| 4 | |

The power of the media

Four reviews of *The Media Machine* by Alexander Grahame

A

The Media Machine attempts to unpick the complex relationships between business, media and politics in the western world. Author Alexander Grahame's 25 years in the news industry enable him to analyse the topic with authority and in great detail. Despite his intimate knowledge of the media's inner workings, however, I didn't come away from the book feeling that I had been party to any great revelations. Without doubt, the main points are eloquently stated, but have all largely been made before in other such studies. His main focus is on how each news title, whether broadsheet or tabloid, subtly manipulates its readers towards a certain opinion. The media's ability to do this gives them great influence over those in power, but hasn't that always been the case? Social media's involvement, however, adds a new dimension, and the author's conviction that its algorithms will create even greater societal divisions are frighteningly plausible.

B

The printed media's ability to seek to control the thoughts, minds and supposedly democratic decisions of their readership, asserts Alexander Grahame in *The Media Machine*, has never had such dangerous consequences as it does today. Few sane people would disagree. According to Grahame, what has complicated this issue beyond recognition is the internet. Astonishingly complex coding now provides each user with news based on what they've previously clicked on and read. His assumption that this will create ever deeper and more heated disagreements within populations, however, is not backed up with any convincing evidence. Despite this, Grahame's arguments throughout the book are put forward with the degree of assurance you'd expect from such a well-respected journalist. Although the idea of press exploitation of people's attitudes and beliefs has been written about on many occasions before, the other countless fresh insights included in the pages of *The Media Machine* make it well worth reading.

C

The main emotion I was left with after reading Alexander Grahame's *The Media Machine* was concern. He paints a believably bleak picture of what humanity has in store thanks to the seemingly endless number of news feeds available to us on our devices, and the effect that this may have on social integrity. Grahame comments so perceptively on this and many other contentious issues that I had never even considered that I eventually lost count. My sense of unease is caused in part by how persuasively the claims made within the book are put across. The conviction with which Grahame writes is impressive. One small irritation is that too much space is given to how much power traditional news titles have over their readers, and hence who they want to win in an election. This has clearly been the case for many decades, if not centuries, yet to my knowledge no society ever fell apart because its media expressed a variety of opinions.

D

Interesting though it is, Alexander Grahame's new book will probably seem to most readers more like a revision aid for a media studies degree than a ground-breaking vision of the media, politics and power. Its principal attempt to be ahead of the times relates to its focus on the internet-age interference with citizens' thinking through various social platforms. Whilst this practice undoubtedly occurs, Grahame's conclusion that it has pushed whole societies to the edge of conflict is hard to have faith in. What had me nodding in agreement, however, was his frightening analysis of the sheer number of votes that can be changed when one of the big national news titles decides to change their political allegiance. This was the only section of the book in which I felt Grahame had a thorough grasp of the issue he was dealing with. Elsewhere, it was unclear whether he actually believed in his own arguments.

TEST

- In Reading and Use of English Part 7 you read one long text which has six gaps in it.
- The missing paragraphs that fill these gaps are written below the text, but not in the correct order.
- There is also a seventh paragraph which does not fit any of the gaps in the text – this is called a distractor.

- You have to decide which of the seven paragraphs fits each of the six gaps.
- To do the task, you need to understand the flow of a text, and understand how sentences refer back to earlier ideas in the paragraph or text, and forward to ideas which follow.
- Each question is worth two marks.

Practice task

1 Read an extract from an article about the rules of good behaviour in restaurants. Two paragraphs have been removed from the extract. Choose from the paragraphs (A–C) the one which fits each gap (1 and 2). There is one extra paragraph which you do not need to use.

The new rules of dining out

The modern restaurant scene is more casual and popular than ever before. Formal etiquette is, thankfully, history. But in this newly democratic realm there are still ways in which we can behave for the good not just of our fellow diners, but also restaurant staff and the venues we love.

With most restaurants facing tough trading conditions, no-show bookings that leave tables empty may make the difference between profit and loss. Should customers need to cancel, simply letting the restaurant know as early as possible so it can reallocate the table is surely not too much to ask.

1	

Many restaurants resent **having to ask** but feel they have no choice. 'I was nervous about doing it,' said Helen Davies, manager of the Happy Frog Restaurant. 'It made me feel as though I was running a travel agency, but it's been a great deterrent. The no-shows stopped immediately.' Helen also has a very clear view about another issue close to both staff and customers' hearts: tipping. 'There must be a clear, honest and open system so that everyone involved knows what the score is,' she says.

2	

Customers are meanwhile advised to tip however they see fit, but shouldn't feel that they need to start trying to understand **the machinations of a business** every time they eat out. Perhaps the sooner others follow one restaurant's policy of increasing staff wages and discouraging tips, the better.

A **The need for one** arises not only from recent scandals concerning restaurant owners keeping all the money allotted for service on credit card bills, but also from reports that some waiters are disingenuously asking for their 10–20 percent in cash in order to avoid sharing it.

B While this is all very admirable, there's much talk within the restaurant trade of the need to bring in new legislation to protect both staff and customer interests. Were this to become a reality, issues such as these would become rarer.

C However, many are failing to provide even **this basic courtesy**, leading increasingly to restaurants demanding credit card details when booking and charging if prospective diners fail to appear without explanation. It is not personal. It is survival.

How did you do?

2 Check your answers.

3 Find phrases a and b in missing paragraphs A–C. Match them with the words and ideas they refer back to in the paragraph they follow in the article.

a 'this basic courtesy'

b 'The need for one'

4 Find phrases a and b in the article. Match them with the words and ideas they refer back to in the missing paragraph they follow.

a 'having to ask'

b 'the machinations of a business'

Strategies and skills

Using content clues

To decide whether a sentence fits a gap, you need to understand how a long text is organised. Ways of linking sections of text include the use of pronouns, linkers and other discourse markers, paraphrases in adjacent paragraphs and the addition of examples and other means of expanding on ideas.

1 Look at the bold phrases in the second part of each extract (1-6) below. Match them with the words or ideas they refer back to in the previous sentence.

> **TIP:** Some pronouns and reference words can refer backwards or forwards to a whole idea, not just a single word.

2 Look at the words in bold in the extracts again.

Which ones refer to

a concepts? _____

b places? _____

c things? _____

d qualities? _____

e activities? _____

_____

1

After four hours walking in torrential rain, I wouldn't have been wetter if I'd thrown myself in a lake. I reminded myself never to come on an expedition like this again.

But **I undoubtedly will**. I tend to have the same thought during any difficult moment while I'm away.

2

There were so many of the huge crabs making their way through the forest that it took extreme vigilance on my part to avoid treading on them.

This careful consideration, however, was not reciprocated and I could feel hard, sharp feet on my shoes and ankles the moment I stopped walking.

3

Monika's description of the town as a creative watering hole in the centre of a large desert seemed particularly harsh on the surrounding villages.

Many of them, in fact, were home to artists' studios and there was even the odd gallery here and there.

4

The scientists have been programming the robots to carry out a range of domestic tasks in order to demonstrate how adaptable and useful they can be.

As I watch, one expertly **manipulates a dustpan and brush to clean up a broken plate**.

5

It's fairly safe to say that most people have little idea of which direction they're facing when placed in unfamiliar surroundings. Deciding whether it's north, south, east or west would be little more than a guess.

People in certain societies, however, instinctively know their orientation in relation to **the points of the compass**, even in rooms without windows.

6

At the time of construction, the theatre was considered a masterpiece of modernist architecture. It was thought such a futuristic building would never date.

Clearly, we see the world through different eyes these days as **the style no longer lives up to its name**.

3 Choose the sentence (A or B) that follows on from each extract. How do you know?

1 Many think that, at best, it's actually just a strategy to reduce costs and boost sales rather than a genuine attempt to help save the planet. These days, saying how green you are pays.
   A Given the behaviour of many multinationals to date, it's hard to rule out such a cynical view.
   B This is one of the reasons why the industry is praised by many environmental campaigners.

2 Kinsella was curious about more or less everything and everyone she encountered, a characteristic that is clearly demonstrated by the variety of subject matter in her novels.
   A Indeed, each one of them has the same overall structure and flow.
   B While one tells of the life of a scientist, the next is about a child refugee.

3 Life on the island soon settled into a routine of sorts, one which would most probably have looked chaotic to outsiders.
   A It followed the ebb and flow of life rather than sticking to a rigid format.
   B They were made to feel welcome as soon as the boat arrived on the beach.

4 The creature lifted its huge head, took one look at the researchers who had set up their camera nearby, yawned and then promptly went back to sleep.
   A You don't need a doctorate to work out that this species is unbothered by human presence.
   B This documentary was an immediate success and has been shown on TV around the world.

SPEAKING BOOST

Discuss or answer.

1 How do you feel about public speaking in English? How would you prepare?
2 Do you tend to follow the rules or are you rebellious?

Understanding the structure of a text

A paragraph that fits a gap often adds more information to something that has been mentioned before, or may introduce a new idea which is mentioned again in the following paragraph.

4 Choose the correct paragraph (A–F) to fit each of the gaps (1–6).

> **TIP:** The correct sentence for a gap often adds a similar or contrasting idea to the previous sentence.

The performing arts should not only be available to children from better-off families. **(1)** _____ Some schools, unfortunately, have already started cutting them from the curriculum.

The debate about whether students should have compulsory art lessons has continued for years. **(2)** _____ As, of course, is the fact that the number of art teachers being trained is on a steady decline.

It's extraordinarily difficult to make it as a professional artist. **(3)** _____ I've no wish to knock this profession, but surely they should be given a chance, however slim it may be.

Funding for the arts has declined at a time when public interest has actually grown. **(4)** _____ There are other domains in which similar trends can be observed.

The price that the work of the world's more renowned artists is now fetching is ridiculous. **(5)** _____ These state that it's how much people are willing to pay that fixes the value rather than beauty.

But, of course, every artist has their own theory about the source of their creativity. **(6)** _____ Others focus internally, looking to tap into some deep inner resource.

A Without a conclusion ever having been reached in the argument, some education authorities have quietly removed the obligation of schools to provide them. This is of great concern.

B An example of this is the struggle facing the once well-resourced national film industry. In an era when cinema audiences are rising, financial support is heading in the opposite direction.

C How can anyone put their hand on their heart and say that one person's work is thousands of times better than another's? It's an absurd idea based on capitalist principles, not artistic merit.

D State education, therefore, should allow universal access to them. However, drama and music tend to be the first things to go when budgets get tight.

E In Greek mythology, it was thought to derive from the Muses, three goddesses who could be turned to for inspiration. This evolved for some into a certain special person whose presence sparks ideas.

F A result of this is that students who are highly gifted artistically are pushed towards teaching. The possibility of attaining anything else is, to all intents and purposes, denied them.

5 Read paragraphs A-F in Ex 4 again.

Which one(s)

1 explains a statement from the previous paragraph?

2 gives a single example of an idea from the previous paragraph?

3 reaches a conclusion based on an opinion in the previous paragraph?

4 gives the first in a sequence of two examples?

6 Match each sentence about the future of work (1-6) with the correct similar or contrasting idea (A-F) which follows it. Use the pronouns and reference words to help you.

1 The scenario in which someone spends their whole career in a single job has virtually disappeared.

2 The automation of certain roles has accelerated remarkably this century.

3 Some think we'll all end up, in effect, self-employed but working as though we're employed by a single company.

4 The difference between the pay of those at the bottom and at the top has grown consistently of late.

5 I can foresee the continuation of the trend for increasing numbers of employees working from home.

6 The point at which we retire has to increase, given how we're living in good health to a greater age.

A There must be some things, however, that even the most complex machine cannot do.

B Nevertheless, there will be many, especially those close to reaching that age, who object.

C There must soon come a point when both governments and low earners say enough is enough.

D Loyalty to one company or organisation seems as old-fashioned as travelling by steam engine.

E This not only cuts down on a company's costs but also, surprisingly, increases worker productivity.

F There's already growing resentment against this working relationship, so I can't see it becoming a reality.

7 Choose the correct phrases to link each second sentence to the first.

> **TIP:** The missing paragraph may add extra details about something that has already been mentioned before, or it may give a reason for something or an example. It is important to recognise how different phrases link ideas in texts.

1 And, of course, many associate the expansion of university education with a reduction in quality. **Although this may be true / Another factor to consider is** to an extent, there's no evidence that this is the case in the majority of instances.

2 Various studies have shown that the body clock naturally changes as we reach adolescence. **Instead of this / This explains why** teenagers wake up late – it's not due to laziness; it's because of their internal chemistry.

3 Many employees continue to work while surrounded by distracting background noise. **Doing so / This means that it** has been shown to be harmful in the long term to individuals' mental health.

4 Many urge parents to drastically limit the screen time their children are able to have. **A perfect example of this / A perhaps unexpected result of this** is that parents rediscover the fun activities that they come up with as alternatives.

5 Research into the dolphins' behaviour is still in its early stages. **What's already become obvious / A very good reason for this** is that it's far more complex than even the most experienced scientists guessed.

6 Expecting profits to grow year on year is simply not sustainable. **One possible explanation of this is / I would therefore propose that** we need a completely new approach to growth and consumerism.

SPEAKING BOOST

Discuss or answer.

1 Describe the plot from the most recent book you read or film you saw.

2 How would you define a good story?

You are going to read an article about cycling in the Netherlands. Six paragraphs have been removed from the article. Choose from the paragraphs A–G the one which fits each gap (1–6). There is one extra paragraph which you do not need to use.

A   Her sentiments encapsulate the motivation behind the drive to get people out of their cars and into cycling and public transport. The goal is to make sure using these methods of transport is as straightforward and comfortable as possible.

B   This bold claim acknowledges the fact that cycling addresses not only congestion in cities but also the mental and physical health of their residents. It brings communities together and helps the environment. This perhaps explains the weight of the enthusiasm behind it in the Netherlands.

C   An essential part of the strategy she outlines is the development of cycling facilities at rail terminals. The national railway service is currently investing tens of millions of euros in bike parking to attract motorists from their cars.

D   Many other Dutch cities are following her example by also pushing for increased help with investment from central government. Most are being met with the same positive response, even if the exact amounts involved differ from place to place.

E   This record-breaking development forms part of a strategy in which hundreds of millions of euros are being devoted to enhancing cycling facilities across the Netherlands. It's a country that's so fervent about its two-wheelers that it is applying to the United Nations to add cycling to its inventory of cultural heritage.

F   Over a century later, 125,000 cyclists go through its centre to reach work, school or the station. It's no surprise then that the world's largest bike park sits perfectly in this global cycling city.

G   In the largest conurbations of Amsterdam, Rotterdam, The Hague and Utrecht, however, cycling is more common. In addition, the four main cities are predicted to expand so therefore the need for greener transport is likely to rise, as is demand for public transport.

The rise and rise of cycling

In a nation with more bikes than people, finding a space to park one can be a problem. The Dutch city of Utrecht is unveiling an answer at its railway station on Monday morning: the world's largest multi-storey parking area for bicycles. The concrete-and-glass structure holds three floors of gleaming double-decker racks with space for 12,500 bikes, from cargo bikes that hold a whole family to public transport bikes that are available for rent.

1	

This obsession for all things bike-related is deeply embedded in national political policy. 'We are striving to make it a cyclists' paradise and there's still much to be done,' said Stientje Van Veldhoven, a junior infrastructure minister. 'I'd like us to make better use of what I call this secret weapon against congestion, poor air quality in cities and climate change that is also good for your health and your wallet.'

2	

Key to achieving this aim, according to Van Veldhoven, is that 'it needs to be very easy to park your bike as close to the train as possible – and you don't want to be looking for half an hour for a space.' According to the Dutch Statistics Office, across the nation 60 percent of all trips to work in the Netherlands are made by car and just a quarter by bike.

3	

'In the next ten years, 500,000 more people will come to urbanised areas, and if all of those people bring their car then we are going to have massive congestion,' said Van Veldhoven. 'So investment in public transport, cycling lanes and cycle parking facilities is crucial to keep this area that's essential for our national economy moving.'

4	

According to its spokesman, Geert Koolen, 'We have over one million passengers a day and in our bigger cities more than half arrive at the station by bike. At Dutch stations there are some 490,000 parking spaces for bikes.' Utrecht is at the forefront of promoting cycling as part of a 'healthy urban living' policy. 'We are counting on biking as a healthy and sustainable form of transport for a growing city,' said the deputy mayor, Victor Everhardt. 'Cycling is in the genes of people from Utrecht and in 1885 it built the Netherlands' first bike lane.'

5	

The scale of Dutch investments shows cycling is about more than just the issue of transportation, according to BYCS, a social enterprise behind a network of international cycling schemes. 'The bike park in Utrecht shows you need massive investments into cycling infrastructure: parking, cycle lanes and great architecture, but we believe this is one of the most impactful things a city can do,' said its strategy director, Adam Stones.

6	

But some experts sound a note of caution. Although the Fietsersbond, a Dutch cycling organisation, warmly welcomes the investment, it warns that it is irritating and counterproductive when bike parks are combined with a no-tolerance policy to on-street parking – as in central Amsterdam, where 'wild' parked bikes are confiscated. 'I am not a fan of this,' said its director, Saskia Kluit. 'Parked bikes give the street liveliness and movement, and if you want the benefit of the cyclist shopping, it's better if they can stop anywhere they want.'

ABOUT THE TASK

- In Reading and Use of English Part 8, you read one long text which is divided into different sections, or up to six (but usually four) shorter texts all on the same topic.

- There are ten questions to answer. These take the form of either questions or statements about information or ideas in the text or texts.

- You have to match each question or statement with the correct section of the long text, or the relevant short text.

- Questions or statements can be about detailed information in the text, or about the writer's attitude or opinion.

- Remember that the information or opinions will be phrased in different ways in the questions or statements and the text.

- Each question is worth one mark.

Practice task

1 You are going to read an extract from an article about surfing in northern California. For questions a–e, choose from the sections in the article (A or B). The sections may be chosen more than once.

Which section

a mentions a specific aspect of weather that surfers would hope for?

b says that the effects of climate change aren't welcomed by the majority of people?

c suggests that surfing is a risky activity wherever it is done?

d states that what is causing changes at Mavericks has an influence all around the world?

e reveals that weather changes at Mavericks are unpredictable?

How did you do?

2 Check your answers.

3 Match the highlighted sections of text from the first paragraph of the article (1 and 2) to the questions in Ex 1.

4 Choose the correct words and phrases to complete the sentences.

1 The highlighted sections **use / don't use** the same words as the options.

2 The correct meaning is given in **a few words / a larger chunk** of the text.

3 You sometimes have to work out from **your own knowledge / the context** which paragraph the option matches.

5 Read section B of the article again. Highlight the sections of text which relate to questions a, c and e in Ex 1.

6 Answer the questions.

1 Do the answers occur in the same order in the text as in the questions?

2 How do we know that the text suggests surfing is risky everywhere?

3 Which words and phrases help you work out that the weather is unpredictable at Mavericks?

A rare benefit of **climate change**

A Mavericks is one of the world's most famous surfing spots. Located on the San Mateo County coast in northern California, surfers from far and wide flock to Mavericks, drawn by some of the biggest (and most dangerous!) waves in the world, which regularly come to shore there. Its popularity as a surfing destination has grown further in recent times thanks to an unusual ally: climate change. A weather phenomenon known as El Niño is causing changes to local weather patterns. [1]El Niño is a naturally occurring weather cycle which can affect climactic conditions on both a local and a global scale. Its consequences are thought to be becoming more intense and more frequent as a direct result of human-induced climate change. [2]While these variations in weather patterns are bad news for many, the increased regularity and proximity to shore of El Niño-related storms is providing a more frequent, and more powerful, supply of waves for surfers in this part of northern California.

B Before novice surfers worldwide start buying tickets to northern California in order to ride their dream wave, it's worth noting that even the most seasoned surfers have had difficulties taming the sea conditions there. Garrett McNamara, a professional surfer who once held the world record for riding the biggest wave, injured himself while surfing at Mavericks after being hit by a massive wave. As when practising their sport in any location, surfers at Mavericks should proceed with caution and listen carefully to advice from locals who understand the sea and weather conditions better than anyone. While El Niño provides the attractive waves that surfers crave, it can also bring the wrong kind of winds. Ideal conditions at Mavericks include light winds from the north, which help surfers glide nicely down the face of a huge wave. Anything other than that can be dangerous, and the rapid alteration which brings about these perfect conditions for surfing can suddenly vary just as swiftly in the opposite sense.

TEST

Strategies and skills

Identifying paraphrase

Information in a text is usually phrased quite differently from the corresponding details in the questions. You therefore need to scan very carefully to find the answers, especially as the details in the question may be mentioned in more than one section.

> **TIP:** More than one section might mention the idea in the question. Some of these are distractors (incorrect information) that might tempt you into putting the wrong answer. You need to review all of the information relating to that idea to work out which is the correct answer.

1 Match each question (1–8) with the correct paraphrase (a–h).

In which paraphrase does the reviewer

1 make a comparison with the author's other work?

2 criticise the author's depth of research?

3 show agreement with one of the author's claims?

4 suggest that some of the topics the author includes in the book are strange?

5 comment on the geographical scope included in the book?

6 give the opinion that the author has been influenced by the work of other people?

7 wonder whether Tierney would be equally good at writing about other topics?

8 speculate how the author decided on the sequence of the chapters?

a I found little I could argue against when it came to Tierney's contentions regarding political bias in the media.

b It's admirable that Tierney has chosen contexts from around the globe to illustrate his points, rather than sticking close to home.

c There's little apparent logic to the order in which the sections appear. I can only assume he chose this by drawing them out of a hat.

d While Tierney undoubtedly writes beautifully, he appears to have spent little time finding factual support for the claims he makes.

e Perhaps Tierney's authorial skills might be put to just as effective use in creating works on social justice or capitalism.

f Although it bears a vague resemblance to Tierney's previous titles, he has made great progress as a writer, stylistically.

g I feel that Tierney's book owes a particular debt to two of the twentieth century's most perceptive political commentators.

h I'm sure that Tierney had a motive for choosing to write chapters on sport and television. What this was is quite beyond me.

2 Highlight the sections of the paraphrases (a–h) in Ex 1 that give you the answers.

3 Read the two texts about setting up a business and answer the questions.

A What I'd stress as an absolute necessity is borrowing as little as you possibly can to get set up. Had I followed my own advice, my first business venture would never have failed. It ended up being a valuable lesson, but not one I'd wish on others. It's also worth bearing in mind all the conflicting evidence you'll find online about the best way to start up a business. If I'm not convinced that it's written by someone who has actually done it and succeeded, I tend to ignore it. It's incredibly easy to write about theory, but another thing entirely to have put it into practice. Finding the right staff can also be a steep learning curve. I would estimate that I've employed four staff I'd rather have not bothered with for every one that really knew what they were doing. There's a lot to be said for following your own instincts when you're doing this. Value someone who is genuine over someone who talks a lot but has little to actually say.

B The biggest mistake people make at the beginning is assuming that their business will be flourishing within a few weeks of opening. This does happen, of course, but only to a small minority of start-ups. The others generally fall into one of two categories: they either follow the long, steady road to profitability or the long, slow decline into failure. You'll soon know which road you're on if you trust your instincts. What I'd also emphasise is the need to get some enjoyment out of the process. It's inevitable that a lot of hours and worry will be involved at first, but try to avoid letting it overwhelm you. Try to see the difficulties you're bound to face as challenges and opportunities to learn rather than impossible problems. Build in time for other out-of-work activities too. After all, one of the aims of setting up your own business is to provide you with more freedom, not less.

1 Find a section about trusting or following your own instinct in each text. What do these relate to in each case?

2 Which text matches with this statement?

'You should believe what your feelings are telling you about how well your business is likely to do.'

3 Which text matches with these statements? Highlight the relevant section of text for each one.

a I was unsuccessful at business before I finally succeeded.

b Spend time away from your business.

c Trust only those who have achieved what you're attempting to do.

d My success rate at one important aspect of running a business hasn't been very good.

e It's a good idea not to be overly optimistic to start off with.

4 Read the two texts about ways of making money for charity and answer the questions which follow.

A I had a great deal of fun raising money. I decided that I'd do something really eye-catching, as I felt that would attract more donors. I also thought people would be liable to give more if they felt there was an element of risk to what I was doing. That's why I settled on doing a parachute jump, and it certainly seemed to bear fruit as I made well over £5,000. I'm an introvert so the prospect of pressuring people for money was quite alarming, but I soon developed what was almost like a script, which somehow gave me more confidence when I was explaining what it was all about. The event itself was terrifying as I've been afraid of heights for as long as I can remember. It's a bit of a paradox in a way, as I'm absolutely over the moon that it's done, yet I have this nagging desire to go and do it all over again.

B My starting point for choosing what to do to raise money was simple: what would make the most and be simple and cheap to organise and carry out? I elected to do a seven-day cycle ride from one end of the country to the other. I already had pretty much everything I needed to do it so there were minimal costs involved. I also felt that doing an endurance event, which might be difficult for most members of the general public, would encourage donors to be more generous. I don't think there was a single part of the whole exercise I didn't enjoy. I work in sales, so I'm used to persuading people to part with their money. I'm also a very keen cyclist and had wanted to undertake something like that for years but could never really justify taking that much time out. Generating income for a climate change charity campaign provided just the justification I needed to take it on, and I have no regrets for having done so.

1 What did each writer think would make people donate more?

2 Who thought that an activity which incorporated personal danger would bring in more money?

3 Which writer
   a thinks their professional experience made part of their task easier?
   b devised a way to help them overcome a natural tendency?
   c mentions what the proceeds of their fundraising would be used for?
   d explains why it took so long to do the activity they chose?
   e describes a confusing outcome of their charity work?

4 Highlight the relevant section of text for each question in 3 (a–e).

SPEAKING BOOST

Discuss or answer.

1 What would you give up or dare to do to help combat climate change?

2 Why do you think there are so many climate change deniers despite the scientific evidence?

Avoiding distraction

In Part 8, you don't need to read each text carefully before you look for the answers to the questions. A more effective method is to use your skimming and scanning skills to focus on finding the information you need.

> **TIP:** Skim the sections or texts quickly first, then read each question in turn, then scan the sections or texts again to find the relevant information to answer the questions.

5 Scan the text. Complete the following tasks quickly.

1 Highlight where the writer mentions receiving praise.

2 Explain in your own words what the writer says about the praise.

3 Highlight where the writer identifies a problem with their own attitude.

4 Explain in your own words what the writer says about this problem.

The interview could have gone better, to be honest. I'd prepared every last detail in the days running up to it, but somehow just couldn't perform to the standard I was hoping for. I guess that's the downside of setting yourself such high expectations: you're never likely to be able to meet them in reality. The chair of the panel commended me on how I'd done on the way out of the interview room. I found it quite difficult to work out whether she actually meant it or if it was something she said to every candidate, no matter how well they'd performed.

> **TIP:** Remember that there may be information about the same topic in two or more of the sections or texts. The incorrect ones are distractors and may distract you away from the correct answer.

6 Scan the text. Complete the following tasks quickly.

1 Highlight where the writer identifies the methods of rebuilding ancient objects.

2 Explain in your own words what the writer says about how this was done.

3 Highlight where the writer mentions a reason for reaching a conclusion about something.

4 Explain in your own words what the writer says about this.

It wasn't the first occasion I'd done research in the field, but this project was the most comprehensive when it came to organising and collating what we found. We were digging in what appeared to be an ancient palace of some sort. The size of the building and the nature of what we were finding in it meant it was unlikely to be anything other than a home to the wealthiest and most important residents of the city. As each piece of metal or broken pot was extracted from the ground, a whole team of researchers descended. It was cleaned, photographed and had its details uploaded onto the project database within a matter of minutes. More senior researchers then set about piecing together the fragments into more complete items, both electronically and in reality.

7 Scan the three sections of the extract below about going back to a place from the writer's childhood. Find the information in questions 1–6 quickly.

In which section (A–C) does the writer

1 comment on an observation made by adults during his childhood?
2 describe how a walk from one place to another seemed as a child?
3 give a possible reason for wanting to return to his old house?
4 suggest he got into trouble with someone when he was a child?
5 mention a motivation for spending a long time in someone's house?
6 doubt his own ability to do something?

RETURNING TO MY
roots

A Recently, I revisited the village where I spent the first nine years of my life for the first time since we moved away. There's nothing remarkable about that, I guess, but it somehow felt like a highly significant journey; a coming of age. I've reached that point in my own life when I find myself reflecting on my childhood a great deal. Perhaps the birth of my first child acted as a trigger for my thinking back. So, one sunny April morning, I found myself parking at the bottom of the small hill where I used to live. I lived in the house at the top, but approaching it by car felt wrong. I needed to walk past each of the three houses below mine slowly, as I had 25 years before, contemplating each of the friends who used to live in them. I wondered if any of them still lived there, and whether I'd have the courage to knock on the doors to find out.

B What struck me most forcefully at first was how small it was. My recent recollections took place in a land of giant houses with endless fields beyond. Now I was faced with a row of ordinary looking homes that certainly bore a resemblance to what I remembered, but were on a totally different scale. The wheat field opposite, where I'd spent many a happy Saturday playing hide-and-seek and escaping the attention of the farmer, usually unsuccessfully, had been replaced by a new housing estate. The field at the top was still there, but the opposite side of it appeared to be only a stone's throw from my old house. Crossing that field had felt like a major expedition when I was eight. There was a part of me that just wanted to climb back into my car and go home, yet a stronger, clearer voice was urging me to start climbing the hill, as I had done countless times so many years ago.

C I began the slow ascent. First came the Moodys' house. Memories of a birthday party there flooded back, stuffing as much cake as I could into my mouth before heading into the back garden to play. Then there was the Woods' place. They had a model railway that I had spent hours admiring. And finally, the Batemans', where my best friend George lived. Every day after school, we'd end up at one or other of our houses, out on the street together or in the fields. Our parents used to joke that there was an invisible piece of string joining us together. Yet as soon as my family moved away, we lost touch and moved on to new adventures, almost as though none of what came before had ever happened. Then, finally, I was outside our old house. The tree my mum had planted in the front lawn was certainly a whole lot bigger. I stood there, unable to move.

Understanding implication

Sometimes an exact meaning is not stated directly or paraphrased in the text, but you can infer it: other information makes it clear what the text is saying.

8 Read the extracts (1–6) and choose the option (A–C) that you can infer from what each writer says.

1   It was the time of the year when the days start to lengthen and the cold edge that had been present in the wind for the previous four months gently softens to something almost resembling warmth. Whenever I passed a mirror, I would catch myself smiling.

The writer
A   has enjoyed the past few months of warmer weather.
B   is pleased that the wind has finally stopped blowing.
C   has had their spirits lifted by the change of season.

2   If you've only ever seen the island on a map, it appears to be relatively close to the nearest land as there's only a centimetre of blue between them. A six-day journey there in an old fishing boat, however, soon put me straight on that particular belief.

The writer says that
A   the island was more isolated than they imagined.
B   they weren't sure how to get to the island.
C   the map of the area around the island was inaccurate.

3   The number of likes that the video received followed the inevitable pattern: a surge in the first few days followed by a slow descent thereafter. As much as I willed it otherwise, it refused to go miraculously viral.

The writer was
A   surprised by how well received the video was to begin with.
B   disappointed by the overall popularity of the video.
C   confused by the video's unusual profile of online likes.

4   Then the reality hit me: not only would there never again be a safe and predictable pay cheque at the end of the month, but I also had little or no idea how to actually run the farm I had just bought.

The writer is
A   looking forward to earning more than previously.
B   annoyed about something they have been sold.
C   uncertain about a decision they have made.

5   The ticket inspector had turned an unusual shade of red. Unless I'm much mistaken, he appeared to be staring at the roof of the carriage and counting slowly and silently to ten.

The ticket inspector
A   was working out how much a passenger had to pay.
B   was worried about the state of the train carriage.
C   was angry and was trying to calm himself down.

6   We watch nature documentaries with wonder as they show how, in the absence of language, different species signal to one another using colour. Doing so saves lives, for example, when a potential predator is spared being poisoned by the bright colouration of toxic prey. Little do we realise that our own lives are just as dependent on colour.

The writer suggests that
A   people don't fully appreciate the importance of colour.
B   people don't really understand how nature works.
C   people aren't sufficiently grateful for being able to use language.

You are going to read an article in which five writers give advice about getting a book published. For questions 1–10, choose from the writers (A–E). The writers may be chosen more than once.

Which writer makes the following statements?

It's important that the story develops quickly.	1 ☐
Being rejected happens to all first-time novelists.	2 ☐
An effective main character must have certain characteristics.	3 ☐
I considered having the book printed myself but eventually decided not to.	4 ☐
You should send your book to certain publishers first.	5 ☐
I got some essential advice at a chance meeting.	6 ☐
I'd recommend avoiding imitating other authors' styles.	7 ☐
A book must have at least one memorable element.	8 ☐
I found the perfect person to comment on my book as it was being written.	9 ☐
Some publishers are more concerned about risk than others.	10 ☐

Getting your first novel published

Are you a writer hoping to get your first novel published?
We've asked five experienced writers to give some tips on how to go about it.

Writer A

Getting your first novel published is always hard. Publishers these days have to be absolutely convinced that a book will make money before they take it on, especially if they haven't got a best-selling author contracted to them or published a series based on the same popular hero, and therefore have little spare cash to play with. Most writers have spent at least a year putting a book together, almost always while holding down another job at the same time in order to pay the bills. It's honestly worth investing an extra couple of months in editing it yourself and getting it to as good a state as you possibly can. It's staggering the number of improvements you'll find, and anything that helps to win over a difficult-to-please publisher will be time well spent. And prepare yourself to be disappointed many times over; it's an inevitable part of the process for everyone.

Writer B

When my first novel was finally accepted for publication, I'd already sent it to at least twenty publishers. Knowing whether it'll be accepted by the first or the fiftieth, or not at all, is an impossibility. What you need to ensure is that at least one aspect of your novel – plot, characters (especially the main ones), context, style – provides something totally original. If so, it will stick in the mind of the publisher far more than something that's relatively formulaic. They have very little time to read the work that's submitted to them, because they receive a lot and you can't generally read a novel in a few hours. It's also worth being aware that different publishing houses are known to focus on particular genres of fiction, so carefully research who is most likely to publish the type of book you've written and prioritise them.

Writer C

I was convinced my first novel was worthy of publication and was perplexed as to why I wasn't getting any response from publishers. Then, out of the blue, I got talking to someone at a party who acts as an agent for authors and she pointed out the necessity of including a covering letter with the manuscript, which I'd consistently failed to do. The next publisher I sent the book to snapped it up, so it clearly worked. What I was most proud of in my first and subsequent novels was the pace of the action. I'd heard that one of the main reasons publishers turn books down is that things move at too pedestrian a pace. I must admit that as a reader I soon lose interest in novels like that, so I go along with using this among their criteria for selection.

Writer D

I prefer reading and writing the kind of novel that develops gradually and subtly, so found it hard to accept when publishers said in their rejection letters that readers would only go for a fast-moving thriller, and not for a novel such as mine. I eventually found a publisher who shared my way of thinking and my debut novel was published last year. It's crucial to be true to your own way of writing rather than adapting it to appear like someone else's simply to get into print. I'd heard that a lot of people were self-publishing work, so thought about heading down that path for a while. Not knowing anyone whose novel had become successful that way was what put me off in the end. I'm pleased now that I decided to stick with the traditional route.

Writer E

I almost fell off my chair in shock when the third publisher I'd sent my novel to said yes. I'd heard so many horror stories of authors working their way through every single publisher in the country and getting nothing but refusals from them all. Most of these poor writers ended up publishing it themselves via printing companies they'd found online. The key to my success was having someone read and critically appraise my work as I wrote it. It's essential that this isn't someone you're particularly close to, as that way they won't be too careful about hurting your feelings. What I'd also recommend is that the central figure in the novel has to create their own destiny and not be someone who just goes along with events and things that happen to them. Every great story has this at its core.

TEST

- Writing Part 1 is compulsory, so you have no choice in what you write about.
- The task asks you to write an essay on a given topic.
- The task includes a question or statement with three bullet points that relate to it.
- You are then given a set of three opinions about the question or statement, one about each of the bullet points.
- You have to discuss two of the bullet points in your response.
- It is essential to include ideas that are relevant to the topic.

- You can include the two opinions you are given about the bullet points you choose, but you do not have to. You can also add new opinions of your own.
- You should organise your essay into clear paragraphs and have an introduction and a conclusion.
- Your essay should be written in a formal or neutral style.
- You should try to use a variety of vocabulary and language structures.
- You need to write between 220 and 260 words.

Practice task

1 Read the essay task and write a first draft of your essay.

Your class has watched a documentary on the impact of tourism on a city. You have made the notes below:

Concerns about the impact of tourism on a city

- economic dependence on tourism
- quality of life for residents
- the environment

Some opinions expressed in the documentary:

'We want industries other than tourism to thrive.'

'The city's always so busy!'

'Air pollution and litter are becoming a real problem.'

Write an essay discussing **two** of the concerns about tourism in your notes. You should **explain which issue is more important**, giving reasons in support of your answer.

Write your answer in **220-260** words in an appropriate style.

How did you do?

2 Read the example essay and notes below and compare it with your draft.

3 How could you improve your draft?

The first paragraph is a general introduction which gives a brief summary of the topic.

The third paragraph discusses the second of the bullet point issues that you chose to write about. This will often be a contrast to the other one, so you can put forward both sides of an argument.

Linking words introduce contrasting ideas.

Tourism is one of the fastest growing industries worldwide, generating vast amounts of money for cities that prove popular with tourists. However, as well as the benefits that it brings, tourism can also have undesirable consequences.

The main argument used to defend large-scale tourism is how much wealth it brings to the local area. The principal beneficiaries are hotels, shops, restaurants, museums and local transport operators. Whilst tourism can benefit the area, it can also lead to the local economy becoming dependent on one sector, rather than a broad range of industries.

Additionally, although tourism provides jobs for local people, it can negatively affect their quality of life. Cities that are popular with tourists are busy all year round, so residents must cope with constantly crowded roads and public transport systems. The popularity of the city pushes up prices, not only for day-to-day goods such as food and clothing, but also for housing. So, although residents may make money as a result of tourism, they have to spend more because of it.

On balance, it could be argued that tourism has more positive consequences than negative. The wealth it brings is beyond doubt. However, efforts should be made to relieve the hardships faced by local people as a result. Controlling housing costs, for example, would be a step in the right direction.

226 words

The second paragraph discusses the first of the bullet point issues that you chose to write about.

The writer adds reasons to support their opinions.

The final paragraph is the conclusion.

In the conclusion, the writer gives their opinion on the issues that were discussed.

Strategies and skills

Structuring an essay

Structure your essay clearly so that the reader is taken logically through your ideas. Your introduction should engage the reader and outline the issues you will be discussing. Don't include specific details, as these should be included in the main paragraphs.

1 Read the exam task below and choose the best introduction (A-C).

> Your class has attended a panel discussion on increasing government funding for certain university courses. You have made the notes below:

> **Which university subjects should receive increased government funding?**
> - business studies
> - art
> - teacher training
>
> Some opinions expressed in the discussion:
> 'Business is the future of employment in this country.'
> 'Many people see art as a luxury, but I think it's essential.'
> 'Schools should be responsible for training teachers, not universities.'

A Government funding for university courses is essential. This is because without it, very few people would be able to go to university as they would have to pay the whole cost of the course, whether they are studying business studies or training to be a teacher.

B The government has limited resources to spend on education. It must therefore think carefully about which university courses will benefit the country most, and target funds towards these. It's my opinion that business studies is the most appropriate course to increase funding for.

C Governments face a difficult task when deciding which university courses should receive increased financial support. As the world changes, so do the needs of the country. Therefore, careful consideration should be given to how universities can best help meet these needs.

2 Read the opinions expressed in the task in Ex 1 again. Which opinions do you think are most convincing? Which two subjects would you choose to discuss in your essay?

> **TIP:** You can use examples in your essay to support your opinions and to help give reasons for what you discuss.

3 Read the example essay below answering the task in Ex 1 and identify the following features.

1 linking words and expressions
2 passive structures
3 some reasons
4 the writer's opinion about the main issue

Governments face a difficult task when deciding which university courses should receive increased financial support. As the world changes, so do the needs of the country. Therefore, careful consideration should be given to how universities can best help meet these needs.

First of all, let us consider business studies. As many countries move away from manufacturing and towards more service-based industries, the study of business has become increasingly important. The proportion of national income related to business has increased considerably, so preparing more young people academically in this critical discipline would appear to be a sensible strategy.

In contrast, art and other cultural activities have failed to develop in terms of what they offer to the country as a whole. While trained artists are undoubtedly essential for the cultural health of the country, a far smaller number of people are required to fulfil the nation's cultural needs. As the sector has grown little, if at all, it would perhaps be unwise to channel further public money into the subject, especially when looked at alongside growth industries such as business.

In summary, therefore, it would be ideal if funding were increased for every course currently on offer at universities around the country. However, given the financial limitations that the government is working with, any additional financial support should be targeted towards thriving vocational sectors such as business, even if that is at the expense of the arts. The programmes of study that obtain more funding should be the ones which best meet the country's needs.

4 Why are each of the features (1-4) in Ex 3 important in an essay?

5 Read the example essay in Ex 3 again. Choose the correct words to complete the sentences.

1 The essay uses **formal** / **informal** language.
2 There are **several** / **no** contractions.
3 The tone is **serious** / **chatty**.
4 The essay is written for **a general** / **an academic** audience.

Linkers help to structure your ideas by showing whether ideas support each other or give a contrast.

> **TIP:** Remember that different linkers are used in different ways in sentences. Learn how to use each one.

6 Choose the correct linkers to add or contrast ideas in the sentences.

1 **Although / However / Despite** having many friends is essential for a lot of people, others prefer to have just a few.

2 National parks provide an important refuge for wildlife **additionally / in addition to / in addition** being fantastic tourist attractions.

3 The latest technology is often extremely expensive. **While / Nevertheless / Therefore**, those who feel compelled to buy each new model as it appears will end up spending a lot of money.

4 Many people fail the test, **despite / however / even though** they spend many months preparing for it.

5 **Despite / Instead / However** the undoubted benefits that tourism brings, there are many negatives for residents of popular towns and cities.

6 Encouraging students to develop more independence helps them greatly with their homework. **Furthermore, / Too, / As well,** it will prepare them well for university, should they choose to go.

Using phrases to help structure your essay helps to make your ideas clearer to follow.

7 Match the phrases used for structuring an essay (1-14) with the correct functions (a-d).

1	Additionally	a	Introducing the first point
2	All in all		
3	Another reason is	b	Introducing further points
4	Finally		
5	First of all	c	Introducing the last point
6	Firstly		
7	In conclusion	d	Introducing the conclusion
8	Last but not least		
9	Lastly		
10	Moreover		
11	Next		
12	The first reason is		
13	Thirdly		
14	To sum up		

Complex sentences

In formal writing such as essays, try to use complex sentences to make your writing more formal and academic. Use linkers, relative clauses and conjunctions.

8 Join the simple sentences together to make more complex sentences using suitable words and phrases. Use the word in brackets to help you, or choose other ways of linking if you wish.

1 Eating lots of sugar is not recommended. Sugar causes several serious illnesses.

Eating lots of sugar is not recommended _____ causes several serious illnesses. (**since**)

2 Roads in many cities are very narrow. They were designed for horses and carts, not traffic.

Roads in many cities are very narrow, _____ being designed for modern traffic. (**due to**)

3 Money shouldn't be spent on space exploration. It should go towards dealing with environmental issues.

Money should be spent on environmental issues _____ being spent on space exploration. (**rather than**)

4 Many businesses are losing money. They continue to use the same business model.

Many businesses continue to use the same business model, _____ losing money. (**despite the fact**)

5 The book has an original storyline. That's why it's so successful.

The book is so successful _____ such an original storyline. (**because of**)

6 Many museums need extensive investment. They will be forced to close if they don't get it.

Many museums will be forced to close _____ . (**without**)

Using formal language

9 Match the informal sentences (1-8) with their more formal equivalents (a-h).

1 We need to think about what might happen.

2 To start with, I'd like to talk about why this happened.

3 This can really help people to find out more about it.

4 You can do this in lots of different ways.

5 It is difficult for lots of us to do.

6 It takes ages to become good at it.

7 It'll definitely cause the prices to go up really quickly.

8 It's important to give everyone a chance to say what they think.

a Developing expertise in this can take a considerable amount of time.

b Firstly, the reasons for this situation will be discussed.

c Every opportunity should be offered for people to express their opinions.

d There are many different methods for achieving this.

e The consequences must be considered.

f Many individuals find this a challenge.

g Rapid rises in the cost are then inevitable.

h It can be highly beneficial for understanding the issue.

TIP: Use formal words, phrases and structures in an essay, and avoid informal language including contractions.

Impersonal sentences

In an essay, it's better to avoid using *I*, *me*, *we* and *us*. Use impersonal sentences instead, and talk about people and topics in general.

10 Complete the impersonal ways of expressing ideas with the phrases in the box.

> considered to be
> is a fairly widespread phenomenon
> is one proposal
> others have been
> the majority of people

1 Like many others, I find that having a clear aim really motivates me.

Of course, _____ find that having a clear aim is a great motivation.

2 I really think that top sports stars are generally great role models for young people.

Top sports stars are generally _____ great role models for young people.

3 I would consider limiting car ownership to one per family.

Limiting car ownership to one per family _____ that is worth considering.

4 I've done well in a capitalist society but many people haven't been so lucky.

Capitalist societies allow certain citizens to flourish but _____ less fortunate.

5 I don't personally think I spend too much time on social media but many people my age do.

Overuse of social media _____ , especially in some age groups.

EXAM TASK

Read the task and write your essay. You should explain which way is more important, <u>giving reasons</u> in support of your answer.

Write your answer in 220-260 words in an appropriate style.

> Your class has attended a panel discussion on improving people's health nationally. You have made the notes below:

> **<u>Ways to improve people's health throughout the country:</u>**
> * additional gyms and sports centres
> * ban on advertising unhealthy food
> * school lessons on healthy living

> Some opinions expressed in the discussion:
>
> 'People often join gyms but give up going after a couple of weeks.'
>
> 'There are so many adverts for food which isn't good for you.'
>
> 'Parents, not schools, should be teaching children about healthy living.'

ABOUT THE TASK

- In Writing Part 2, you choose one question to answer from a choice of three. One of these may be a proposal. These are formal or semi-formal depending on the context.

- You write a proposal in order to offer solutions to a problem, or put forward a plan or idea for a project of some sort.

- Details of what you are writing the proposal for are given to you in the task. These will include information about who you are writing to and what the proposal is about.

- You must read the information about the proposal very carefully. You will lose marks if you write about the wrong thing.

- The aim of the proposal is to persuade the reader to agree to your solutions or plan. You therefore have to use persuasive language.

- You need to organise your proposal effectively into sections and paragraphs. You should have a clear introduction, a detailed section outlining the content of your proposal and a summary or conclusion at the end.

- You can use headings to clearly define the sections.

- Your proposal should be between 220 and 260 words long.

Practice task

1 Read the task and write a first draft of your proposal. Write 220–260 words in an appropriate style.

> The council in the town where you live would like to fund activities organised by residents for next month's World Environment Day. You decide to write a proposal for the town council, explaining what activity you would like to organise and why, saying how you will organise it, and outlining how the activity could benefit local people.

How did you do?

2 Read the example proposal and compare it with your draft.

3 Complete the boxes in the example proposal with the correct number in the box.

> 1 Give a reason for the final point in the task.
> 2 Summarise the points the proposal will cover.
> 3 Justify why your proposal should be chosen.
> 4 Use emotive vocabulary to persuade.
> 5 Add detail to the second point in the task.
> 6 Respond to the first point in the task.
> 7 Include headings.
> 8 State the reason for writing the proposal.
> 9 Use persuasive language.
> 10 Mention other suggestions in a negative light.

4 How could you improve your draft?

Introduction

The aim of this proposal is to suggest an activity that could take place in the town on World Environment Day. The proposal will include details of the activity, an outline of how it could be organised, and a summary of how it will benefit local people.

The proposed activity

World Environment Day is aimed at raising awareness of environmental issues. I would therefore like to propose organising a march through the town centre. I am convinced that this would be the best possible activity for achieving this aim, as everyone in the town would know about whether they joined it or not. A concert or similar event, whilst a good idea in principle, would affect only those in attendance and would therefore be less effective.

The organisation of the activity

The event would need publicity, which would be done via social media and a poster campaign around the town. Road closures would be necessary, which could be arranged in conjunction with the council.

The benefits

The event will benefit not only local people but everyone around the world. Each small thing that is done to encourage people to take the threat to the environment seriously is beneficial for our precious planet.

Conclusion

I would urge you to consider this proposal favourably, as it would be a fitting and effective means of celebrating World Environment Day as a town, united against the dangers faced by our beautiful world.

239 words

Strategies and skills
Using persuasive language
The point of a proposal is to persuade the reader to go along with your ideas or recommendations. You therefore have to use persuasive language in certain parts of your proposal. Effective writers often use emotive adjectives and adverbs to make their writing more persuasive.

1 Read the extract from a proposal about saving a building. Highlight the adjectives and adverbs that are used to persuade readers.

> Although this unique building requires a substantial amount of work, it is my sincere belief that investing in it will be immensely beneficial to the town. Even in its current state of disrepair, it is a much-loved landmark that would undoubtedly be transformed into a potentially lucrative attraction if it were restored.

2 Complete the extract from a proposal to put a wildflower garden on a piece of college land. Use appropriate emotive adjectives and adverbs.

TIP: Be careful not to repeat adjectives or adverbs in the same text, as this sounds very repetitive and can make it seem like you have a narrow vocabulary.

The space is relatively small but is close to the outdoor seating areas used by students to relax, eat and drink during their breaks. The addition of a **(1)** _____ wildflower garden nearby would have a **(2)** _____ **(3)** _____ effect on their mood and therefore on their performance at college. Having an **(4)** _____ wildflower garden would also be **(5)** _____ **(6)** _____ for the environment and would be **(7)** _____ for providing food for local insect populations.

3 Complete the sentences (1-8) with the words in the box.

> advantages   advise   agree   benefit
> certain   doubt   evidence   grateful

1 I would strongly _____ you to consider my proposals carefully.
2 It would be of great _____ to everyone if my proposals were accepted.
3 We would be extremely _____ if you gave our proposals serious consideration.

4 I am absolutely _____ that the ideas I have proposed would help the college.
5 I have no _____ whatsoever that these proposals would improve the appearance of the town.
6 I am sure that you will _____ that inviting parents to the talent show is a good idea.
7 These are just two of the many _____ that putting our ideas into practice would bring.
8 There is _____ to suggest that starting the school day later would improve student performance.

4 Rewrite the sentences to make them more appealing and persuasive.

1 I hope you like my ideas.
2 Thank you for reading my proposals.
3 I think new sports facilities would be good.
4 How about organising an exchange with students from another country?
5 Having a sports day would be good because young people will enjoy it.
6 The museum is a good place for international students to visit.

5 Match each additional way of being persuasive (1-5) with two of the examples (a-j).

1 Exaggerating
2 Using rhetorical questions
3 Using repetition
4 Using emotive words
5 Using inclusive language

a And isn't it the case that more customers using the café is exactly what everyone would want?
b We all know the joyful effect that hearing the beautiful sound of children's laughter has.
c I doubt anyone in the country would disagree with this proposal.
d I would argue that more choice means more users, and more users means a much greater profit.
e I am sure that we are all aware of the advantages that having such facilities brings.
f There are hundreds of reasons why having a big concert would be the best idea.
g Wouldn't it encourage a far healthier student population if the sports facilities were free?
h We all want our friends, our fellow residents and our children to be able to walk safely in the city centre.
i My proposal would take an appalling and ugly area of land and turn it into a small piece of paradise.
j Residents would use it for meeting friends, and meeting those you love, after all, is so important.

Writing effective introductions

You always need to write an introduction to a proposal.

6 Read these statements about a good introduction and decide whether they are true or false.

A good introduction should

1 give a brief summary of the content of the proposal.
2 always be just one sentence long.
3 include details about each of the points in the task.
4 avoid the use of your own opinions.
5 give several reasons why you decided to write the proposal.

7 Read the introductions (1–3) to the exam task below. Complete the sentences (A and B) with what is wrong with each one.

> The council of the city where you live has asked residents for ideas on how to encourage more students to use public transport. You decide to write a proposal for the city council explaining what your idea is, outlining how it will work in practice and saying how this will encourage students to use public transport.

1   This proposal is about providing free transport in the city to all full-time students, which is a great idea for getting them onto public transport. It will give loads of information about why it's such a good thing.

   A   Some of the language used in the introduction is _____ .
   B   It includes the writer's _____ , which is not good in an introduction.

2   The aim of this proposal is to outline the reasons why students should be allowed to travel for free.

   A   The introduction is too _____ .
   B   It doesn't include all of the points from the _____ .

3   Dear Sir/Madam,
I am writing to you to suggest giving free access to public transport as a means of encouraging more students in the city to use it. I will include details of the student 'smart cards' and electronic readers that would make this work at a practical level. I will also say that this recommendation is likely to prove effective, and will explain why.

   A   The introduction is written as though it's a _____ and not a proposal.
   B   It includes too much _____ in response to the points in the task.

TIP: Use formal or semi-formal words, phrases and structures in a proposal, appropriate to the context and the reader. Avoid informal language including contractions.

Writing effective conclusions

Proposals must include a conclusion. This summarises the content of the proposal, urges the reader to follow your advice, suggestions or recommendations, and provides a memorable ending to it.

8 Choose the correct option to complete the three conclusions.

In summary, I would **(1) widely / strongly** recommend that you accept my proposals for improving the school canteen.
(2) Doing / Having so will greatly enhance the dining experience for students and enable the school to produce healthier meals and **(3) nevertheless / therefore** better-performing learners.

I would **(4) entirely / wholeheartedly** recommend following my proposals for spending the money. Club members would greatly **(5) appreciate / respect** the new equipment, which would last for many years **(6) to come / to arrive**.

I have **(7) reason / knowledge** to believe that the suggestions outlined in this proposal constitute the best possible **(8) method / course** of action. Following this advice is sure **(9) to lead to / to direct to** a happier population and an increase in satisfied visitors.

EXAM TASK

Read the task and write your proposal. Write your answer in 220–260 words in an appropriate style.

> Your cycling club wants to encourage new people to join. The club president would like members to come up with ideas for an event that would attract new people. You decide to write a proposal outlining your idea for an event, giving details of the event and explaining why you think it would be successful in attracting people to the club.

Write your **proposal**.

ABOUT THE TASK

- In Writing Part 2, you choose one question to answer from a choice of three. One of these may be an email or a letter. This may be formal or informal.
- You usually write the email or letter to reply to one you have received, or in response to an advertisement or notice you have seen.
- Your email or letter could be to a friend, a colleague, a potential employer, a college principal or a magazine editor, etc.
- In the task you may have to respond to questions in an email or letter, or give information in response to an advertisement, for example a job application.

- You should address all of the points in the task.
- It is important to write your email or letter in a style appropriate for the person you are writing to. If you know the person well, you should use an informal style. In other situations, you should use semi-formal or formal language.
- You should organise your writing into clear paragraphs, and use the appropriate conventions for opening and closing your email/letter.
- You should write between 220 and 260 words.

Practice task

1 Read the task and write a first draft of your letter. Write 220-260 words in an appropriate style.

> You have received a letter from an English-speaking friend who lives in your country.

… Some friends from home are coming to visit me next month. They'd love to go and see a big event of some sort while they're here. They're not bothered what kind of event – sport, music, theatre, anything – but would like to see something that really reflects the character of your country.

I don't know what to suggest so I'd like your advice, please: what to see, where to see it and why?

Cheers,

Rick

Write your letter in reply. You do not need to include postal addresses.

How did you do?

2 Read the example letter below and compare it with your draft.

Hi Rick,

It's great to hear from you. How are you and your family?

You must be looking forward to seeing your friends. It would be lovely to meet them – I'm sure we'd get on well.

I'm really into sport, and I'd say the best event you could take them to would be the Tour de France which lasts for three weeks next month. There really isn't any sporting event that's more French!

In case you've never heard of it, it's the toughest professional cycling road race in the world. The cyclists cover more than 3,500 km, including ascending some of the steepest roads in France. Even if sport isn't really your thing the atmosphere is incredible, so it's a great day out.

It's best to see the race in the mountains. The cyclists pass more slowly going uphill, and the racing there is more exciting. To choose the best place, visit the website – it shows you the exact route and times.

You'll get the most from it if you take a picnic and arrive very early in the morning. If not, you won't find a good place to watch from. You'll be amazed what happens as the cyclists approach – everyone starts shouting and urging them on! The determination on the face of the racers is so inspiring!

I hope that's helpful. Would it be OK if I came with you?

All the best

233 words

3 Complete the boxes in the example letter with the correct number from the box. You will need to use one of the options twice.

1 Use informal expressions in the body of the letter.
2 Refer to the email you received from Rick.
3 Answer Rick's first question.
4 Answer Rick's second question.
5 Give reasons for your suggestions.
6 Use appropriate phrases to begin and end your email.
7 Explain why you've made your choice of event.
8 End your email by referring back to your reason for writing.
9 Include some personal information at the start.

4 How could you improve your draft?

TEACH

Strategies and skills
Using correct register

As with any of the writing tasks in the C1 Advanced exam, you will need to write in the correct register. This changes depending on your target reader. For the email/letter task this will be formal, semi-formal or informal.

1 Complete the table with the examples of different registers in the box.

> I found it somewhat difficult to believe.
> It was hard to believe.   I couldn't believe it!
> I'm really sorry 🙁
> I can only apologise for the mistake.
> I would really like to apologise.
> It was very nice to see you.   Good to see you.
> It was a great pleasure to meet you.
> There is every reason to be optimistic.
> Look on the bright side.
> There's positive as well as negative.

informal	semi-formal	formal

2 Rewrite the formal sentences using informal language.

1 It is with great regret that I must inform you that I am unable to attend the event.

2 I am writing to you to request a meeting at which we could discuss the problem.

3 I have a great deal of experience of working in supervisory roles.

4 Would it be possible to visit your school at some point in the near future in order to observe a class?

5 I would be extremely grateful if you could send me your latest price list at your earliest convenience.

6 Many thanks for attending the recent event to open the new sports centre.

3 Rewrite the informal sentences using formal language.

1 Please can you sort this broken computer out soon?

2 I haven't been to your city for ages.

3 I'm getting in touch because the 8.20 train to London this morning was an hour late – again! 🙁

4 Sorry to hear you've been poorly – get well soon!

5 Why are you always late for work?!

6 Sorry, but I can't come to your wedding.

Using formal language

Sometimes, the letter/email task requires you to write using formal language.

4 Read the exam task below and write a first draft in response to it.

> You see the following job advertisement on a website, *Summer Vacancies*:

We are currently seeking English-speaking people to work as Activity Leaders at our summer camps for young teenagers. At the summer camps, students take part in classroom-based work, especially to improve English language skills, and a range of outdoor activities such as cycling, canoeing and climbing.

If you are interested, please apply by email to Ms Angela Holmes. In your application, tell her whether you'd prefer to lead classroom or outdoor activities, what experience you have of doing this, and saying what personal qualities would make you the perfect choice for this role.

Write your email to apply to work at a summer camp. You do not need to include email addresses.

Write your answer in 220–260 words in an appropriate style.

5 Use the checklist below to assess your own email.

Have you

1 started your email with a formal greeting?

2 written a short introductory paragraph, explaining why you are emailing?

3 responded to all three of the requests in the email above?

4 written a short final paragraph to conclude the email?

5 used an appropriate way of ending a formal email?

6 used formal language throughout your email?

7 written between 220 and 260 words?

6 Read the example response to the task in Ex 4. Which elements in the checklist has the writer failed to include?

👤 **From:** Marek
Subject: Activity Leader Application

Hi Angela,

I am writing to you to apply for the position of Activity Leader, which was recently advertised on the Summer Vacancies website.

I am particularly interested in working as an Activity Leader for the outdoor activities at the summer camps. I've done lots of outdoor stuff, like climbing, hiking, mountain biking, canoeing and running. I not only have extensive experience of taking part in these activities, but also in passing on my skills to others. For example, I am a member of both climbing and mountain-biking clubs. At the former, I train others in the basic abilities needed to ascend and descend the climbing wall, and also take newer members on outdoor climbs and supervise them. At the latter, I regularly lead rides through the countryside around my home town, some of which are quite challenging.

I'd be brilliant at this because, although I am only nineteen years old, I am a mature and responsible individual. I love working with younger teenagers as they have a wonderful energy and curiosity. I feel I am good at encouraging them to use these qualities in a positive way. My aim is to be a good role model for them by acting in a responsible manner at all times.

All the best,

Marek

---

7 Highlight five examples of informal language in the example email.

8 Rewrite the five highlighted examples of informal language in a more appropriate way.

> **TIP:** Use formal words, phrases and structures in a letter of application, and avoid informal language, including contractions.

9 Complete the final paragraph that was missing from the example answer in Ex 6. Use the words in the box, adding a capital letter where necessary.

> convenience   hearing   hesitate   respect   should

I look forward to **(1)** _____ from you at your earliest **(2)** _____ . **(3)** _____ you require any further information in **(4)** _____ of my application, please do not **(5)** _____ to contact me.

Common expressions used in formal language

Formal letters and emails often contain fixed chunks of language that can be memorised and used in other letters.

10 Match the informal expressions (1-7) with their more formal counterparts (a-g).

1 See you soon!
2 I'm just dropping you a line to …
3 I've done loads of …
4 Nice to hear from you!
5 Sorry I was …
6 Can't wait to see you!
7 You'll notice from my CV that I've …

a I have extensive experience of …
b I must apologise for …
c Many thanks for your email.
d I look forward to meeting you.
e Yours faithfully
f As you will see in the attached CV …
g I am writing to you regarding …

EXAM TASK

Read the task and write your email to apply to volunteer. You do not need to include email addresses. Write your answer in 220-260 words in an appropriate style.

> You see the following notice on a website, *Research4U*:

> We are looking for English-speaking volunteers to go on an expedition into the Amazon rainforest to collect data for a research project. Applicants should have an interest in the environment and be capable of spending several weeks in an isolated area of a tropical rainforest.
>
> If you are interested, please apply by email to Ms Sharon Jarvis (s.jarvis@research4U.net). In your application, include details of your interest in the environment, say what personal qualities you have that would make you the perfect choice for this role and explain what you would hope to gain from the expedition.

Write your **email**.

TEST

TEST

- In Writing Part 2, you choose one question to answer from a choice of three. One of these may be a review.
- The purpose of a review is to describe something, give opinions about it, make recommendations and give reasons to support them.
- You are told who you are writing the review for; this may be for an English-language magazine, newspaper or website.
- You are given a topic for the review, and some ideas to write about or questions to discuss. For example, you may be asked to write a review of a film, a game, a place, an event, a product or a service, such as a shop or restaurant.

- It is important to write your review in an engaging and interesting way. The reader needs to understand exactly what you are reviewing and what you think about it. You need to give examples and reasons to support your opinions.
- Your review should be organised into clear paragraphs, with an introduction and a conclusion.
- You should describe the subject of the review in the introduction, and reasons why you would or would not recommend it for other people in the conclusion.
- You should use a wide variety of informal and semi-formal vocabulary and language structures.
- You should write between 220 and 260 words.

Practice task

1 Read the task and write a first draft of your review. Write 220–260 words.

> You see the following announcement on a website, *Perfect TV*.

Reviews wanted

Send us a review of the best TV drama series you've seen in the last few years.

What was it about the series that makes it so entertaining? Which characters do you particularly like?

Write your **review**.

How did you do?

2 Read the example review and compare it with your draft.

3 Complete the boxes in the example review with the correct number from the box. You will need to use one of the options twice.

> 1 Give your recommendation clearly.
> 2 Answer the first question.
> 3 Support your opinion with reasons and/or details.
> 4 Name the series that you're reviewing.
> 5 Try to engage the reader from the start, e.g. with a rhetorical question.
> 6 Use linking words or phrases to connect your ideas.
> 7 Explain what the drama is about, without giving too much detail.
> 8 Answer the second question.

4 How could you improve your draft?

A GREAT TV DRAMA

Who can resist a good TV drama? I know I can't. The best one in recent years, in my opinion, is called *Village Life*. Now in its second series, it allows us to see inside the homes, lives and minds of the inhabitants of the small village of Chesterton.

The central character is a policewoman called Rachel, who arrives in Chesterton thinking there will be little crime and that she'll be able to take it easy in her final years before retirement. How wrong she turns out to be! She slowly realises that many villagers are involved in something not entirely legal and sets out to investigate.

What's especially enjoyable about the series is the complex plot, as it always keeps the viewer (and Rachel!) guessing as to what will happen next. We are introduced gradually to the residents of the village, who all add a new and unexpected twist to the story. My favourite is the owner of the mansion, who comes across as something of an idiot but uses his image to hide the fact that he's up to no good. However, there are many other personalities to keep you entertained and the acting is, without exception, excellent.

I would highly recommend *Village Life* to anyone who enjoys quality drama which combines mystery and tension with a great deal of humour and affection for the characters. Although it's supposedly a crime drama there's nothing to upset younger viewers, making it a perfect programme for the whole family.

249 words

Strategies and skills
Using descriptive and dramatic language

A review should be entertaining as well as informative. One way to do this is to use plenty of highly descriptive and dramatic language (but not too much!). This will convey the writer's message as effectively as possible but also attract and interest the reader.

> **Tip:** You can use examples in your review to support your opinions and to add detail to what you discuss.

1 **Read the sentences from different reviews. Choose the word or phrase (A–C) that completes each one in the most descriptive and dramatic way.**

1 There's a _____ section of the play which will have you roaring with laugher.
   A very funny   B highly amusing   C pretty good

2 If you love _____ thrillers then this is the film for you.
   A frightening   B really scary   C spine-tingling

3 I soon became totally _____ by the complex rhythms and melodies of the album.
   A absorbed   B interested   C attracted

4 I must admit that I found the game's higher levels _____ impossible.
   A utterly   B fully   C very

5 Viewers will be _____ into a magical world of strange and fascinating creatures.
   A carried   B moved   C transported

6 The film has some _____ scenes in which we learn about Sam's tragic past.
   A quite emotional   B incredibly moving   C extremely sad

7 While there's _____ action, the play maintains your interest throughout.
   A comparatively little   B not much   C only a bit of

8 Unfortunately, the film becomes _____ soon after it has started.
   A quite dull   B rather boring   C somewhat monotonous

2 **Match the words (1–8 and a–h) to create compound adjectives and nouns.**

1 absent   a jerker
2 mean   b provoking
3 tear   c baked
4 kind   d spirited
5 sun   e breaker
6 time   f minded
7 thought   g saver
8 record   h hearted

3 **Complete the sentences using the compound adjectives and nouns from Ex 2.**

1 The documentary was a _____ exploration of the environmental problems we're all facing.

2 The film's opening memorably shows a man walking across a _____ desert.

3 The book is a _____ , selling more copies than any other non-fiction title ever.

4 The novel's central character, _____ inventor Delius Hooke, has trouble remembering anyone and anything!

5 The tragic ending makes the film a real _____ .

6 The app is a genuine _____ , allowing you to set meetings and contact everyone involved within minutes.

7 The hero, Titus, is saved by a _____ woman who takes him to a safe hiding place.

8 A _____ villain (as most villains are!), Captain Granite is determined to take over the world.

In less formal reviews, simple opinions and ideas can be made more complex and entertaining for readers. To do this, they can be exaggerated a little, or more controversial language can be used. For example, 'The programme was boring' might become 'I've never fallen asleep so quickly as when I started watching this programme.'

4 **Rewrite the sentences to make them more complex and entertaining.**

1 Actually, it's a very useful app that everyone should get.

2 Only go and see this film if you've really got nothing else to do.

3 It was the best concert I've ever been to.

4 There isn't much to do in the holiday resort.

5 The acting in the play was absolutely amazing.

6 The restaurant serves the best food in the area.

Engaging the reader

In a review, you use different functions. You describe, explain, give examples and opinions and then, finally, recommend. These will help you engage the reader throughout your review.

5 Read the extract from a review. Match the sentences labelled 1–10 with a function (a–g). The functions can be used more than once.

a describing

b engaging readers

c explaining

d giving an example

e giving an introductory summary

f giving an opinion

g recommending

(1) If you're looking for a great evening out, then why not give *Party Politics* at The Palace Theatre a try? (2) It contains plenty of serious political observations, yet will make you roar with laughter too.

(3) The play is set in a small town and the action takes place during an election. The central character is a political candidate and we follow his adventures as he does all he can to persuade people to vote for him. (4) One of the funniest involves a dispute with an old lady who, when he knocks on her door, thinks he is a robber and chases him away with a stick. (5) What makes it funnier is that the whole event is captured by a film crew and broadcast all over the world!

(6) It's hard to choose a single thing about the play as its most impressive feature. If I had to go for just one, I think it would be the script. (7) It's brilliantly observed political satire, although the performances it draws from the cast are almost equally superb. (8) Written by the ever-reliable Miranda Carter, it's certainly amongst the best of her work to date.

(9) I would suggest that anyone with even the slightest interest in the absurdity of politics should go and see *Party Politics*. (10) I guarantee that you won't be disappointed.

It is important that you include a recommendation in your review that is clearly stated and tells readers exactly what you think.

6 Choose the best word to complete the recommendations below.

1 I **might** / **would** definitely recommend this book to anyone who likes serious crime fiction.

2 I **strongly** / **greatly** advise anyone with an interest in classical music to listen to this album.

3 Those who love platform games should **utterly** / **undoubtedly** give this game a try.

4 I **completely** / **wholeheartedly** recommend this restaurant to anyone who loves great traditional food.

5 **Unless** / **Because** you actively enjoy wasting three hours of your precious time, avoid this film.

6 I promise that no one will **miss** / **regret** buying this product: you'll wonder how you ever lived without it.

Structuring a review

A review should be clear and easy to follow, and each paragraph should have one main idea.

7 Read the short paragraphs below (1–6). What is the main idea? Choose the correct option (A or B).

1 The book is an in-depth analysis of the reasons behind the most recent global economic crises. Its author backs up all of the arguments she makes with detailed, reliable data.
   A The book was well-researched.
   B The book was quite controversial.

2 While the main character comes across as authentic, few of the supporting roles do. This leads to the whole film ending up a little difficult to believe.
   A Most of the acting in the film wasn't very good.
   B The characters in the film were largely unconvincing.

3 As you walk in, you're immediately struck by how bright and relaxed the café seems. There isn't a single dark shade in the entire place. Even the floor and counter are made from pale wood.
   A The way the café is decorated.
   B How the café was built.

4 The period of the artist's work covered in the exhibition is not, to be honest, his best. Had there been more of a variety from throughout his career, my rating would have been higher.
   A Criticism of the choice of paintings in the exhibition.
   B Criticism of the quality of the artist.

5 The gameplay takes you through a series of landscapes where you can hunt for secret treasure and gather useful materials. The amount of terrain to explore will keep you occupied for weeks.
   A Praise for the appearance of the game.
   B Praise for the complexity of the game.

6 I get the sense with most official biographies that I'm reading a rather unexciting, cleaned-up version of the subject's life. That's definitely not the case with *Inside Billy Frost*.
   A Comparing *Inside Billy Frost* negatively against better biographies.
   B Suggesting that *Inside Billy Frost* is more true-to-life than other biographies.

8 Read the exam task and the example review. Complete the review with the words and phrases in the box. Add a capital letter where necessary.

> as well as   could   however   if   issue
> literally   occasionally   sound

> You see the following announcement in an English-language magazine.

REVIEWS WANTED

Have you bought something for your home that you've found particularly useful? This could be a gadget, an item of furniture, etc. If so, why not send us a review of it?

Why has the item been so useful? Does it have any negative features? Who would you particularly recommend it to?

Write your **review**. Write your answer in **220–260** words in an appropriate style.

My helpful friend

A I have a friend who buys the most up-to-date electronic devices and then somehow turns any conversation around to the subject of how great her latest gadget is. **(1)** _____ familiar? I got so fed up with her going on about her digital assistant that I decided to buy one just to shut her up!

B For those who don't know, a digital assistant is an electronic box that sits in your home and does things for you when it's told to. Useful things, like putting the heating on or playing your favourite music. I was incredibly sceptical, thinking that I wouldn't use it at all once the initial excitement and novelty had worn off.

C **(2)** _____ , the longer I've had it, the more uses I've actually found. **(3)** _____ the heating and music it now wakes me up, gives me news reports and weather forecasts, traffic and travel updates, announces the scores of my favourite sports teams, reminds me about important events ... I **(4)** _____ continue, but I may end up becoming just as irritating as my friend!

D The only **(5)** _____ with my new electronic buddy is that it **(6)** _____ misunderstands my accent. I speak to it in English and it seems I don't pronounce everything to my new friend's satisfaction!

E I'd recommend this device to **(7)** _____ anyone. You don't need to be very knowledgeable about technology to use and install it and will soon find more things to do with it than you can imagine. **(8)** _____ it can convince me of its charm, I'm sure it will convince you too!

9 Complete the table to summarise the content and purpose of each paragraph of the example review.

paragraph	summary of content	purpose
A		
B		
C		
D		
E		

Most paragraphs begin with a sentence which introduces what the rest of the paragraph is about. This is called a topic sentence.

10 Highlight the topic sentences in each paragraph of the example review. In each case, does the whole sentence introduce the topic or just part of it?

Using adjectives that indicate opinion

Using a variety of value adjectives makes a review more interesting to read, and makes it easier for the reader to understand exactly what you think.

11 Complete the table with the adjectives in the box.

> appalling   average   disastrous   fabulous
> inadequate   inferior   luxurious   mundane
> pleasurable   repetitive   shabby   sparkling
> splendid   tedious   terrific

strongly positive	positive	neutral	negative	strongly negative

12 Look at the lists of adverbs and some adjectives (1–8). Cross out the quantifier that does not collocate with the adjective and noun in bold.

0 completely   absolutely   ~~fully~~   **splendid soundtrack**
1 certainly   relatively   somewhat   **shabby dining area**
2 exceptionally   vastly   extraordinarily   **tedious scenes**
3 thoroughly   totally   perfectly   **inadequate lighting**
4 actually   genuinely   truly   **terrific acting**
5 utterly   quite   slightly   **appalling taste**
6 delightfully   definitely   beautifully   **sparkling performance**
7 above   over   below   **average entertainment**
8 mildly   thoroughly   terribly   **pleasurable experience**

Read the task and write your review. Write 220–260 words in an appropriate style.

> You see the following announcement on an English-language website.

Reviews wanted

If you've visited a museum that you've particularly enjoyed, then why not post a review of it on our website?

What makes the museum so special? What did you particularly enjoy learning about? Who would you particularly recommend it to?

Write your **review**.

ABOUT THE TASK

- In Writing Part 2, you choose one question to answer from a choice of three. One of these may be a report.
- Reports are usually written for someone in authority, so they are formal or semi-formal depending on the context.
- You write a report to present facts and ideas about something, give your opinions and make recommendations.
- Details of what you need to include in the report are given in the task, including who the report is for and what it is about.

- You must read the information that's given to you about the report very carefully. You will lose marks if you write about the wrong thing.
- You need to organise your report effectively into sections and paragraphs. You should have a clear introduction, a detailed section giving factual information, a section which makes recommendations, and a conclusion at the end.
- You can use headings to clearly define the different sections.
- Your report should be between 220 and 260 words long.

Practice task

1 Read the task and write a first draft of your report in 220-260 words.

> Your college wants to improve its sports facilities. You have been asked by the college principal to write a report about them. In your report, you should evaluate the current facilities at the sports centre and make recommendations for improving them.

Write your report.

How did you do?

2 Read the example report and compare it with your draft.

3 Complete the boxes in the example report with the correct number from the box.

> 1 Provide a reason for making recommendations.
> 2 Use a linker to introduce a contrasting idea.
> 3 Introduce negative information which will be used constructively in the recommendations.
> 4 Provide detailed factual information about the sports centre's current facilities.
> 5 Use a linker to connect to the previous paragraph.
> 6 Outline the reason for writing the report.
> 7 Give an overview of the details in the topic sentence.
> 8 Use a linker to add a further recommendation.
> 9 Summarise the benefits of the recommendations.
> 10 Soften the language by adding hedging words (*quite, rather,* etc.) when criticising.

4 How could you improve your draft?

Introduction

The aim of this report is to give an overview of the facilities provided by the college sports centre and to give recommendations about how it could be improved.

The current facilities

There is a relatively narrow range of sports facilities at the college. The sports centre provides a multi-purpose hall in which users can play badminton, table tennis, five-a-side football, basketball and volleyball. Due to space restrictions, only one of these sports generally operates at any one time.

In addition there is a gym advertised by the college as being 'fully equipped'. However, there are only ten machines in total, comprised of four different types which are somewhat out of date.

Outside, two fenced all-weather areas can be used for hockey and football. There are no grass pitches. There is also a large car park which remains virtually empty for the majority of the week.

Recommendations

The current facilities are clearly inadequate as only a small variety of sports are available, due to a lack of appropriate space. I would therefore strongly recommend converting the greatly underused parking area into additional facilities. The construction of a second hall there would enable multiple sports to operate simultaneously. Up-to-date gym equipment should be purchased. Additionally, I would advise the creation of further outdoor playing facilities, namely tennis courts and grass multi-use pitches.

Conclusion

Should the above recommendations be implemented, the sports centre will not only become more popular among current students, but will also attract many new students to the college.

247 words

Strategies and skills

Structuring a report

It is important to divide a report into distinct sections. Adding a heading for each section helps make it clear what each one is about.

> **TIP:** Be careful to avoid putting your opinion in the section of the report where you are giving factual detail. You can make general observations but not clear opinions or recommendations.

1 Read the exam task and the extract from the example report. Choose the best heading (a–g) for each of the three sections in the extract. There are four headings you do not need.

> You have just been on a tour of a big football stadium with your college class. Your teacher would like you to write a report about the tour, describing what your class saw and outlining any negative aspects of the tour. Explain whether you would recommend the tour for other college classes, and what changes you would suggest making to it.

(1) _____

The students all gathered at the visitor centre, where they were shown a video about the history of the club. The cups and awards the club had won were all on display in there. The tour itself then started, beginning at the highest part of the stadium. Looking down on the pitch, the whole building seemed enormous, especially as there were no spectators there at the time. The highlight was seeing the changing rooms. It was easy to imagine the excitement in there just before a game, and the joy, or disappointment, afterwards.

(2) _____

Students were generally pleased with the tour but several negative comments were made. The most widespread complaint was that the tour moved too quickly, giving students little time to enjoy each stage. A small number of students were not happy due to having no interest whatsoever in football, but this is perhaps to be expected.

(3) _____

I would definitely recommend this tour to other college groups. The great majority of those present stated that they preferred the stadium tour to other recent college trips to the City Museum and the recycling centre. There will always be a small minority who have little interest in the subject or focus of the trip, whether it is a science museum or a film studio.

a   Suggested changes
b   Suitability for other classes
c   Introduction
d   Description of the tour
e   Conclusion
f   Problems with the tour
g   Recommendations regarding behaviour

2 Look again at the extract from the report in Ex 1. Answer the questions.

1   In section 1, do you think the writer mentions everything they saw on the tour? Why? / Why not?

2   Identify the three places the writer mentions visiting on the tour.

3   In section 2, what does the writer see as the most important negative aspect?

4   In section 3, what point does the writer make about people saying they didn't like football?

5   Choose the best introduction for the report (A–C).

A   This report aims to outline the reasons for choosing to visit the football stadium recently. It will also make recommendations for alternative locations for the next class trip.

B   The aim of this report is to give an overview of the recent class trip to the football stadium and to compare student enjoyment with that of previous trips.

C   The purpose of this report is to describe the highlights of a recent football stadium tour, identify any less enjoyable features and to identify its suitability for future outings.

3 Read the response to the final part of the task in Ex 1: 'what changes you would suggest making to it'. Complete it with the words in the box.

> case   highly   most   perhaps
> so   subsequent   terms

In **(1)** _____ of changes, I would **(2)** _____ recommend asking the guide on future tours to slow down the pace of the visit **(3)** _____ that students can really make the **(4)** _____ of seeing each part of the stadium. **(5)** _____ the school only booked a tour of a certain length, in which **(6)** _____ I would suggest that a longer tour were booked for **(7)** _____ visits.

4 Write a conclusion for the report in Ex 1.

5 Complete the sentences from reports with the words and phrases in the box. Then decide if each sentence could be used in an introduction (I) or a conclusion (C).

aim of   conclusion   general   identifies
intends   summarise

1 The _____ this report is to evaluate student attitudes to places to eat out in the city.

2 To _____ , a large majority of students think that there are insufficient takeaways.

3 This report _____ to highlight positive and negative features of eating out in the city.

4 People are, in _____ at least, dissatisfied with the prices of many of the city's restaurants.

5 The _____ I would reach is that the variety of food available is inadequate.

6 This report _____ the current range and quality of eating establishments in the city.

Referring to research

Referring to research findings can make your report sound more accurate and authentic.

Tip: You can invent some research that will support your report findings. No one will check if this is true or not!

6 Match the sentence halves to make sentences you can use to refer to your research.

1 I conducted a face-to-face survey
2 I interviewed users of the library
3 According to most customers
4 A questionnaire on bus usage
5 The majority of respondents

a was given to around 100 passengers.
b of more than 40 local residents.
c I spoke to, prices have increased significantly in recent months.
d indicated that they were satisfied with the range of shops.
e and asked them a range of questions about the services it offers.

It sounds convincing if you mention numbers or proportions of people when you refer to research that you have done.

7 Complete each second sentence with one word so that it has a similar meaning to the first.

1 Only one or two people complained that the prices were too high.

Only a small _____ of people complained that the prices were too high.

2 I interviewed 50 people and 40 of them wanted shops to open later.

Four _____ of people interviewed reported wanting shops to open later.

3 No one I asked was happy with the music in shops.

Music in shops proved to be a problem: _____ of those interviewed were happy with it.

4 Eight out of ten people liked the idea of having more space for shopping bags on buses.

_____ percent of those surveyed were keen to see increased space for shopping bags on buses.

5 Almost everyone would like there to be more clothes shops in town.

The vast _____ of people would like a greater number of clothes shops in the town centre.

6 Eleven of the twenty people in my survey disliked the city centre traffic.

Slightly more than _____ of the people surveyed complained about the city centre traffic.

Using formal language

Reports generally contain formal language.

8 Complete each second (formal) sentence with a suitable phrase in the box so it has a similar meaning to the first (informal) sentence.

> cause of dissatisfaction
> fortunate enough   has proved
> in favour of   insufficient funds
> seriously concerned that

1 Almost everyone hated the high ticket prices.
The high ticket prices were a major _____ amongst theatre-goers.

2 Parents with children really love the café.
The café _____ especially popular amongst parents with children.

3 Some people are very worried that buses won't come so often.
Some people are _____ the frequency of bus services will be reduced.

4 There wasn't enough money to pay for student transport.
Students complained that there were _____ to pay for their transport.

5 Luckily, we saw lots of animals on the walk.
We were _____ to see a wide variety of wildlife during the walk.

6 Everyone loved the idea of doing a sponsored run to get the money we needed.
Everyone was _____ doing a sponsored run to raise the required amount of money.

Using passive constructions is a good way of making the language in a report more formal.

9 Complete the sentences using a passive form of the verb in brackets.

1 Insufficient tasks _____ (give) to participants during the work experience programme.

2 The most frequent criticism that _____ (mention) was a lack of supervision by managers.

3 The company _____ (consider) to be one of the best employers in the local area.

4 Participants on the scheme _____ (expect) to behave in a professional manner.

5 It _____ (suggest) recently that paying for the participants' travel would be a good idea.

6 Overall, the work experience scheme _____ (not think) to be a success.

Making recommendations

Part 2 report-writing tasks often ask you to make recommendations.

10 Choose the correct verb forms to complete the recommendations.

1 I would strongly advise **offering** / **to offer** customers a refund if their food takes too long to prepare.

2 I suggest **to organise** / **that we organise** a party as an excellent way of welcoming the international students to the college.

3 I would highly recommend **to put** / **putting** details of the event on social media as soon as possible.

4 Free gifts could **be given** / **to give** out as a way of attracting potential customers to the new shop.

5 The furniture and the way that the café is decorated **should make** / **should be made** more appealing to attract more young customers.

6 Above all, **I would propose** / **it would be proposed** investing in really effective advertising.

EXAM TASK

Read the task below and write your report. Write your answer in 220–260 words in an appropriate style.

> You have just returned from a three-week trip to an English-speaking country organised by the private language school you attend.
> The director of the language school has asked you to write a report about the trip. In your report, you should evaluate the study programme you did while you were there, comment on the accommodation and suggest any changes you would recommend for next year's trip.

Write your **report**.

- In Listening Part 1 you listen to three short dialogues, each with a different topic focus.
- There are two multiple-choice questions on each of the dialogues.
- Each question has three options, and you must choose the correct one based on what you hear.

- The questions can be about the purpose or function of the conversation, the main idea of what the speakers are talking about, or what they agree or disagree about.
- The questions can also be about one or both of the speakers' opinions, attitudes or feelings.
- You will have time to read the questions before you hear the recording, and you will hear each dialogue twice.

Practice task

1 🎧 **L01** You will hear a conversation between two teachers who are discussing the idea of using rap music in teaching. For each question, choose the best answer (A–C).

1 How does the woman feel about using rap music in her own lessons?
   A convinced of its educational value
   B cautious about over-using it in class
   C concerned about students' reaction to it

2 The man mentions an activity he did with students about rap music in order to
   A make a point about rap music's ability to engage learners.
   B suggest some learners may benefit more than others.
   C question the validity of a teaching method.

How did you do?

2 Check your answers.

3 Read the audioscript for Ex 1 question 1. Match each highlighted part with the topic of one of the options (A–C) in question 1.

> … **¹**but they're generally far more up for new methods of learning than teachers, in my experience. So, there was little chance they'd find it a waste of time. **²**It's too early to tell whether it's as good as other ways of developing their understanding, but **³**I want to avoid a mistake I always make, which is to include a new technique I've learnt in every class. The novelty soon wears off and students get as fed up with it as the old ones.

> **TIP:** There will always be incorrect information in the recording that relates to two of the three options. These are known as distractors. As you listen, rule out the incorrect information as well as choosing the correct answer.

4a Read the audioscript for Ex 1 question 2. Match each highlighted part with the topic in one of the options (A–C) in question 2. One option has two sections connected to it.

> I had a class discussion about rap a few weeks ago. **¹**What took me aback was the passion it generated throughout the group. **²**I half expected it not to work as a whole-class activity, as **³**I thought the minority who have no interest in it would withdraw from the debate. They had just as much to say as its greatest advocates, though, **⁴**which suggests it's a powerful vehicle for getting across the things we want to teach.

4b Which highlighted part of the audioscript gives you the answer to Ex 1 question 2? Why are the other options wrong? Answer the questions to help you.

1 Does the man think that his activity was unsuccessful?

2 Does he think that some students were left out of the discussion?

Strategies and skills

Understanding attitude and opinion

Speakers will rarely state that they are going to offer an opinion. You must therefore listen carefully to identify when the opinion is given. In addition, the language used in the options will always be paraphrased in the recording.

> **TIP:** In the exam, you have some time before each conversation to look at the options for each question. Use this time to familiarise yourself with the options and prepare yourself for what you are likely to hear.

1 🎧 **L02** **Listen to some speakers (1–3). What is their attitude or opinion? Choose the correct option (A–C). Highlight the section of the audioscript where the correct option is paraphrased.**

1   The glossy leaflet describing how great it would be was some distance from the reality, I'm afraid. I was seriously hoping that a course with as many sessions as this one would be able to explore the issue in the kind of detail I enjoy. However, the opposite was the case.

What did the man think of the course?
A   It was too long.
B   It lacked depth.
C   It met his expectations.

2   In my day, school seemed to reward those who were good at academic theory and didn't address the needs of those who were good at practical applications. I was in the latter group, of course, and although I suppose some staff tried to make the lessons as interesting as they could, I still left with very little to show for it, despite many years of consistent effort.

When talking about her schooldays, the speaker reveals
A   her respect for the teachers.
B   regret at not having worked harder.
C   resentment with the education system.

3   In some ways, the majority of modern movies are extremely clever. They contain both visual and verbal in-jokes that appeal in different ways to different age groups. What's turned me away from going to the cinema so often, though, is that the idea of 'good guy is threatened by a powerful bad guy but eventually wins' has become almost universal. I just really crave something that doesn't use that same tired formula.

What does the man think about most new movies?
A   They share a common theme.
B   They lack a moral message.
C   They contain unconvincing dialogue.

2 🎧 **L03** **Listen to some speakers (1–3). What is their attitude or opinion? Choose the correct option (A–C). This time, you do not have the audioscript to help you.**

> **TIP:** You will hear each speaker twice. Use the second time you listen to check your answers.

1   When talking about the new gym she uses, the woman is
A   impressed by the equipment.
B   critical of how it's managed.
C   surprised at the cost.

2   What does the man say about his new boss?
A   She has a lot of relevant experience.
B   She consults with staff effectively.
C   She organises her time well.

3   In the woman's opinion, travel companies are offering ecotourism
A   to improve their corporate image.
B   to broaden their product range.
C   to increase their profits.

SPEAKING BOOST

Discuss or answer.

1   What do you think 'critical thinking' is? How important is it?

2   What's the best way to tackle fake news?

Identifying purpose and function

3 Read what the speakers (1–8) say. What are they doing? Choose the correct option (A, B or C).

1 'They had every intention of paying but if the ticket office was closed and the machine was out of order, what else were they supposed to do?'

  A advising   B defending   C describing

2 'It might be an idea for you to think about what training you'll need in the next few months and come up with a list.'

  A suggesting   B requesting   C explaining

3 'If the management devoted as much energy to putting what we recommended into action as they do to writing reports about it, we wouldn't be facing this dilemma.'

  A emphasising   B recommending   C complaining

4 'Personally, I think that kind of music would be right up your street and, after all, the tickets are only £10.'

  A accepting   B persuading   C highlighting

5 'As soon as I'd told you I'd be able to finish the work on time, the director asked me to meet some clients and take them out for lunch, so it's going to be a little late, I'm afraid.'

  A justifying   B offering   C reassuring

6 'So the play's about a woman who was separated from her twin sister at birth. It explores all the ways it has affected her and her determination to find her twin.'

  A summarising   B identifying   C demanding

7 'I'd seriously think twice about taking the car out in this weather. Even where there isn't snow on the road, there's black ice, which you can't even see.'

  A emphasising   B warning   C agreeing

8 'That's incredibly kind of you – it's such a privilege to witness two people who are clearly in love getting married. I'm actually going to be away on holiday when that's all happening, though.'

  A refusing   B praising   C enquiring

Identifying feeling

4 🎧 **L04** Listen to some speakers (1–8), and decide how they feel. Choose the correct option (A–C).

> **TIP:** Remember that a word such as 'insecure' can have a slightly different meaning in a different context. As you listen, make sure that you think about the context and not just about the word itself.

	A	B	C
1	frustrated	insecure	protective
2	respectful	impatient	astonished
3	content	bitter	self-conscious
4	determined	desperate	dissatisfied
5	eager	irritated	realistic
6	stubborn	arrogant	suspicious
7	sympathetic	unsure	enthusiastic
8	doubtful	concerned	impatient

SPEAKING BOOST

Discuss or answer.

1 Do you think we would be more productive if we studied or worked fewer but longer days?

2 What's your most productive time of day? Can you think why this might be?

Identifying agreement

5 Read six short conversations. Do the speakers agree or disagree?

1 **A:** The new system means anywhere that serves food is inspected every year and has to put a sticker in the window saying what their hygiene rating is. It's a great idea.

  B: I worry that establishments will make sure everything's perfect when the inspectors are there, though, then do exactly what they want for the rest of the year.

2 **A:** Gym membership's never what it seems. I thought I'd be able to go whenever I wanted, but there are apparently limitations on the times I can use it in the terms and conditions.

  B: Those documents are so long that no one ever bothers to read them, and then everyone gets caught out by some regulation at the bottom of page seven.

3 **A:** I didn't actually have very high expectations of the course, but have been thoroughly impressed by how it was run and by how much of the content will be useful for work.

  B: I've actually put some of the principles we discussed in several of the seminars into practice already and I'm keen to implement others when I have more time.

4 **A:** The book falls into the trap of many popular psychology titles in that it overgeneralises what people are like, so they end up being put into broad categories.

  B: That's a common approach, and one which many readers tend to like. I found that most of the chapters managed to steer clear of doing anything like that, though.

5 **A:** In my opinion, studying philosophy's as relevant today as it's always been. If anything, given the increasingly volatile world we live in, it could even be made a mandatory school subject.

  B: I can certainly see the benefit of getting students to think about things a little more deeply. Forcing it universally onto the curriculum is perhaps going a little too far.

6 **A:** City living's slowly become more intense, to my mind, but because the changes are relatively gradual, few people living there actually notice.

  B: I'm sure residents would say the cities they live in are pretty much the same as ten years ago, apart from a few cosmetic changes, which isn't the case to an objective observer.

L05 You will hear three different extracts. For questions 1–6, choose the answer (A, B or C) which fits best according to what you hear. There are two questions for each extract.

Extract One

You hear a scientist being interviewed about plastic pollution.

1 What is the man doing?

  A explaining how the problem can be solved

  B identifying who is primarily to blame for the problem

  C emphasising that the problem must be addressed

2 Why does the man use the examples of plastic bags and bottles?

  A to support the main point he's making

  B to highlight a popular misconception

  C to introduce a new argument

Extract Two

You hear two friends talking about a place where they spent a lot of time as children.

3 The woman is reluctant to return there because

  A she's worried it will ruin her memories of the area.

  B she'd rather not meet some of the people there.

  C she's convinced she won't like how it's changed.

4 How does the man respond to the woman's concerns?

  A He attempts to persuade her to go anyway.

  B He suggests they're unlikely to be valid.

  C He admits he feels the same way as her.

Extract Three

You hear two scientists talking about food hygiene in restaurants.

5 They both think that

  A current laws are insufficient.

  B more inspections are needed.

  C owners don't take the issue seriously.

6 How does the woman feel about advising the government on food hygiene issues?

  A uncomfortable at how critical she needs to be

  B frustrated by the response to her suggestions

  C cautious about appearing overenthusiastic

- In Listening Part 2, you listen to one long monologue. The speaker is usually giving a presentation or talk on a particular subject.

- There are eight sentences, each one with one gap. You listen and complete these gaps in the sentences with a word or a short phrase.

- The sentences provide a kind of summary of what the speaker says, and are in the same order as the information you hear.

- You won't hear the actual sentences on the recording as they paraphrase the information given by the speaker.

- Most answers are concrete pieces of information, such as nouns, although the sentence may tell you about the speaker's opinion or attitude towards the topic.

- You must complete the gap with the exact word or words you hear, not a paraphrase, and the words you write should fit the sentence grammatically.

- You'll have time to read the questions before you hear the recording, and you'll hear the recording twice.

Practice task

1 🎧 **L06** You will hear a student called Darren Jones giving a presentation about gold. For questions 1-4, complete the sentences with a word or short phrase.

FACTS ABOUT **GOLD**

Darren says that gold is found in a **(1)** _____ , unlike most other metals.

Darren points out that gold **(2)** _____ found in caves are evidence that humans used gold 40,000 years ago.

Darren mentions that **(3)** _____ is the country that produces the majority of gold these days.

Darren was surprised to learn that quite a lot of gold is used in the **(4)** _____ industry.

How did you do?

2 Check your answers.

3 🎧 **L07** A student wrote the wrong answers for Ex 1. Look at their answers, then listen again. Decide why you think they made these mistakes.

Darren says that gold is found in a **(1)** ___mine___ , unlike most other metals.

Darren points out that gold **(2)** ___coins___ found in caves are evidence that humans used gold 40,000 years ago.

Darren mentions that **(3)** _the United States_ is the country that produces the majority of gold these days.

Darren was surprised to learn that quite a lot of gold is used in the **(4)** ___building___ industry.

TIP: There will usually be incorrect information in the recording that can fit in each of the gaps. This is known as distraction. As you listen, rule out the incorrect information as well as choosing the correct answer.

TEACH

Strategies and skills
Identifying cues

Each question will have a cue in the recording before or after you hear the answers. Each cue will tell you where the answer for that particular question is.

1 Read the sentences from a Part 2 Listening task in which someone called Leila is talking about an animal called a golden tree frog. Highlight the key words and phrases that cue the answer and show what you are listening for.

THE GOLDEN TREE FROG

Leila's research focuses on the
(1) _____ of the golden tree frog.

Leila says that golden tree frogs are now largely confined to two (2) _____ in Trinidad.

Leila says golden tree frogs are now listed as (3) _____ on international conservation scales.

Leila uses the word (4) _____ to describe the golden tree frog's flight.

2 Match each phrase (a–e) with one of the sections you highlighted in Ex 1 that has a similar meaning. There is one phrase that you do not need to use.

a   … they glide through the air from tree to tree …

b   … their distribution is now limited to …

c   … so we were there to try and provide that …

d   … the frogs we saw were largely females …

e   … golden tree frogs have recently been re-categorised as …

3 🎧 **L08** Now listen for the cues you have identified in Ex 1. Complete the sentences in Ex 1 with a word or short phrase. You will hear the speaker twice.

SPEAKING BOOST

Discuss or answer.

1   What do you think is more important for civilisation: competition or collaboration? Think about advancement and entertainment.

2   Do you think competitiveness is something you are born with? Is it a trait we should encourage in children?

Understanding specific information and stated opinion

Knowing the kind of word you need to listen for will help you to identify it.

> **TIP:** You must always try to spell the word or phrase you write correctly.

4 Read four sentences from four different tasks. Decide whether each sentence should be completed with a verb, a noun, an adjective or an adverb. Use each kind of word once only.

1   Helen uses the word _____ to describe how she feels about living on a houseboat.

2   Jim says that _____ is the key quality that anyone considering solo sailing needs.

3   Everyone Maddy worked with was a volunteer except for the person who _____ the bands.

4   Neil describes rainfall in the area as being _____ lower than in the past.

5 🎧 **L09** Read and listen to the audioscript for Ex 4 question 1. Look at the highlighted adjectives. Which one does Helen use to describe how she feels about living on a houseboat? What do the other adjectives describe?

While I was pretty content for quite a while living in the house I was in prior to buying the houseboat, I began to feel restless. It was as though I always thought I should be somewhere else, and was quite the opposite of how well-balanced I am now I'm actually living on the water. I was terribly excited once I'd had the idea, but then got really worried about finding the perfect houseboat!

6 🎧 **L10** Listen to the recording for Ex 4 question 2. Tick the qualities in the list that Jim mentions. Which one does he say is the most important?

1 character	☐	4 experience	☐
2 discipline	☐	5 optimism	☐
3 drive	☐	6 strength	☐

7 🎧 **L11** Listen to the recording for Ex 4 question 3. Which of the verbs in the box does Maddy use to describe what volunteers did? Which one describes what the person who was paid did?

> booked   filmed   introduced   organised

8 🎧 **L12** Listen to the recording for Ex 4 question 4. Which adverbs does Neil use? What does each one describe? Which one is the answer?

Identifying and eliminating distractors

Working out which information provides the answer and which information is a distractor is an important skill.

TIP: Don't be distracted if you hear a word and also see it in an option – think about what the speaker is actually saying.

9 Read the sentences for the first part of an exam task in which a TV weatherman called Tony Halstead talks about his work. What kind of word will go in each gap?

1 Tony says that _____ is the most interesting aspect of his job.

2 Tony dislikes _____ , although he has to do it for his work.

3 Tony appeared on screen with _____ for his most unusual forecast.

4 Tony has had to have training in _____ since he started his job.

10 🎧 **L13** Now listen to and read the first part of the recording. What is the answer to Ex 9 question 1? Highlight the distractors in the audioscript.

I've been a professional TV weatherman for about eight years now. The novelty of being recognised wore off quite a while ago, so it's actually the variety that still gets me to work every day with a smile on my face. I present from a whole range of places, not just the studio, you see. Studying weather patterns, of course, is always fascinating. I've been doing that for so long now, though, that there isn't much I haven't seen before.

11 🎧 **L14** Listen to the rest of the recording and complete Ex 9 questions 2–4. What distractors are there for each one?

EXAM TASK

🎧 **L15** You will hear an archaeologist called Laura Holden talking about a project she's involved with which is mapping an ancient city in Cambodia called Angkor. For questions 1–8, complete the sentences with a word or short phrase.

Angkor **Mapping** Project

Laura says her interest in
(1) _____ eventually led her to choose a career in archaeology.

Laura's friendship with someone who worked as a **(2)** _____ helped her become involved with the Angkor project.

Laura explains that **(3)** _____ were the best means of getting above Angkor in order to take images.

Laura's project used special
(4) _____ to create the images of Angkor.

As soon as Laura saw an image of a
(5) _____ , she realised the project would be a success.

Laura's role on the project was to create
(6) _____ of parts of Angkor.

Laura compares Angkor to a
(7) _____ when describing how big the city really was.

Laura believes that **(8)** _____ was responsible for the decline of Angkor.

ABOUT THE TASK

- In Part 3, you listen to a long text which lasts around 3-4 minutes. This is usually an interview, with an interviewer and two interviewees. It can also be a discussion between two speakers, briefly introduced by a third speaker.

- There are six questions, each with four options to choose from.

- Each question relates to a specific part of the recording, and is introduced by the interviewer.

- The questions on the page follow the order you hear them on the recording. The answers come from what the interviewees say, not the interviewer.

- The questions test your understanding of detailed arguments and the speakers' attitudes, feelings and opinions.

- Questions may also test the function or purpose of what one or both of the interviewees is saying.

- Some questions might focus on specific details in the recording, and others might ask you to understand the gist or main idea of what the speaker is saying.

- One or two questions involve understanding the interaction between two speakers, for example agreement or disagreement between the two interviewees, or a shared opinion or experience.

- You'll have some time to read through the questions before you hear the recording, then you'll hear the recording twice.

Practice task

1 🎧 **L16** You will hear an interview with two estate agents called Harriet Brown and Andrew Miller talking about setting up their own businesses. Choose the answer (A, B, C or D) which fits best according to what you hear.

1 What does Harriet say about the decision to set up her own business?
   A She sought a lot of advice before making it.
   B She was motivated to make it by a difficult relationship.
   C It was something she'd thought about for a long time.
   D A series of events led her to think it was the right thing to do.

2 Andrew admits to being unsure about choosing a location for his business because
   A his financial situation limited his options.
   B he didn't have a clear idea of what to look for.
   C there were so many possibilities to select from.
   D he didn't want to upset existing estate agencies.

3 Harriet and Andrew agree that the first few months after starting their businesses
   A are hard to recollect in detail.
   B seemed to pass very quickly.
   C were a period of great excitement.
   D involved working extremely long hours.

How did you do?

2 Check your answers.

3a Read the audioscript for Ex 1 question 1. What is question 1 testing? Choose A, B or C.
   A opinion   B feeling   C detail

Well, I've always felt that the idea of 'home' and having a safe space to relax and unwind is such an important concept. I guess that's why I got into the profession. I'd already gained lots of experience in selling houses before I even thought about going it alone. [1]Had there been tension with my boss, the decision would have been made for me, of course, but we got on pretty well. Even so, in the few weeks after I'd decided, [2]there was no way I could pick her or my other colleagues' brains for tips on how best to do it – I didn't want anyone there to know what I was planning. [3]Then, a few days after I'd received a big bonus at work, some suitable premises became available in the town I'd just moved to, so I thought 'it's now or never!' [4]I was expecting to have to wait ages for everything to fall into place, but I was up and running before I knew it.

3b Match the the highlighted sections (1-4) in the audioscript with the topic of one of the options in question 1 (A-D).

3c Which part gives you the correct answer? Why are the other options wrong?

4a Read the audioscript for Ex 1 question 2. What is question 2 testing? Choose A, B or C.
   A feeling   B gist   C opinion

I'd already agreed a loan with the bank at a pretty favourable rate, which opened up a much wider range of potential premises. I'm a bit of a perfectionist, so I set about finding somewhere that met absolutely all of my criteria. This didn't exist, of course, and I was faced with this long list of other options, none of which seemed totally suitable. I eventually picked one almost at random, as I was so fed up with trying to decide. There was another similar business just down the road from it. Rather than worrying about whether two could succeed in the same street, I thought 'business is business' and went for it anyway.

4b Make notes about what Andrew says in relation to each of the options in question 2. Which part gives you the correct answer? Why are the other options wrong?

Strategies and skills

Identifying agreement and disagreement

When listening to a Part 3 discussion, you may need to decide what the participants agree or disagree about. Both speakers discuss the same point in turn, so you have to keep in mind what the first speaker says in order to decide if the other person agrees or disagrees.

1 Read Ex 1 question 3 of the Practice task again, which tests agreement. Match phrases that Harriet says about each option (1–4) with what Andrew says about each of them (a–d).

Harriet

1   I wouldn't be able to tell you now even a fraction of what I did.

2   … although the days seemed to fly by …

3   My expectations were that it'd be a really thrilling time. After all, what could be more exhilarating than running my own estate agency!

4   I was spending as much time as I could at the office …

Andrew

a   … the first few months seemed to last for years!

b   … I'd avoid the trap that many new business owners fall into of being at work all day every day to begin with.

c   … my memory of it all is a little hazy.

d   My lasting impression of that time is of finishing one thing and immediately moving onto the next, without time for serious reflection or to catch my breath …

2 In which of the matched pairs in Ex 1 do both phrases have a similar meaning?

> **TIP:** There will always be incorrect information in the recording that supports the three incorrect options. This is known as distraction. As you listen, rule out the incorrect information as well as choosing the correct answer.

3 🎧 **L17** Read and listen to three extracts from Listening Part 3 tasks. What do they agree about? Choose the correct option (a or b).

1   **A:** There needs to be a total re-think on transport in the city, and I mean total! As it stands, the car is king, and there's no culture of looking out for cyclists, which frightens people who would otherwise ride to and from work. Nonetheless, some cities have managed to transform this almost overnight.

   B: Drivers' lack of concern for bike riders is certainly what's kept me and a lot of others off our bikes, but I think you're being incredibly optimistic about how quick it would be to solve the problem.

   a   people's attitudes to cycling and cyclists
   b   the speed at which people's attitudes can change

2   **A:** I think we've reached the upper limit of how much medical research we can actually afford – I mean, there aren't endless reserves of money available. We'd make significant progress if these resources were targeted much more carefully.

   B: The processes for choosing who's entitled to receive financial support are already time-consuming and rigorous enough. We're definitely up to the maximum of the share of budgets that medical research should receive, though.

   a   the quantity of medical research that should be funded
   b   how decisions are made about which medical research to fund

3   **A:** The study showed that when upbeat, rousing classical or pop music was played in the factory, output actually rose, whereas the reverse was true for calmer or more sombre music. Interestingly, workers reported feeling more lively and content whatever the music was. That's surely true.

   B: It was such a small-scale, short-term study that I wouldn't read much into it, certainly when it comes to efficiency on the production line. Having something to break the repetitive nature of that kind of work is bound to lift your spirits, though, even if you don't really like what's being played.

   a   certain types of music enhance productivity
   b   listening to music while at work improves mood

4 🎧 **L18 Listen to the extracts and choose the correct answer (A-C).**

1 The speakers disagree that reducing government support for charities leads to
   A greater efficiency in how charities are run.
   B a higher level of public donations.
   C public resentment against the state.

2 The speakers disagree about
   A the nutritional quality of school meals.
   B whether some pupils should pay for school meals.
   C the portion sizes of school meals.

3 The speakers disagree about
   A how well-equipped the training centre was.
   B how well the teacher dealt with the students.
   C how interesting the content of the course was.

4 The speakers disagree about
   A the impact of the internet on people's social skills.
   B the degree to which the internet is useful in education.
   C the speed at which people expect problems to be solved.

SPEAKING BOOST

Discuss or answer.

1 What do you think of virtual, online communities? How are they different from non-virtual communities?

2 What do you think an 'echo chamber' is on social media? What effect do you think it might have?

Understanding feeling

It is important to understand what a speaker thinks about something, although they may not express it simply and clearly.

5 🎧 **L19 Listen to the extracts (1-6). For questions 1-6, choose the best answer (A-C).**

1 The speaker thinks that the author
   A has provided extremely detailed arguments.
   B has arrived at opinions without convincing evidence.
   C has focused more on the supporting data than on opinion.

2 The speaker thinks that opponents of homeschooling
   A base their attacks on its credibility on insufficient examples.
   B are unwilling to accept how effective it can sometimes be.
   C make inaccurate observations about teaching standards.

3 What point does the speaker make about the film?
   A There are some unusual characters.
   B The special effects are highly impressive.
   C It's different to most other films in its genre.

4 The speaker believes that the majority of professional athletes
   A are overpaid.
   B are good role models.
   C are skilled on social media.

5 The speaker thinks that behaviour on trains
   A is much the same as it always was.
   B has deteriorated in recent years.
   C is gradually improving after having declined.

6 What does the speaker say about his online course?
   A Employers see it as less valid than a traditional course.
   B Doing it required a lot of technical skills.
   C Its flexibility was as much a problem as a benefit.

Dealing with paraphrase

The language used in the recording will always be different to the wording in the questions and options. This is called a paraphrase.

> **TIP:** In the exam, you hear the speaker twice. The first time you listen, just put a pencil mark against the option you think is correct. The second time, check all the options again and confirm your answer.

6 Match the sentences that have a similar meaning (1-5 and a-e).

1 There aren't anywhere near as many as that.
2 A balance needs to be struck.
3 This goes against conventional wisdom.
4 It was a complete lie.
5 There are some criteria that must be met.

a Nothing could be further from the truth.
b Most people believe something different.
c The number is a great deal lower than you quoted.
d Certain qualities are necessary.
e There should be a sensible compromise.

7 Complete each second sentence with a word from the box so that it has a similar meaning to the first sentence.

> hold   hope   matter   mind
> moderation   room

1   I soon lost interest in listening as the song was rather dull.

   The track wasn't original enough to _____ my attention for long.

2   I needed ideas so decided seeing some art would be a good idea.

   I went to the exhibition in the _____ of finding inspiration.

3   The doctor told them not to eat so many sweet things.

   They were advised to eat sugary foods in _____ .

4   The actors were told that their performance really wasn't good enough.

   The director told the cast that there was a lot of _____ for improvement in their acting.

5   I'm certain he'll arrive soon, but I just don't know when.

   It's only a _____ of time before he gets here.

6   I did all I could to reassure her that it would be OK.

   I tried everything to put her _____ at rest.

EXAM TASK

L20 You will hear an interview in which a journalist called Yasmin Harvey and a research scientist called Guy Jameson are discussing new technology. For questions 1–6, choose the answer (A, B, C or D) which fits best according to what you hear.

1   What does Guy say initially pushed him towards working in the technology field?

   A   the prospect of creating highly lucrative devices
   B   a powerful desire to continue learning new things
   C   a wish to be employed at the cutting edge of science
   D   the need to please influential people in his life

2   Why does Yasmin choose to define the word 'technology'?

   A   to check her understanding of the interviewer's question
   B   to suggest it's a commonly misunderstood term
   C   to emphasise its importance to society
   D   to clarify her own thoughts on the issue

3   What does Guy suggest about government funding to support technological developments?

   A   It tends to target what's exciting and not what's useful.
   B   It's all based on the likely profits they will make.
   C   High-status academic institutions get more than their fair share.
   D   The application process for it is extremely demanding.

4   What is the focus of Yasmin's forthcoming book on technology?

   A   an overview of scientific creativity
   B   case studies of important developments
   C   an analysis of approaches in different locations
   D   evaluations of the methods of notable scientists

5   When asked about the control of new technology, Yasmin and Guy agree about

   A   how easy it will be to impose any limitations.
   B   the likely response from high-tech industries.
   C   who should be responsible for overseeing any restrictions.
   D   the amount of regulation that should be in place.

6   Which aspect of future technological development do Yasmin and Guy disagree about?

   A   channelling more research into environmental concerns
   B   the private sector becoming the primary source of research funding
   C   increased cooperation between research teams worldwide
   D   how replacing employees with machines will affect society

ABOUT THE TASK

- In Listening Part 4, you listen to five short monologues on the same topic.
- Each monologue is given by a different speaker describing their thoughts and opinions about the topic.
- There are two tasks, each of which is about a different aspect of the same topic.
- You are given two lists, one for each task. Both lists have eight different options.

- As you listen, you match the correct option from both lists to each speaker.
- You use each option only once, and there are three extra options in both of the lists that you do not need to use.
- The tasks test your understanding of attitude and opinion, and you need to listen to the general meaning (or gist) of what each speaker is saying.
- You'll have time to read the options before you hear the recording, and you'll hear the recording twice.

Practice task

1 🎧 **L21** You will hear three short extracts in which people are talking about doing long solo journeys.

TASK ONE

For questions 1-3, choose from the list (A-E) the reason each speaker gives for choosing to go on the journey.

TASK TWO

For questions 4-6, choose from the list (A-E) how each speaker feels about the journey now.

While you listen you must complete both tasks.

A to escape from a boring routine
B to face up to a long-held fear
C to raise money for a good cause
D to rise to a challenge from a friend
E to test the limits of physical ability

A eager to try a different way of travelling solo
B satisfied to have achieved their aims
C keen to share similar journeys with others
D surprised by people's reaction to the achievement
E grateful to have survived the experience

Speaker 1 [ ] 1

Speaker 2 [ ] 2

Speaker 3 [ ] 3

Speaker 1 [ ] 4

Speaker 2 [ ] 5

Speaker 3 [ ] 6

How did you do?

2 Check your answers.

3a Read the audioscript for Ex 1 speaker 1. Look at the highlighted phrases (1–3). Which topic in the options for Task One (A-E) does each highlighted section relate to?

It wasn't as though I decided to sail solo across the Atlantic one day and was sailing the next. It took ages to prepare and I needed help from many other people. **¹Thankfully, my employer was sympathetic,** probably because they thought doing **²an immensely dangerous and physical challenge ³to financially support a good friend who was seriously ill** was an acceptable excuse! I'd never done anything like that before and had certainly never spent such a stretch of time on my own. It's given me a taste for it actually, so I wouldn't say no to having a go at something comparable in the near future, just perhaps not in a boat.

3b Which of the highlighted phrases (1–3) gives you the correct answer for Task One? Why?

TIP: You may hear more than one option mentioned in the recording, but the reason and the way the person feels will not be the same as in the option. These are called distractors.

4a Highlight the sections of text in Ex 3a which relate to options for Task Two. Which topic in the options (A-E) does each highlighted section relate to?

4b Which of the sections you highlighted gives you the correct answer for Task Two? Why?

5a Read the audioscript for Ex 1 speaker 2. Look at the highlighted sections. Which topic in the options (A-E) for both Task One and Task Two does each highlighted section relate to?

¹My friends weren't sure what possessed me to cycle across Australia on my own. ²I really thought they'd change their tune once I'd done it, but they still think I was mad to take it on. While it's true that **³there were a few moments that could've turned nasty,** things like that always turn out OK. A common theme amongst those who've done something similar is that **⁴they're seeking something that's as different to the mundanities of day-to-day existence as possible.** My motivation was more personal. **⁵I'd always avoided spending time by myself. The longer this went on, the more intimidating a prospect it became. The bike ride seemed like a perfect way to overcome that.**

5b Which highlighted sections give you the answers for the two tasks?

6a Read the audioscript for Ex 1 speaker 3. Highlight the sections which give the answers and the distractors for Task One. Underline the same things for Task Two.

I walked from the far north east of North America to the far south west. It all started when the friend who was best man at my wedding poked fun at me for being so unfit. He said I'd never be able to walk more than 20 km, so I just thought up the most ridiculous way imaginable to do it. I actually got a lot from it, so my intention now is to repeat the walk, but across South America instead. It'd be fun if a few of us decided to do it this time, not just me. I'm glad I did it, even though the time it took me was a little outside what I was hoping for.

6b Which is the correct option for each of the tasks? How do you know?

TEACH

Strategies and skills
Understanding the main point

In Listening Part 4, it's important to understand the main point that each speaker is making. You may need to be able to do this for two different topics in a single monologue.

1a Read the extract from a Part 4 speaker about attending a training course. Choose the option (A–F) which best summarises the main point the speaker is making about why they attended.

> Never having done anything like payroll training before, I was actually surprised by how much I got out of it. While having it on my company training record certainly won't do my chances of getting a position with a bit more responsibility any harm, it also allowed me to get out of the office for a day a week for a few months, which is really why I signed up for it.

A to improve their prospects of promotion
B to add to their existing skills
C to make important business contacts
D to try something completely new
E to impress a colleague
F to break the normal work routine

1b Which other options are mentioned? Why are they wrong?

> **TIP:** The speakers will also refer to some of the other options, but there will always be a reason why these options are incorrect. As you listen, rule out the incorrect information as well as choosing the correct answer.

2a 🎧 **L22** Listen to two more speakers talking about why they attended a training course. Which of the options (A–F) in Ex 1a best summarises what they say?

2b Which other options does each speaker mention? Why are they wrong?

3 🎧 **L23** Read and listen to this extract from a Listening Part 4 task. For both tasks, choose the correct answer (A–E) to answer the question.

> It's been a more complicated process than I was expecting, as moving away from family was tough, but my first impressions of the place are largely positive. I still have the occasional doubt as to whether I should've stayed, but I didn't have much choice in the end as my boss said that my skills were needed here. I'm a city girl at heart and this place just feels a little bit small to settle down in in the long term. Don't get me wrong! There's lots going on here and it's a popular place, but the prices of property and the cost of living reflect that. I'm hoping that I'll soon have a bit more say in where I end up, once I'm a bit higher up in the company.

TASK ONE
What is the speaker's reason for moving to a new town?

A to take up a new job
B to have a change of scenery
C to allow a relationship to develop
D to save money
E to be in a more relaxed environment

TASK TWO
How do they feel about their new town now?

A doubtful they made the correct decision
B uncertain how long they'll stay
C delighted to have met so many people
D surprised by how rapid settling in has been
E disappointed by the atmosphere

4a 🎧 **L24** Listen to another speaker on the same topic as in Ex 3. What is the correct option (A–E) for both Task One and Task Two?

4b Which other options does the speaker mention? Why are they wrong?

SPEAKING BOOST

Discuss or answer.

1 If you get lost, do you usually ask for help or work out where you need to go by yourself?

2 How important is it to have direction in your life? Do you always have a plan?

Understanding gist

Understanding gist involves working out the overall meaning, even though it is not directly stated in a text.

5 Read the extracts and answer the questions.

I needed to save money, but the inability I'd shown to do so throughout my life immediately sprang to mind. I resolved to change, starting the process by skipping the morning coffee I picked up at the station each morning on my way to work. The weekend takeaway meals had to go too, as did the cakes and chocolate that had always been a feature of my weekly shop. It was far from the instant fix that the lottery promised, but I was at least guaranteed to be able to put away what I needed, if not as quickly as I might have wanted.

1 What strategy did the speaker adopt to save money?
   A replacing expensive items with cheaper ones
   B making small sacrifices over a long period
   C buying lottery tickets instead of buying luxury items

2 In saving money, the speaker demonstrates
   A a lack of self-control
   B an inability to change their behaviour
   C a degree of self-knowledge

When my book finally came out, there was a flurry of things I was contracted to do, such as media interviews and readings at various places around the country. What I'd pictured in my mind's eye as a period of relative calm, savouring the acclaim I thought being a published author was sure to bring, turned out to be something resembling a three-hour commute to and from work with a one-hour period of nerve-racking but enjoyable activity in between.

3 What surprised the speaker when her book was published?
   A the realities of being a successful writer
   B how little time she got to spend with readers
   C the number of invitations she received

4 What is the speaker's attitude to travelling to events?
   A She thinks journeys pass quickly.
   B She enjoys the anticipation.
   C She sees it as a chore.

6 Match the extracts (1–5) with the speaker's opinion (a–e).

1 After being in the movie business for so long, you'd think he'd have put in at least one decent performance by now.

2 Clearly there's something in his genes as he's the third generation of McTavishes to have been deservedly nominated for an Oscar.

3 Although I've no great desire to see less of him on-screen, I've a feeling that he'd shine just as brightly behind the camera as in front of it.

4 Reviews of films that he's appeared in seldom mention his abilities at all, even though he steals every scene he's ever appeared in.

5 He may be good at what he does, but if I have to see his face peering out from the screen once more this year, I may well stop going to the cinema altogether.

a He comes from a family of talented actors.
b He's underrated as an actor.
c I'm bored of seeing him in films.
d He's a very poor actor.
e He would probably make a good film director.

Interpreting opinions

It is important to understand what a speaker thinks about something, although they may not express it simply or clearly.

7 Read the extracts (1–6) in which speakers are talking about what has helped them to succeed. Match them with the opinions (a–f).

1 Without being able to predict how customers think, I'd never have got to where I am now.

2 I've never met anyone at the top level of my profession who's shy.

3 Most of my lessons have been based on my own failures.

4 The only route I could see to get where I wanted to be was via academic excellence.

5 There's something within me that always wants to be at the next level up from where I am.

6 I put my own success down to finding out how others who went before me got to where I want to be.

a learning from their own mistakes
b being highly self-confident
c having a need to constantly improve
d understanding other people well
e reading about how others have got to the top
f studying to a very high level

8 🎧 L25 Listen to five short recordings in which people talk about having a gap year between school and university. Choose the option (A–H) which best matches the opinion of each speaker.

A There were some unexpected advantages.
B I realised that I needed a break from education.
C I'm not sure I even want to go to university now.
D It's given me a much clearer idea of my future.
E Being older than other students doesn't worry me.
F I wish I'd made better use of the time.
G It seemed to pass incredibly quickly.
H I feel quite distant from my school friends now.

Speaker 1 ____
Speaker 2 ____
Speaker 3 ____
Speaker 4 ____
Speaker 5 ____

Identifying attitude and feelings

To identify how a speaker is feeling, you may need to listen for phrases you can link to an option.

9 Read the options (1-5) from a Part 4 task and the two sentences, A and B. Both sentences refer to the topic of the option, but only one matches the feeling. Choose the sentence (A or B) that best matches the feeling in the option.

How did each speaker feel about organising a public event?

1 astonished by the amount of work involved
   A I knew beforehand it'd be a challenge, but was taken aback by just how much of one it ended up being.
   B Taking it on certainly led to me learning a lot about how to delegate work to others in a diplomatic way.

2 confused by the regulations regarding public events
   A A friend who happens to be a solicitor was helping me, so I didn't need to concern myself overly with the red tape.
   B I could really have done with a law degree to fight my way through all the paperwork that needed to be completed.

3 supportive of everyone who helped
   A The stage manager did a fantastic job of dealing with the security guards, some of whom were uncooperative to say the least.
   B I really can't fault a single individual who was involved in the staging of the event; there seemed to be no weak links in the chain.

4 modest about their part in the event's success
   A The public response was amazing but it wouldn't have been possible without every single member of the team that helped to stage it.
   B Reading the fantastic reviews on social media made me feel so proud of what I'd achieved in such a short space of time.

10 🎧 **L26 Listen to five speakers talking about their attitudes towards bad decisions they have made in the past. Match what each speaker (1-5) says with an option (A-H).**

A I learnt a lot from it.
B I think anyone else would have done the same thing.
C I should have got more advice before making it.
D I had enough knowledge to know better.
E I regret that it affected so many other people.
F I found out quickly that I'd made the wrong choice.
G I was persuaded to make it by someone else.
H I had no option but to decide quickly.

Speaker 1 ____
Speaker 2 ____
Speaker 3 ____
Speaker 4 ____
Speaker 5 ____

Correcting mistakes

If you choose one wrong option, you may make a mistake with other answers because you have already used that option once.

> **TIP:** The first time you listen, just put pencil marks against the two options you think are correct. The second time, check all of the options again, and confirm your answer.

11 🎧 **L27 A student has answered the task below. Listen to the speakers and decide which answers are correct and incorrect. Correct any that they got wrong.**

You will hear four short extracts in which people are talking about taking up a new sport. For questions 1-4, choose from the list (A-F) what has allowed each speaker to progress at their new sport. For questions 5-8, choose from the list (A-F) what has surprised each speaker about their new sport.

TASK ONE

What has allowed the speakers to progress?

A knowledge of similar sports
B a supportive club
C watching other people do it
D natural talent
E many opportunities to practise
F effective coaching

Speaker 1	A	1
Speaker 2	B	2
Speaker 3	F	3
Speaker 4	C	4

TASK TWO

What has surprised the speakers about their sport?

A how much stamina it requires
B the cost of the equipment
C how many people do it locally
D public interest in watching it
E how competitive participants are
F the technical skill required

Speaker 1	D	5
Speaker 2	A	6
Speaker 3	E	7
Speaker 4	F	8

EXAM TASK

🎧 **L28 You will hear five short extracts in which people are talking about starting new jobs.**

While you listen you must complete both tasks.

TASK ONE

For questions 1–5, choose from the list (A–H) each speaker's early impressions of their new job.

A	challenging in a positive way
B	a relaxed environment to work in
C	great chances for promotion
D	a good level of responsibility
E	a really positive staff attitude
F	excellent facilities for employees
G	seemed to have a thorough induction
H	an innovative organisation

Speaker 1 ⬜ 1
Speaker 2 ⬜ 2
Speaker 3 ⬜ 3
Speaker 4 ⬜ 4
Speaker 5 ⬜ 5

TASK TWO

For questions 6–10, choose from the list (A–H) what each speaker has found difficult about their new job.

A	prioritising different tasks
B	managing the heavy workload
C	contacting certain colleagues
D	commuting to and from work
E	getting used to new systems
F	having confidence in their own ability
G	finding their way around the premises
H	learning who is who

Speaker 1 ⬜ 6
Speaker 2 ⬜ 7
Speaker 3 ⬜ 8
Speaker 4 ⬜ 9
Speaker 5 ⬜ 10

ABOUT THE TASK

- In Speaking Part 1, the examiner asks you some questions about you and your opinions.
- This allows you a little time to settle into the test before you do more challenging tasks.
- It tests your ability to use general social and interactional language.
- The first few questions ask for information about you. The following questions ask for your opinions about everyday topics.
- The examiner will ask you and your partner questions individually.

- Tell the examiner if you don't understand any of the questions, but remember that you can only ask for repetition, not explanation.
- Listen to what your partner says, because you can comment briefly on this if the examiner then asks you the same question.
- You shouldn't talk to your partner in this part, so remember not to interrupt them, or agree or disagree with what they are saying.
- You should give interesting answers, but don't speak for too long.
- This part of the test takes about two minutes.

Practice task

1 🎧 **S01** Listen to these Speaking Part 1 questions. Think about the best way to respond to them, then answer them.

How did you do?

2 Read the questions from Ex 1 again and some answers to them (A–C). Choose the best answer for each question.

1 Where are you from?
   A Venezuela. It's in South America.
   B I'm from a city called Bucharest, which is the capital city of Romania.
   C I've lived the whole of my life in a large city called Valencia, which is on the south-east coast of Spain. It has a population of around two million people.

2 What do you do?
   A Well, I work and then in the evenings I usually I go out with my friends. I play quite a lot of sport too, especially at weekends.
   B I'm a receptionist.
   C Currently, I'm studying for a degree in politics and history at university, and I also work part-time in a café at weekends.

3 How long have you been studying English?
   A I started when I was eight years old, I think, and studied it all through secondary school, so for about ten years now – I really enjoy it.
   B I have classes twice a week, on Monday and Wednesday evenings, and each one lasts for two hours, so four hours a week in total.
   C Nine years altogether.

4 What do you most enjoy about learning English?
   A We often have class discussions and debates in English about lots of different topics, most of which are really interesting. They're usually very lively and great fun to take part in.
   B I really need it for my job. The people I email and talk to don't speak the same language as me so we use English instead.
   C Definitely not writing or grammar exercises!

5 What did you most like about the area where you grew up?
   A I think it's one of the best places in the world. I love it.
   B I liked the city, the different facilities there, and I also loved the beach, the landscape and the climate.
   C I really liked the fact that it's a small city – not so big that it's stressful, but big enough that you have everything you need and can get to know people quite well.

6 How important is it for you to earn lots of money?
   A For many people it's very important, which is why they get jobs that guarantee they'll make a lot of money, even though they might not be that interested in the work. For others, it's the job satisfaction that's more important than the salary.
   B I want to make enough to be able to live on, of course, but I'm not especially interested in getting rich for the sake of it. Particularly if it means doing something I don't really enjoy.
   C Not very. The field I'm aiming to work in isn't very well paid, so it's quite fortunate really.

7 Which famous person would you most like to meet?
   A I think it'd be pretty interesting to meet an astronaut like Tim Peake or Chris Hadfield. I'd want to know how it felt being in space and whether they were scared or not during the mission.
   B I'd be worried about being disappointed. I mean, what if your hero turned out to be someone you didn't actually like very much?
   C Cristiano Ronaldo, I guess. I love football and he's the best player.

8 What do you hope to be doing in ten years' time?
   A My dream would be to have my own fashion design company. I'd like to specialise in men's fashion. I don't know how realistic that is, to be honest, but that's ideally what I'd like to be doing.
   B I'll probably be teaching English somewhere, maybe in another country. I hope so.
   C Ten years is a long time to think into the future, especially as I quite often don't know what's going to happen next week!

3 What is wrong with the other answers in Ex 2?

Strategies and skills
Extending your answers

> **TIP:** If you practise adding phrases to your answers which allow you to give reasons and add information, this will encourage you to say more.

1 Complete the responses to Part 1 questions with the words in the box.

> addition   fact   hard   opportunity   other   plan

1   It's _____ to choose just one place, but if I had to, I'd say that visiting Japan would be top of my list. It seems like such an interesting country in so many ways: the landscape, the people, the cities – everything!

2   On the one hand, there wasn't a great deal to do in the area where I grew up because it was a small village, but on the _____ hand, it was very safe as there weren't any busy roads at all.

3   I have several news apps on my phone that I use to get notifications about interesting stories. In _____ to that, I watch the news on TV in the evening as it tends to go into more detail.

4   Given the _____ , I'd definitely learn how to scuba dive. I'm fascinated by what lives under the water and I think seeing it first-hand rather than on documentaries would just be amazing.

5   If everything goes to _____ , I'm going to study mechanical engineering at university. Once I've finished that, I'll find a really good job with a major company, either here or in another country.

6   I'd say that the person I admire more than anyone else is my dad, due to the _____ that, despite balancing a demanding job with family life, he's always so positive, which is not something many people manage.

2 What question do you think each person was answering?

3 In what way does each speaker extend what they say?

Adding examples

4 Choose the correct option to complete the responses to Part 1 questions.

1   I use lots of different methods for keeping in touch with friends, actually. **For instance / As well as that**, I spend an hour or so a day on social media.

2   We went to some really interesting places while we were there, **then again / such as** the royal palace and the gardens.

3   I didn't especially enjoy joining in the sports **like / as** football and tennis that my friends used to play.

4   A lot of the things we do in class, **perhaps / say**, giving presentations and reading out our work, are really good for developing my confidence.

Giving reasons

5 Complete the sentences with the words for giving reasons in the box.

> due   grounds   owing   reason
> result   seeing   start   view

1   Richard couldn't climb the mountain _____ to being very unfit.

2   Valerie gave up learning English for the _____ that she didn't have time.

3   They didn't go for a picnic as planned _____ to the wind and rain.

4   In _____ of how much work he had to do, Marcin decided to start work early.

5   The level of the river was lower than usual as a _____ of the recent dry weather.

6   Gina refused to go on the _____ that it was too dangerous.

7   I'm unlikely to get the job _____ as I don't have any relevant experience.

8   I can't go to the cinema tonight. I've got too much homework for a _____ .

There are other ways of adding reasons using a single word.

6 Complete the answers with ideas of your own.

1   What new things would you like to learn in the future?
    I'd really like to learn more languages **since** …

2   Which of your teachers at school will you always remember?
    I'll never forget my music teacher at secondary school **as** …

3   How important to you is it to have a healthy lifestyle?
    It's extremely important to me **because** …

4   If you could try any sport you've never done before, what would you choose?
    I'd definitely choose … **as** …

7 Complete the answers to the questions using ideas of your own. Give examples, reasons and other information.

1   Is there a film you've particularly enjoyed seeing recently?
    Yes, the one I've most enjoyed in the last few weeks was …

2   What would your ideal holiday be?
    Well, my favourite type of holiday is …

3   How important is it to have friends who share the same interests as you?
    I think it's fairly important, but …

4   Would you say you're a well-organised person?
    I'm not sure I'd exactly describe myself as that, but …

TIP: It's good to think about the types of questions you may be asked, but never rehearse answers. It shouldn't sound like you prepared them before the exam.

8 🎧 **S02** Listen to some students responding to the questions in Ex 7 and compare your answers with theirs.

Using a range of language

It is important not to repeat words too much, and to use a range of language.

9 Replace one of the highlighted words in each sentence with the words in the box.

accomplish   affordable   exceptionally   hysterical   illustrate
imaginative   immediately   substantially

1   Transport where I live is quite cheap. It's cheap to travel anywhere in the city.

2   I admire her because she's extremely hard-working, and also she's extremely generous.

3   Some days it feels as though I achieve very little when I actually achieve a lot.

4   I like to be creative in my free time. I'm actually quite a creative person.

5   I like keeping fit a lot more than I used to, so I do a lot more exercise than before.

6   It's hard to explain what I mean, so perhaps it's better to explain it with an example.

7   The last film I saw was very funny indeed. Everyone in the cinema clearly thought it was funny.

8   I got a job just after leaving university, and then got my first flat just after that.

Asking for repetition

If you have not heard or fully understood a question, you can ask the examiner to repeat it.

TIP: Remember that the examiner can only repeat the question to help you, not rephrase it.

10 Match the beginning of a request to repeat the question (1–6) with its ending (a–f) to make phrases you can use to ask for repetition.

1   I'm sorry, but would you mind

2   Could you please

3   I'm not sure what you

4   I'm afraid I

5   Sorry, but is it possible

6   I beg your pardon, but

a   to repeat the question, please?

b   saying that again, please?

c   I'm afraid I didn't catch what you said.

d   repeat the question, as I didn't hear it properly?

e   didn't hear the question – sorry!

f   said, I'm afraid.

EXAM TASK

🎧 **S03** Read and listen to the questions. Answer them so that they are true for you.

First of all, we'd like to know something about you.

* Where are you from?

* What do you do there?

* How long have you been studying English?

* What do you most enjoy about learning English?

* Do you prefer spending time with a large group of friends, or just one or two? (Why?)

* What's the best thing about the town or city you live in? (Why?)

* Who was the biggest influence on you when you were a child? (Why?)

* Would you prefer to have a job you really enjoy or one which pays very well? (Why?)

* Do you think you spend too much time on the internet?

* How do you hope to use your English skills in the future?

* Is there a festival or celebration you particularly enjoy? (Why?)

* What's the most interesting aspect of trying new things?

- In Part 2, you have to speak alone for about a minute. You should not help your partner, or interrupt them in this part.

- The examiner gives you three pictures, and tells you what they have in common. The examiner then reads out a task related to the pictures for you to do.

- You must choose two of the three pictures, which you will then talk about.

- You must compare the pictures you have chosen and carry out the task the examiner has asked you to do.

- The task involves talking about two issues related to the pictures.

- The two questions which make up the task are written on the paper above the pictures.

- After you have compared your two pictures and carried out the task for one minute, the examiner will ask your partner about your pictures for about 30 seconds.

- You also have to answer a question about your partner's pictures, so listen carefully to your partner while they are speaking.

- You should always answer these questions based on what you can see in the pictures.

Practice task

1 Look at the pictures below. They show pairs of people performing in different situations. Compare the pictures, and say why the people might have chosen to perform in these situations and how the people might be feeling.

Talk about them on your own for about a minute.

> - Why have the people chosen to perform in these situations?
> - How might the people be feeling?

How did you do?

2 Think about your own answer to the task.

Did you
- compare the pictures?
- answer the questions?
- talk about the people in the pictures?
- talk for about a minute?

3a 🎧 S04 Listen to two students (A and B) doing the task in Ex 1 and answer the questions.

1 Do they compare the pictures or just describe them?

2 Do they answer the questions, and talk about both pictures?

3 Do they talk just about the people in the pictures or about other things too?

3b Which student gave the better answer? Why?

4 Think about your own response again and compare it to the students' responses. Try the task again, this time using the checklist in Ex 2.

Strategies and skills
Comparing

When comparing pictures, mention both what is similar and what is different about each picture. Balance your answer by talking about one point of similarity or difference in both pictures, rather than talking about each picture separately. Where possible, extend the comparisons through your answers to the specific questions, in order to make your answer more coherent.

> **TIP:** Examples of things that might be the same or different include the setting (inside/ outside, city/countryside, sunny/raining), the context (formal/informal, amateur/professional) and the people (serious/relaxed, alone/with others), etc.

1 Read the exam task and look at the pictures. Think about how they are similar and different.

2 Complete the sentences comparing and contrasting the pictures.

1 The main similarity between the pictures is _____ .

2 What the two pictures have in common is that _____ .

3 In the first picture, _____ whereas in the second one _____ .

4 A significant difference between the pictures is _____ .

5 The people having the discussion in the first picture _____ .

> **TIP:** Remember that you need to spend time responding to the questions as well as comparing the pictures, so manage your speaking time carefully.

3 Look again at the questions above the pictures. Write four sentences for each picture, two for each of the two questions.

4 🎧 **S05** Listen to a student doing the whole task. Did they have the same ideas as you?

Your pictures show people discussing things in different situations. Compare the pictures, and say why you think the people are discussing things in these situations, and how easy or difficult it might be to take part in the discussion.

> • Why might the people be discussing things?
> • How easy or difficult might it be to take part in the discussion?

Speculating

The questions in Part 2 give you the opportunity to use complex language, and to speculate about the people in the pictures: why they are there, how they are feeling, etc.

> **TIP:** Remember that you should only talk about the people in the pictures, and not about yourself.

5 Look at the picture below. It shows people working in a team. What could you say in answer to each of the two questions? Make sentences beginning with these phrases.

- They might be …
- I would guess that …
- It's possible that …
- It could be the case that …

- I'd imagine that they are …
- I suppose that …
- I'd assume that …

> - Why might teamwork be important in this situation?
> - How difficult might working in a team be in this situation?

6 🎧 S06 Listen to two students answering both questions. Did they have the same ideas as you?

> **TIP:** Remember to compare and contrast the two pictures before you move on to answering the questions.

Structuring a long turn

Linkers help to structure your answer by showing whether ideas support each other or give a contrast. When you are talking about the pictures you should connect your ideas using linking words.

> **TIP:** Remember that different linkers are used in different ways in sentences. Learn how to use each one.

7 Look at the exam task. Choose the best words to complete the student's answer so that it is organised clearly.

¹First of all / Principally, I'd like to talk about the similarities and differences between the two pictures. In the first picture, we can see three students who are learning about creating and operating robotic machinery. There's no teacher present so they seem to be experimenting and investigating on their own. **²To contrast / In contrast** with the other picture, which shows students listening to a lecture, this is a very hands-on way of learning practical skills. The first learning activity is taking place in a classroom or robotics workshop, **³whereas / although** in the other picture, it's in a large lecture hall.

The teaching in the lecture theatre involves a lot of listening for students. Learning in the robotics workshop, **⁴on the other hand / for that reason**, is much more about doing. Learning through lectures is a good way for many students to get information about quite theoretical subjects. **⁵Therefore / However**, learning in a workshop will greatly develop students' practical skills.

I imagine that learning through doing, **⁶as is the case / as you'd expect** in a workshop such as in the first picture, would be far more interesting **⁷when related to / when compared to** simply listening to what someone says, looking at what they show you on a screen and just writing it all down.

Your pictures show students learning in different ways. Compare the two pictures and say how students can benefit from these different ways of learning, and how interesting they might find learning in these ways.

- **How can students benefit from these different ways of learning?**
- **How interesting might they find learning in these ways?**

Answering the follow-up question to your partner's long turn

When your partner has finished talking about their pictures you will be asked a follow-up question about them. This asks for your opinion about what is shown in the pictures.

> **TIP:** This question is an extension question to your partner's task. You can improve your answers by giving reasons and examples, but don't speak for too long.

8 Read the follow-up questions (1–4) and the first part of two student responses (A and B). Which response is best? Why?

1 Which of these ways of learning do you think is most successful?
   A I'd prefer the one in the first picture because I learn better that way.
   B I think it depends on what kind of person you are. For example, …

2 In which situation do you think teamwork is most important?
   A In my opinion, I don't think a restaurant kitchen could operate without teamwork because …
   B The chefs in the restaurant kitchen.

3 Which kind of discussion do you think is most useful?
   A I'd go for the political debate because it helps to inform people about important issues, such as …
   B I think the discussion amongst friends in a café is so much more fun because …

4 Which of these events would be most rewarding for the performers?
   A I actually believe that the people watching the football will get more satisfaction, especially if the team that they're supporting wins.
   B My guess is that the footballers would gain a greater sense of satisfaction, as long as they put in 100 percent effort during the game.

Dealing with unfamiliar vocabulary

You may have to talk about something you have forgotten the words for, or you may not know the word you need. It's important to have some strategies in place if this happens. This will give you time to think and recover.

9 Complete the sentences with the words and phrases in the box to form expressions you can use if you are not sure of a word.

> come back to me   give me a moment
> gone blank   not totally sure
> should know   think of what it is

1 Just _____ and I'll be able to remember the word for it.

2 I'm sorry, but my mind's _____ . Ah yes, it's called a yacht.

3 Oh, I can't remember the name for it. It'll _____ in a second.

4 I'm _____ if this is the right word for it, but I think it's a screwdriver.

5 I realise I _____ the name for this, but I just can't remember it now.

6 I know the word but I just can't _____ at the moment.

🎧 **S07** Listen and complete the exam task.

Candidate A, it's your turn first. Here are your pictures. They show people helping others in different situations. Compare two of the pictures, and say how difficult you think it might be to help someone in these situations, and how you think the people who are helping might be feeling.

- How difficult do you think it might be to help someone in these situations?
- How do you think the people who are helping might be feeling?

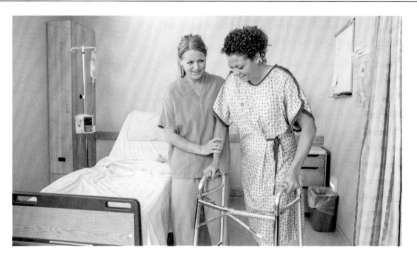

Candidate B, which of these ways of helping do you think people would be most grateful for?

Candidate B, here are your pictures. They show people attending important events. Compare two of the pictures, and say what the people might find enjoyable about attending these events, and how difficult you think the events might be to arrange.

- What might the people find enjoyable about attending these events?
- How difficult do you think the events might be to arrange?

Candidate A, which of these events do you think would be the most expensive to organise?

TEST

- In Speaking Part 3 you and a partner have to do a collaborative task with two sections.
- The examiner explains the context of the task and then gives you a question to discuss.
- This question appears in the centre of a diagram and has five written prompts around it. These prompts give you points to consider and are related to the central question.
- You have a short time to look at the task before you need to start speaking.
- You have about two minutes for your discussion of the question and prompts.

- You do not have to speak about all of the prompts, and you can add ideas of your own.
- The examiner stops you after about two minutes and asks you a second question, which is related to the topic you have been discussing. This question is not written down, and you are asked to reach a decision with your partner.
- You have about a minute for this. It doesn't matter if you and your partner are unable to agree on a final decision; it's your discussion that is important, and there is no right answer.

Practice task

1 🎧 **S08** Look at the Part 3 task and listen to the examiner explaining the task. Think about how each of the prompts relates to the central question, and what you would say about each of them.

> Now I'd like you to talk about something together for about two minutes. Here are some things that people think about when they are considering whether to study in another country, and a question for you to discuss. First you have some time to look at the task.
>
> Now talk to each other about **how important these things might be for studying successfully at university abroad**.

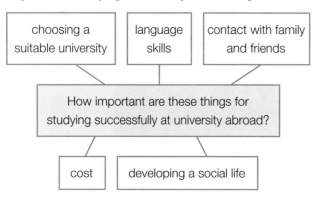

choosing a suitable university | language skills | contact with family and friends

How important are these things for studying successfully at university abroad?

cost | developing a social life

> Now you have about a minute to decide **which of these things is most important in order to study successfully at a university in another country**.

2 🎧 **S09** Listen to a student talking about the first part of the task and respond to their comments. Mention the following things when you hear numbers 1–3. Make sure you link what you say to Student A's previous comment.
1 the need to choose a country which has a respected education system
2 the necessity of choosing a country where the language spoken will be useful for your future plans
3 how important it is to stay in touch with friends and family

How did you do?

3 🎧 **S10** Listen to two students doing the first part of the task in Ex 1. Do they have the same ideas as you, or do they mention different ones? Tick the points that the two students make in their discussion.
- The value of a qualification depends on where it comes from. ☐
- It's better to go to an English-speaking country. ☐
- Being unhappy will affect your ability to study. ☐
- Having money worries will affect your education. ☐
- Working at the same time as studying is a bad idea. ☐
- A good social life can help you learn about a country's culture. ☐

4 🎧 **S11** Listen again to the students doing the first part of the task. Answer the questions.

Do they
1 ask one another what they think?
2 give their own opinions?
3 give examples and reasons to support their opinions?

5a 🎧 **S12** Listen to the students doing the second part of the task. Do they reach a decision? If so, what is it?

5b 🎧 **S13** Listen to the second part of the task again. Tick the phrases that one of the students uses to change their opinion and agree with the other.
- I see what you mean. ☐
- I hadn't really thought of it like that. ☐
- I agree with your choice. ☐
- I think I'll accept what you say and change my mind. ☐
- I'll go along with what you said. ☐

6 Try the task again, using the checklist in Ex 4.

Strategies and skills

Interacting in a two-way conversation

Part 3 should be an interactive, two-way conversation in which both speakers give and ask for opinions, comment on their partner's points, agree, disagree, etc.

> **TIP:** Avoid giving all your opinions on the question and all of the prompts in one go. Make the conversation interactive throughout.

1 Complete the table with the expressions in the box.

> From my perspective …   How do you feel about …
> I appreciate what you're saying.   However …
> I'm not convinced that's true …   My view on this is …
> So, what are your thoughts about …
> That's a really clear way of explaining …   Well, if you ask me …
> Wouldn't you agree that …

asking for opinions	giving opinions	referring to your partner's points

As well as giving opinions, you should try to support them with reasons and examples, as this raises the level of the discussion. It also helps your partner by giving them ideas to respond and react to.

2 Read the exam task and the prompts. Complete the sentences below by adding reasons or examples.

> Here are some things that people can do to have a relaxing break from work or study, and a question for you to discuss.
>
> [listening to music]   [meeting friends]   [going for a walk]
>
> [What are the advantages and disadvantages of having a relaxing break in these different ways?]
>
> [having something to eat]   [checking your phone]

1 As far as I'm concerned, meeting friends during a break isn't a great idea because …

2 If you ask me, going for a short walk during a break is a great way to relax. For example, …

3 I'm not convinced that having something to eat is always a good idea because …

4 My thinking is that listening to music is a perfect way of winding down during breaks, because …

5 It seems to me that a light snack is a great idea during a break. For example, …

6 My opinion is that checking your phone isn't always the best thing to do, because …

3 🎧 **S14** Listen to students discussing the task and answer the questions.

Do they
1 ask for each other's opinion?
   Tick phrases they use from Ex 1.
2 give reasons and examples for their own opinions?

4 🎧 **S15** Listen again and compare their reasons with your ideas.

Evaluating, referring, reassessing

Before you agree or disagree with your partner, you can summarise and/or check what they have said. This is a good way to make sure you fully understand their point of view.

> **TIP:** You should explore each point fully with your partner before moving on to the next.

5 Complete the beginnings of these sentences with the words in the box. They form phrases you can use to summarise and check.

> by   clarifying   correctly   said   saying
> thinking   trying   understood

1 So if I understood you _____ , what you meant was …

2 Are you _____ that you think …?

3 Just to make sure I've fully _____ what you said, …

4 So _____ saying that, do you mean that …?

5 And _____ about what you said about …

6 Are you _____ to say that you agree with …?

7 When you _____ that you think …

8 Would you mind just _____ the point you made about …?

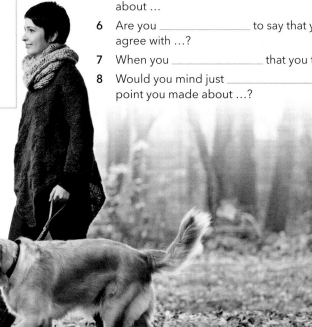

Agreeing and disagreeing

You can either agree or disagree with your partner during Part 3. This often generates lots of discussion. You should use ways of showing how much you agree or disagree with your partner.

> **TIP:** Remember that there are no 'right' or 'wrong' answers in any of the Speaking Part 3 tasks. You are judged on your ability to use English, not on your opinions!

6 Read the opinions and decide whether the responses (A–C) are generally agreeing or disagreeing with them. Then, rank them from strongest agreement or disagreement (1) to weakest (3).

1 Choosing whether to move house or not is probably the most difficult decision anyone will ever have to make.
   A I can't say I agree, although it's definitely very important.
   B You'll just know whether it's right or not, so it's not hard at all.
   C I suppose it might be but it probably depends on the person.

2 Using less electricity is probably the most useful way for people to help the environment.
   A I've always believed that to be the case.
   B It possibly is, but I'd try other ways first.
   C It should help to make a difference.

3 IT literacy is undoubtedly the most important skill employers are looking for.
   A I think it's probably one of them.
   B But surely that depends on the job you're applying for.
   C I'd strongly argue that communication skills are more highly valued.

4 The best way to measure someone's success is to look at the job they do.
   A I'd definitely go along with what you say on that.
   B Sure, but there are other ways that are almost as good.
   C It needs to be considered alongside other things.

5 The primary consideration when choosing a university is the quality of the teaching.
   A Don't you think location is just as, if not more, important?
   B I would actually put that at the bottom of my list.
   C That or the facilities in the local town or city, maybe.

Negotiating towards a decision

It's important that you discuss your decision in detail, so make sure you don't decide too quickly.

> **TIP:** It doesn't matter if you don't reach a final decision in the time given, or can't agree on it. It's the language you use that counts.

7 Match the sentence halves in each category.

Negotiation towards a decision

1	What do you	a	this is the most important one?
2	Do you think this one's	b	this one as being …
3	Shall we choose a different one	c	feel about …
4	So are you telling me that	d	then, if we don't agree on …
5	Well, I think we can both	e	say we don't think …
6	Let's rule out	f	the most important?

Reaching agreement on a decision

1	We both feel that	a	the conclusion that …
2	So we've come to	b	final decision about …
3	I think we've finally arrived	c	opinion that …
4	So we've definitely reached our	d	problem-solving as being …
5	We've both decided on	e	at a decision about …
6	We're both of the	f	problem-solving is …

Expressing inability to reach a decision

1	I'm very sorry, but we can't	a	going to agree about …
2	We've both ended up with	b	to make a final decision about …
3	I don't think we're ever	c	we'll ever agree on …
4	We really haven't found it easy	d	a different opinion on …
5	I think that we'll just have to	e	agree on …
6	I think it's really unlikely that	f	agree to disagree about …

8 🎧 S16 Complete the dialogues (1–4) with suitable phrases from Ex 7. Then listen to check your answers.

1 **A:** OK, so having discussed all the options, we really need to make a decision. Do _____ ?
   B: Yes, I think we're _____ problem-solving is the most important.
   A: Great, so that's decided that, then.

2 **A:** OK, well let's _____ the most important, then, shall we?
   B: Yes, because neither of us thought that was significant. Actually, I don't _____ which one's most important.
   A: No, probably not.

3 **A:** OK, so are _____ ?
   B: Yes, definitely, and I think you were saying the same thing, weren't you?
   A: I was! Great! So we've both _____ the most important.

4 **A:** So, shall _____ that?
   B: OK, but I think that we'll _____ which is the most important.
   A: Yes, I think we've got very different opinions about it, haven't we?

S17 Listen and complete the exam task.

Now, I'd like you to talk about something together for about two minutes.

Here are some events which can have a significant effect on people's lives and a question for you to discuss. First you have some time to look at the task.

Now, talk to each other about **how much these events might affect people's lives.**

becoming famous	passing your driving test	receiving a lot of money

How much might these events affect people's lives?

starting your first job	moving abroad

Now you have about a minute to decide **which of these things has the most significant effect on people's lives.**

- In Speaking Part 4, the examiner asks you and your partner questions that are related to the topic you discussed in Part 3. These questions develop the topic in different ways, and you should give your opinion on what you are asked.

- There is no specific number of questions you may be asked, because it depends on how much you say about each one. Part 4 usually lasts for about five minutes in total.

- The examiner may ask you and your partner individual questions, or ask you to discuss a question together.

- Even if your partner has been asked an individual question, you can still add your own opinion and develop a discussion.

- It's a good idea to refer to what your partner has said if you are adding to their answer.

- You should try to use complex language and justify your opinions by adding reasons or personal examples.

- There is no right answer to any of the questions, so you should just say what you think. Try to give full answers if you can.

Practice task

1 🎧 **S18** In Part 3, you have been discussing skills that are important for the workplace. Now the examiner will ask you some further questions about the topic.

Read and listen to the questions. Make notes on what you would say in answer to each one.

1 Do you think that certain people are naturally much better at certain workplace skills than others? (Why? / Why not?)

2 Do you think work experience programmes would be beneficial for students who are still at school? (Why? / Why not?)

3 Which do you think is more important for being successful in the workplace: knowledge and qualifications or experience? (Why?)

4 Who do you think should pay for workers to develop new skills in their jobs: the employer or the employee? (Why?)

How did you do?

2 🎧 **S19** Listen to students giving their own answers to the questions in Ex 1. Were their ideas similar to yours?

3 🎧 **S20** Listen again to the students answering Ex 1 question 1. Answer the questions.

1 Do they give examples to support their ideas?

2 Do they agree or disagree with each other?

4 🎧 **S21** Listen again to the students answering Ex 1 question 2. Which points do the two students make in their discussion?

1 Schools put more emphasis on preparing students for academic study than for work.

2 I was ready for the world of work when I left school.

3 Schools are good at developing general skills needed in many jobs.

5 🎧 **S22** Listen again to the students answering Ex 1 question 3. Answer the questions.

1 Do they ask one another what they think?

2 Do they give their own opinions?

3 Do they give examples and reasons to support their opinions?

6 Read the students' answer to Ex 1 question 4. Highlight the phrases the students use to

1 refer to what their partner has said

2 agree

3 disagree

B: Oh, the employer, definitely. They're the ones who will benefit the most from the employee developing the new skills, so I think it's only fair that they should pay for the training.

A: I'm not so sure, you know … I mean, suppose an employer spends thousands of pounds or dollars or whatever training an employee on how to use a particular piece of software. Then after a few weeks, the employee uses the new skills they've gained to get a better-paid job with another company. The first employer has basically lost all of the money they've invested in that employee.

B: Well, I'd go along with you in that it's not fair on the employer, but maybe they should have paid the employee more and it wouldn't have happened … No, seriously though, companies can put it in employees' contracts that if they leave within a certain time after they've received some training, they have to pay the money back.

A: That's a really good idea, actually.

7 Look again at what the students said in their answer to question 4.

1 What reason does Student B give for thinking the employer should pay for training?

2 Does Student A agree or disagree with him?

3 What example does Student A give for their opinion about who should pay?

4 What idea does Student B come up with to protect employers?

5 What is Student A's reaction to Student B's idea?

Strategies and skills
Justifying your opinions

In Part 4, as well as giving opinions you should try to support your views with reasons and examples, as this raises the level of the discussion. It also helps your partner by giving them ideas, and something to respond and react to.

> **TIP:** Make the conversation as interactive as possible throughout. To do this, comment on your partner's opinions, agree, disagree, etc., but remember to be polite and respectful throughout the discussion.

1 Match the opinions (1-8) with the reasons and examples which support them (a-h).

1 Tourism brings more benefits to a city than disadvantages.

2 Individuals should take more responsibility for helping the environment.

3 I don't think schools should have to teach children the skills they need in the home.

4 Working from home can never be as efficient as going to a workplace.

5 It's always better to consult your closest friends before you make a big decision.

6 I think it's always better to communicate with people face to face if you can.

7 The way a room is decorated can definitely affect your mood when you're in it.

8 Honesty is the most important quality in a really good friendship.

a Parents and older siblings should show them how to cook and clean and so on.

b There are too many distractions there, so people will do less of what they're paid for.

c If you can't tell each other the truth, you're never going to feel close.

d You'll understand each other much better because of seeing your expressions.

e It creates a lot of jobs, generates revenue and makes the place seem really alive.

f If it's full of bright, fresh colours, you'll feel so much more alive than if it's dark.

g They might have made similar choices themselves so will be able to help you.

h Everyone blames industry and government but does very little themselves.

You should try to add detail and precision to your answers. This raises the level of your responses and makes them more interesting.

2 Choose the correct word or phrase (A–C) to complete the sentences.

1 I think that all schoolchildren should have to play team sports because they develop skills that will be really important later in life, and on _____ they help to deepen friendships.
A top of that   **B** addition   **C** as well

2 Building time to relax into the working day is essential because it improves the quality of your work and, _____ this, gives you an opportunity to informally develop better working relationships with colleagues.
A also   **B** in addition   **C** as well as

3 The internet is definitely the best place to find out about the news because, unlike TV, you can choose which news stories to read about, _____ you can also get different opinions on the same story by visiting different sites.
A it's also true   **B** plus   **C** as well as

4 I'm not convinced that you do have to share exactly the same interests as your friends, because friendship isn't just about what you do together. _____ that, it's actually very unlikely that two people anywhere will have identical interests.
A In addition to   **B** On top   **C** Along

3 Complete the responses with the words and phrases in the box. Add a capital letter where necessary.

> amongst other things   an example   common knowledge
> doing so   instance   only have to

1 I think travel is definitely an excellent way of learning new things. For _____ , you can develop your skills in a new language and find out about the geography of a new country too.

2 I agree that it's possible to have a great holiday without going abroad. To give you _____ , in many countries there are beautiful beaches and great weather, so there's no need to go anywhere else.

3 I think it's a great idea for students to do work experience while they're still at school. It's _____ that they benefit enormously from mixing with older, more mature people and developing skills they'd never learn at school.

4 I believe that litter is becoming a much bigger problem. You _____ look around the streets in a few different cities and towns to know that this is true.

5 It's a great idea to have a gap year before university. _____ will allow you to relax a bit before you start studying again, and maybe travel a bit as well.

6 I really believe that people can learn a lot by reading fiction. _____ , it helps you identify with how other people think and feel, so in fact you learn a lot about yourself.

> **TIP:** You can give a general example to support your opinion to raise the level of your response and give your partner something to respond to.

4 **Read the opinions. Use expressions from Ex 3 and your own ideas to add examples to support each of the views.**

1 I know it's a widely held belief that young people don't read enough these days, but I disagree.

2 I think it's totally true that you can't always believe what you read in the news.

3 No, I don't think that high street shops will disappear completely.

4 It's a very good idea for employers to provide leisure facilities for their staff.

5 I agree that it would be great if there were a bigger variety of programmes on TV.

6 There are lots of benefits that people get from helping others.

Giving personal examples to support your opinions makes your answer more interesting.

> **TIP:** Remember that if you give information about yourself, it does not have to be true.

5 🎧 **S23** **Listen to three students talking, and tick the phrases they use to introduce personal examples.**

- Speaking for myself, … ☐
- I have a friend who … ☐
- On one occasion, I remember … ☐
- To give you an example from my own experience, … ☐
- I have some experience of that myself, actually … ☐
- What really helped me to do this was … ☐

6 **Answer the questions using the three expressions that were not ticked in Ex 5.**

1 Some people say that everyone should be paid the same, no matter what job they do. What's your opinion?

2 How important is it to plan each day carefully when you're studying?

3 Do you think working for a large company gives people more opportunities than working for a small one?

Developing a discussion

It's important to pick up on and extend what your partner has said when they answer a question.

7 **Complete the sentences with the phrases in the box to form expressions you can use to develop a discussion.**

> add something to   also say is   apart from what you hear what you're saying   in addition to interesting argument   make a point one point you mentioned   the complete opposite you a question about

1 If I could, I'd really like to _____ what you've said.

2 Is it OK if I _____ about that too?

3 That's a really _____ you've put forward, but could I just say …

4 I _____ but I'm not sure I totally agree with you.

5 What I'd _____ that …

6 And _____ the ideas you mentioned, I'd also say that …

7 There was _____ that I'd like to say a bit more about.

8 I totally agree with you, _____ said about …

9 I'm sorry but my opinion is more or less _____ of what you said.

10 I'd like to ask _____ one of the things you said.

8 **Read the questions. What could you say in answer to them? Make notes of what you could say in answer to each one.**

> **TIP:** Instead of giving an irrelevant answer to a question you don't know much about, it's better to ask the examiner to clarify or say that you don't really have an opinion. You can also encourage your partner to give the first response to a question that the examiner asks you both.

1 Do you agree that banning all vehicles from city centres is a good idea?

2 Do you think people worry about the environment too much these days?

3 How do you think people can be encouraged to save energy and water?

4 Some people think that the environment is already too badly damaged to fix. Do you agree?

5 Do you think that all countries need to work closely together to solve environmental problems?

9 Read the ideas students thought of to develop their answers to the questions in Ex 8. Match their ideas with the appropriate question. Were their ideas similar to yours?

a   There could be adverts on TV showing ways of doing this.

b   They need to forget their political differences because it's such a big issue.

c   The pollution in them is terrible.

d   The technology already exists to reverse the problems – we just need to do it.

e   It's such a big problem that they should be anxious about it.

f   Any problem can be solved if we put in enough time, money and effort.

g   They could be made cheaper for anyone who uses very little of them.

h   It would certainly make them more pleasant places to live, work and visit.

i   Hopefully their concerns will push them to do more to help.

j   If they don't, it will make the whole problem much more difficult to deal with.

10 🎧 **S24** Listen to two students answering the questions in Ex 8. Which ideas from Ex 9 do they mention?

11 🎧 **S25** Listen again. Which phrases from Ex 7 do they use to develop the discussion?

EXAM TASK

🎧 **S26** In Speaking Part 3, you have been discussing factors which can affect our choice of where to live. Now the examiner will ask you some further questions about the topic.

Listen and answer the questions. Discuss each one with another person if possible.

1   Given the choice of living anywhere in the world, which country or region would attract you the most? Why?

2   Some people choose to live in many different places throughout their lives. Do you think this is a good idea? (Why? / Why not?)

3   Which has a greater influence on someone's life: the home that they live in or the town or city where they live? (Why?)

4   Some people say that the weather in an area influences the character of the people living there. What's your opinion?

5   Some people say that almost everyone will live in cities in the future. Do you agree? (Why? / Why not?)

6   Some people say that living in the countryside is better suited to older people. What's your view on this?

Questions 1-8

For questions 1-8, read the text below and decide which answer (A, B, C or D) best fits each gap.
There is an example at the beginning (0).

Coral reefs

Coral reefs are complex marine ecosystems found **(0)** _____C_____ in tropical seas. They are characterised by their unusual **(1)** _____ of biodiversity. Although they **(2)** _____ only 0.1 percent of the world's oceans by area, 25 percent of the world's marine species are **(3)** _____ there for some or all of their life cycles.

Coral's solid calcium carbonate structure is created by individual organisms called polyps. Although coral polys **(4)** _____ a resemblance to plants, they are in fact animals. Each polyp is packed with microscopic algae, which provide nutrients for the coral in the **(5)** _____ of sugars created through the process of photosynthesis. In **(6)** _____ , the algae receive the carbon dioxide necessary for photosynthesis and a safe place to live.

Coral reefs worldwide are under **(7)** _____ , partly due to rising sea temperatures. When the water temperature reaches a certain threshold polyps become stressed, which causes them to expel their algae. The algae **(8)** _____ around 90 percent of the coral's energy requirements, so without the sugar provided by their algae, the polyps die.

0	**A** greatly	**B** significantly	**C** predominantly	**D** considerably
1	**A** intensity	**B** concentration	**C** focus	**D** consolidation
2	**A** compose	**B** establish	**C** signify	**D** constitute
3	**A** resident	**B** inherent	**C** natural	**D** fundamental
4	**A** reveal	**B** present	**C** expose	**D** bear
5	**A** character	**B** shape	**C** form	**D** appearance
6	**A** return	**B** trade	**C** swap	**D** substitute
7	**A** danger	**B** threat	**C** risk	**D** hazard
8	**A** meet	**B** allow	**C** reach	**D** get

Questions 9–16

For questions 9–16, read the text below and think of the word which best fits each gap. Use only <u>one</u> word in each gap. There is an example at the beginning (0).

Write your answers in CAPITAL LETTERS on the separate answer sheet.

Making art from waste

For many, recycling amounts **(0)** ___TO___ little more than putting plastic bottles into the correct receptacle. Artist Michelle Reader, however, has been making **(9)** _____ of discarded items to create sculptures since as **(10)** _____ back as 1997.

Michelle searches for the raw materials from **(11)** _____ her artworks are made in places such as city dumps, second-hand shops and factories. Not knowing exactly what she'll find is almost as much of **(12)** _____ thrill as creating the sculpture itself. She certainly has no lack of materials to choose from, given **(13)** _____ readily things are thrown away these days. Michelle thrives **(14)** _____ the challenge of the inventiveness needed to transform what she's found into art.

Her best-known work *Seven Wasted Men* depicts a family, and is constructed from three weeks' worth of each person's own waste. It not only emphasises the sheer quantity of rubbish we produce, **(15)** _____ also creates a picture of each family member through the things they throw away. **(16)** _____ or not you like the sculpture, you can't help admiring the artist's ambition!

Questions 17-24

For questions 17-24, read the text below. Use the word given in capitals at the end of some of the lines to form a word that fits in the gap in the same line. There is an example at the beginning (0).

Write your answers in CAPITAL LETTERS on the separate answer sheet.

How do fossils form?

When creatures die, they **(0)** ___TYPICALLY___ decompose completely. Occasionally, however, under a very particular **(17)** _____ of circumstances, they turn into fossils: the prehistoric remains of animals and plants that have been preserved in rock.

TYPE

COMBINE

The perfect conditions for fossil creation are usually found in lakes and seas, as the remains have to be surrounded by water. This explains why fossils of marine species are **(18)** _____ more common than terrestrial ones. For fossils to form, the dead organism must be buried quite quickly, for example in mud or sand. This is because **(19)** _____ to oxygen leads to rapid and complete decay, making fossil formation an **(20)** _____ .

CONSIDER

EXPOSE

IMPOSSIBLE

Over an **(21)** _____ long period of time, the layer of mud or sand that's covering the dead organism becomes thicker. A **(22)** _____ of this is that the deepest levels eventually come under such **(23)** _____ that they gradually turn into rock. Meanwhile, minerals from the water seep into the organism's tissues, causing them to **(24)** _____ . This creates a solid outline of the organism encased in rock – a fossil.

EXCEED

SEQUENCE

PRESS

HARD

Questions 25–30

For questions 25–30, complete the second sentence so that it has a similar meaning to the first sentence, using the word given. <u>Do not change the word given.</u> You must use between <u>three</u> and <u>six</u> words, including the word given. Here is an example (0).

Example:

0 I really don't mind whether the radio is on or off.

DIFFERENCE

It really _MAKES NO DIFFERENCE TO ME_ whether the radio is on or off.

Write only the missing words **IN CAPITAL LETTERS** on the separate answer sheet.

25 Max didn't sleep well even though he was very tired.

SPITE

Max didn't sleep well _____ very tired.

26 It's very hard to understand why the programme is so popular.

CLUE

I really _____ the programme is so popular.

27 The manager reported that more customers than ever were satisfied.

WAS

The manager reported that _____ all-time high.

28 Would you be able to help me lift this heavy table?

HAND

Would you mind _____ this heavy table?

29 'I'll do all I can to finish writing the report today,' promised Ellen.

WHATEVER

Ellen promised she _____ to finish writing the report today.

30 Steven claimed he wasn't involved at all in making the decision.

NOTHING

Steven claimed to _____ making the decision.

Questions 31–36

You are going to read a review of a book about bird migration. For questions 31–36, choose the answer (A, B, C or D) which you think fits best according to the text.

The Long Spring by Laurence Rose

A lyrical diary of the life of migrating birds

In one part of Spain, adult white storks have stopped making the arduous annual trip to and from their winter feeding grounds in Africa. The African savannah is no longer worth it, as they've learnt that the rice fields neighbouring their Spanish rooftop nesting sites provide food year-round. This secret doesn't appear to get passed on in any way to their young who, come autumn, fly south. How they know where to go without parental guidance is unclear. It's one of many mysteries in a migration that each spring sees storks and two billion other avian immigrants arrive on Europe's shores.

These storks are one of the first species that Laurence Rose encounters as he follows the leading edge of spring north, starting in February at the Strait of Gibraltar and finishing in May in Finnmark, Norway, deep in the Arctic Circle. *The Long Spring* is a diary of his travels. Following spring's progress is a delightful concept, encompassing one of the most astonishing migrations on Earth. Who can fail to be moved by the diminutive northern wheatear, for example? Weighing in at around 30 grams, it has been found to migrate more than 29,000 kilometres a year using routes inherited from the last ice age. From cattle egrets to spoonbills, there's a profuse and stellar cast on display in Rose's book.

For more than 30 years Rose has worked for a British bird protection charity, so his knowledge on the subject is beyond question. He is also a classical composer. His ability to identify a bird, not just by a fleeting glance, but by the briefest catch of a note, is stunning. In *The Long Spring* the calls of birds are truly brought to life, described not just phonetically, as in less illuminating books on the subject, but also in terms of their changes of tone. A species called the cuckoo, for example, sings from a major third to a sharp minor third, while the bittern's call can boom as low as 200 hertz, 'a sound like a distant bull'.

These are details to delight a serious bird fanatic. They may also baffle the more casual reader. Rose's overflowing enthusiasm occasionally runs away with him in a manner as relentless and confusing as the march of spring. He describes endangered Balearic shearwaters in flight as 'effortless in their stiff winged air-skiing … the line they follow is an undulating one, like a slow melody made visible, and I realise they are working layers of air in the same way a cyclist might requisition energy from a downhill stretch to supplement the effort needed for the next rise.' You may need a moment to take that in.

On arriving in England, the book is overtaken by Rose's preoccupation with the shooting of a bird called the grouse. His views are unambiguous: grouse hunting leads to the hilly habitats where they live, often called moors or moorland, being stripped of vegetation and diversity in order to make the birds easier to see and therefore shoot. In particular, Rose condemns the persecution of the birds of prey that naturally feed on grouse by those who organise the hunts. While grouse shooting is not historically blameless, it is striking that Rose makes no effort to speak to a scientist or anyone involved in moorland management. A recent study of a grouse moor in Scotland found 103 different bird species, including 11 different birds of prey. This single moor boasted as many breeding pairs of one species, the golden plover, as there are in all of Germany. The report concluded that managing the land for grouse shooting was the key to such biodiversity. That Rose won't engage with a differing scientific viewpoint renders much of his argument ineffective.

Rose ends his journey on the northern tip of Norway in May 2016, watching 'two male redstarts … drawing up their own border, civilly with song.' The final chapter, reflecting on the future of the species he has travelled with, has the backdrop of change within Europe. What will become of the crucial pan-European agreements to protect migratory birds? Surprisingly, he is full of hope, suggesting that the continent's politicians may well replace the agricultural policy that perpetuates wildlife decline with something altogether more beneficial. It reminds me of the white storks he met at the start of his journey, who've changed old habits and are thriving as a result.

31 **What do we learn about white storks in the first paragraph?**

   A   Little is understood about why some adult storks have ceased to migrate.

   B   Instinct in young storks is more powerful than imitating their parents' habits.

   C   The journey that most storks make has become more difficult in recent years.

   D   Storks prefer to make their annual journeys in the company of other birds.

32 **In the second paragraph, what does the reviewer say about *The Long Spring*?**

   A   It includes details about a wide range of birds.

   B   The idea behind the book is better than the actual thing.

   C   Some species mentioned in it are more interesting than others.

   D   The places the author travelled to have been very well chosen.

33 **In the third paragraph, the reviewer says that Rose**

   A   has chosen his latest career direction wisely.

   B   tends to overly complicate descriptions of birdsong.

   C   has developed greatly as a writer since his earlier work.

   D   is effective at combining two areas of expertise.

34 **What is the reviewer emphasising in the sentence 'You may need a moment to take that in.' in the fourth paragraph?**

   A   the importance of the subject matter

   B   the significance of an important opinion

   C   the complexity of the descriptions

   D   the beauty of the language used

35 **What criticism does the reviewer make of Rose in the fifth paragraph?**

   A   He uses a trivial example to make an important point.

   B   His ideas are not put forward in a convincing way.

   C   He is blaming the wrong group of people.

   D   His opinions don't take account of all the evidence.

36 **In the final paragraph, the reviewer draws a comparison between 'white storks' and**

   A   agreements to protect birds

   B   European politicians

   C   agricultural subsidy systems

   D   political change in Europe

Questions 37–40

You are going to read four excerpts from articles in which education experts discuss homeschooling (educating children at home rather than at school). For questions 37–40, choose from the experts A–D. The experts may be chosen more than once.

Homeschooling

A   Tessa Hamilton

There's a surprising amount of controversy surrounding homeschooling. In my thirty years of working in education, twenty of which as a homeschooling advisor, I've never come across anyone who I've felt to be incapable of teaching their children adequately. There are those, of course, who benefit greatly from additional support and training, but if the necessary systems are in place whereby the authorities can scrutinise all homeschool tutors and their students, then I see no reason for concern. What's struck me over and over is how consistently mature homeschooled students seem in relation to their traditionally schooled counterparts. Perhaps the gap would close if schools opted for smaller classes, but funding issues often constrain this possibility. Were it an option, this may also go some way to allowing school students to catch up to their homeschooled peers academically.

B   Virat Bhalla

Many educational commentators point to homeschooled children's exemplary conduct as one of the principal indicators as to how successful it is as an educational strategy. While I can't disagree with their assessment, I'd take issue with its importance educationally. I'd always look to their academic attainment as the truer measure of whether homeschooling is working or not, and there's a growing body of evidence that suggests these children are seriously underperforming in national tests. I think much of the blame for this must be placed at the doors of whoever has taken on the homeschooling of their children. Few of them, after all, are trained teachers, and those found lacking should be prevented from continuing. Insufficient checking up on who is teaching what to whom has also been a factor, and this should be tightened up considerably and made compulsory for all concerned.

C   Elena Collias

In many countries homeschooling is frowned upon, even if it's not actually against the law. This mistrust comes at least in part from occasions on which it's been discovered that those claiming to homeschool are not actually doing what they say they're doing. That's why tight regulation and checking needs to be in place. Personally, I think this should include a prohibition being placed on adults who apply to homeschool their children who are not considered up to the task. After all, teaching is a demanding profession, whether it's done in a school environment or at home. When it's done well, however, there's little doubt that it can work wonders for any student's academic development. A highly positive side-effect is that children schooled in this way tend to be far more sensible and grown-up in their approach to life than those of a similar age in state education.

D   Morio Furukawa

I can see the attraction of homeschooling, especially for those parents whose line of work results in them moving frequently from place to place. However, just as a child who moved to a new school every few months would fall behind their peers academically, so do many of those who are homeschooled. Despite these observations, I'm a great believer in parental choice and would advocate that parents be at total liberty to educate their children as they see fit, without any interference from those in authority. Nor should the state be able to disallow certain people from teaching their children in this way due to perceived doubts about their ability to do so. I'm convinced that everyone can do an adequate job given the necessary support. Students educated in this way never seem to act as responsibly as their state-schooled peers, however, perhaps because of having had fewer opportunities for social development.

Which expert

has a different view to the others regarding the effect of homeschooling on the behaviour of children?	**37**
shares an opinion with D about the educational progress of homeschooled children?	**38**
expresses a different opinion to the others about government monitoring of homeschooling?	**39**
expresses a similar view to B about whether all parents should be allowed to homeschool their children?	**40**

Questions 41–46

You are going to read an article about centralisation in large cities. Six paragraphs have been removed from the article. Choose from the paragraphs A–G the one which fits each gap (41–46). There is one extra paragraph which you do not need to use.

The case for and against a centralised country
The world's megacities attract jealousy – but they also draw in the most talented

I'm on holiday in Umbria, Italy, where the phrase 'rolling hills' makes sense at last. Each of the shapely slopes throughout the region is crowned or footed by a village with its own life and integrity, despite the northern Europeans and their second homes and one freeloading columnist.

Always startling to a visitor from a centralised nation is the dispersal of Italy's glories, not just to the secondary but the tertiary towns, and even those smaller than that. Across the Tuscan border in Arezzo, population 99,000, we tour early Renaissance masterpieces, boutiques commensurate with a larger city and the unusual piazza which featured in Roberto Benigni's Oscar-winning film, *Life Is Beautiful*.

41

Some countries have a large enough population to do both (the USA, Japan). Some are too small to have much choice (Denmark, Singapore). But for those in the 20–100 million population range, there is something of a trade-off between concentration and proliferation.

42

And while residents living in the provinces of both countries chafe at their capitals, the resentment feels less vicious where the capital is smaller, where it is just one multiple larger than the next biggest city, which is only one-half bigger than the next one, which itself barely edges out the next one, and so on.

43

And perhaps they would be wrong. There is a case for concentration too, and it goes beyond municipal arrogance. In previous centuries, nations scrambled for resources abroad. If there is an international race in this century, it is for talent.

44

For a nation, having several wonderful cities will not be enough to tempt the mobile and gifted. It will have to have one city in the elite tier. Three decades since the internet promised the abolition of geography, success in, say, corporate law or consulting or finance still requires at least a stint, if not a career, in one of a small number of world cities. Even as that number grows, it will probably always be a select club.

45

As patriots, they worry about concentration and its discontents in other regional cities. As pragmatists, they know how a country's money is made. Building up one big city makes sense. And if this reads as so much bean-counting, consider this case for the centralised model. A high-ranking official within the European Commission gives a year in 'seething' London the credit for her 'inner freedom' and her habit of 'trying everything'. The sentiment is still heard among young Europeans today. To perform this kind of liberating role, a city does not just need a tolerant culture, which, after all, Hamburg or Berlin also offer. It needs monstrous scale.

46

It is just that in a world of nicely equalised cities we would not have these outsize urban havens, magnetically attracting people who wish to create themselves anew. My stopover in London was as refreshing as a holiday in Umbria. The all-encompassing metropolis or the individuality of regions: most countries have to choose one or the other. Individuals don't.

A Look at the efforts made to break into or stay in it. Dublin already dominates Ireland. Paris already dominates France. And still each nation's ministers are suggesting that their capital takes a share of any business that cities in other countries might lose in the ups and downs of global capitalism.

B Italy arrived at almost exactly this kind of spread by unifying relatively recently in its history. But anyone designing a country from scratch right now would surely choose the same balance over a centralised model.

C The gravity of a megacity of this size will undoubtedly pull the rest of the country out of shape. In a medium-sized nation, critical mass in one place implies a relative deficit somewhere else, leading to a rise in anti-metropolitan resentment elsewhere in the country.

D Justice would seem to argue for the latter. True, there are advantages of size in London that are not evident in Rome in terms of shopping and entertainment, for example. But most Italians probably have access to more and have things closer to hand than the majority of Brits.

E And, to be honest, there's no better way of encouraging this kind of rivalry between regions. The problem is inevitably worse the bigger the size gap between capital and provincial cities gets.

F Flying home from such treasures via London – the colossal scale of it – I wonder which country has it right. Is it wiser to concentrate economic and cultural life in just one city, the better to make it world-class, or to spread it about countrywide?

G Coveted as they are, the ablest people can choose to live in the cities with the very deepest capital markets, the very widest dining options, the very largest hub airports and remuneration terms.

Questions 47-56

You are going to read an article about searching for life on other planets. For questions 47-56, choose from the sections (A-D). The sections may be chosen more than once.

Which section

explains the science behind some possible evidence for life on other planets?	47
suggests that scientific progress related to finding planets has moved very quickly?	48
states that a search has no guarantee of success, despite statistics suggesting otherwise?	49
contrasts two different worlds in order to exemplify a point?	50
gives details of a unique scientific occurrence?	51
describes the limitations of existing technology?	52
uses the study of one type of body in space to explain the benefits of studying another?	53
explains how scientists find out detailed information about other planets?	54
defines an area of space in which life can exist?	55
makes a hypothetical estimate in order to support a point?	56

Is Earth the only living planet?

A

In 1990, as the Voyager 1 space probe pushed towards the outer edge of our solar system, its cameras looked back to snap a series of photographs. Taken at a distance of about four billion miles from Earth, the images form the first and only 'family portrait' of six of the eight planets arrayed around the Sun. In one, the Earth appears as a pinprick of light. This image of our 'blue dot' emphasises its beauty and fragility, imploring us to take care of the only place we know of that harbours life. Yet, in just the three decades since Voyager's backward glance, we have learnt that our neighbourhood scatter of worlds is far from exceptional. In the early 1990s, scientists started to discover planets orbiting stars other than our Sun: exoplanets. Among the thousands of other solar systems catalogued since then, more than 4,000 exoplanets have been identified within them. This is likely to be the tip of a very large iceberg: were each star in our galaxy to have just one orbiting it, there would be 200 billion in the Milky Way alone.

B

The data accumulated to date suggests that at least every fifth star harbours a rocky planet such as Earth at a distance where liquid water could exist on the surface. This distance, where it is not too hot and not too cold for liquid water, is called the 'habitable' or 'Goldilocks' zone. Astronomers are interested in worlds that orbit within that zone because liquid water is essential for life as we know it. The spectrum of light that reaches Earth's telescopes from distant stars carries a 'fingerprint' of the chemicals it has encountered en route. If it has reflected off the surface and/or the atmospheres of other planets, we can learn about the composition of those worlds. The fingerprint from Earth, for instance, shows water, oxygen and methane. The presence of water tells us that the Earth is within its sun's habitable zone; oxygen and methane in combination, meanwhile, provide strong evidence of life. Venus's spectrum, on the other hand, lacks these signs, indicating a world empty of living things.

C

The challenge is to detect spectral fingerprints from great distances. Current instrumentation is capable of obtaining them only from a few large, hot planets; the signal from small, rocky worlds is overwhelmed by the glare of the parent star. But the next generation of telescopes will be able to distinguish finer details. Earth's fingerprint can then be used as a key to interpret those of different exoplanets. Earth's has changed over time; the emergence of life has produced oxygen in large quantities, but this alone is not conclusive evidence of life. There are also geological reactions that slowly produce oxygen molecules. However, detecting it in combination with a gas such as methane would be very interesting indeed. Oxygen reacts with methane to form carbon dioxide and water; the two gases don't hang around for long before they react with each other. So, if we detected oxygen in an atmosphere in the presence of methane, as on Earth, it would mean the oxygen was being produced in large quantities, perhaps by something living.

D

Our search also has the potential to give us insights into our own world. We know how our Sun was born and will die because we observe stars like it at different stages in their evolution. Similarly, if we could find fingerprints from dozens of Earth-like planets at various evolutionary stages, we could piece together more precisely how Earth formed and glimpse a possible future. For example, if we were to see that all older Earths show high concentrations of sulphur dioxide – which we can't breathe – in their atmospheres, it would be worthwhile creating a technology that could filter it out of our own atmosphere. Understanding other planets could also allow us to take better care of our own – though scientific knowledge does not necessarily translate into political will. Even with at least 40 billion other possible Earths in our galaxy, the likelihood of finding life is small. As so often in astronomy, we are at the very limits of what our technology can see. But our chances are good.

You <u>must</u> answer this question. Write your answer in 220-260 words in an appropriate style on the separate answer sheet.

 Your class has watched a panel discussion about ways of boosting interest in the arts. You have made the notes below:

Ways to boost interest in the arts:

- increase government financial support
- more time for arts subjects on school timetables
- more arts programmes on TV

Some opinions expressed in the discussion:

'Governments have cut funding for the arts.'

'Arts subjects add variety to the timetable.'

'Most people find programmes about the arts boring.'

Write an essay discussing **two** of the ways of boosting interest in the arts in your notes. You should **explain which way is most effective** at boosting interest in the arts, **giving reasons** in support of your answer.

You may, if you wish, make use of the opinions expressed in the discussion, but you should use your own words as far as possible.

Write an answer to <u>one</u> of the questions 2-4 in this part. Write your answer in 220-260 words in an appropriate style on the separate answer sheet. Put the question number in the box at the top of the page.

A famous celebrity who used to study at your college recently gave a talk at the college about their life and work. The school principal has asked you to write a report about the talk, describing what the celebrity spoke about, explaining how useful it was for students and suggesting who should be invited to give a talk next.

Write your **report**.

3 You see this announcement on a website, *Tech News*.

> ## Reviews wanted
>
> Send us a review of an app that you have recently started using.
>
> What does the app do? What are the positive and negative features of the app? Would you recommend the app and, if so, who to?

Write your **review**.

The company you work for has an area of unused land next to its buildings. Senior management are thinking of selling the land but have asked staff for their opinions. You think the land should be used to benefit staff. Write a proposal for the senior management, explaining what you think the land should be used for, suggesting what needs to be done to the land and saying how the land could benefit staff.

Write your **proposal**.

Questions 1–6

🎧 **PE01** You will hear three different extracts. For questions 1–6, choose the answer (A, B or C) which fits best according to what you hear. There are two questions for each extract.

Extract 1

You hear two friends discussing the topic of advertising.

1 Which aspect of advertising do the two friends disagree about?

   A how effective it is at selling products
   B how entertaining many adverts are
   C how irritatingly frequent advert breaks are

2 In the woman's opinion, a ban on advertising aimed at children would

   A discriminate against certain companies.
   B have the support of many politicians.
   C create some economic difficulties.

Extract 2

You hear part of a discussion programme in which two journalists are talking about the theatre.

3 What criticism does the man make of some theatres?

   A Their ticket prices put many people off going to them.
   B They only put on plays by well-known writers.
   C Too little is spent on promoting their productions.

4 How does the woman respond to the man's criticism?

   A She questions the accuracy of the information he gives.
   B She suggests that he is focusing on a trivial issue.
   C She gives an explanation for the cause of the problem.

Extract 3

You hear a woman telling a friend about living on a houseboat.

5 What is the woman doing during the conversation?

   A admitting to doubts about living on a boat long-term
   B expressing regret about her choice of boat
   C complaining about others living in nearby boats

6 Why does the man refer to his brother?

   A to support a point the woman has made
   B to reassure the woman about her decision
   C to suggest he's surprised by the woman's opinion

Questions 7-14

🎧 **PE02** You will hear a science student called Sandra Ibbotson talking to a group of fellow students about a research trip she went on to study an animal called the Greenland shark.

For questions 7-14, complete the sentences with a word or short phrase.

Greenland shark research trip

A scientist from **(7)** _____ was responsible for organising the research expedition.

Sandra says that it was her experience of **(8)** _____ that led to her being chosen for the expedition.

Sandra compares travelling on board a ship in bad weather with being in a **(9)** _____ .

The primary aim of the scientists on the trip was to study the **(10)** _____ of Greenland sharks.

Sandra was interested to learn about Greenland sharks' incredibly **(11)** _____ .

Sandra was surprised to discover that **(12)** _____ occasionally form part of the Greenland shark's diet.

Sandra was struck by Greenland sharks' lack of **(13)** _____ when she was diving with them.

Sandra thinks that investigations into **(14)** _____ will eventually benefit from some of the Greenland shark research project's findings.

Questions 15–20

🔊 **PE03** You will hear an interview in which two environmental journalists, Karen Brearley and Ian Gill, are talking about air travel. For questions 15–20, choose the answer (A, B, C or D) which fits best according to what you hear.

15 Karen says that her most recent article on air travel
- A caused embarrassment to other climate scientists.
- B was thought inaccurate by several journalists.
- C had been improved by alterations made by her editor.
- D has caused some readers to alter their habits.

16 Ian refers to sport in order to support a point he is making about
- A the need to introduce limitations to flights gradually.
- B the effects of limiting flights on aviation industry employees.
- C how destructive an increase in flight numbers would be.
- D how energy use in other industries is far greater than aviation.

17 What does Ian suggest about the statistics relating to air travel?
- A They are more complex than the aviation industry admits.
- B They are manipulated by those with a financial interest.
- C They are calculated in an inconsistent way.
- D They are already out of date by the time they are published.

18 When asked about advances in aviation technology, Karen expresses doubt that
- A the speed of change is fast enough to be of use.
- B the research is focused on the most beneficial area.
- C the developments will ever be as good as manufacturers claim.
- D the progress will ever match that of other types of transport.

19 When talking about government policy, Karen and Ian agree that
- A stricter restrictions on aircraft fuel emissions should be imposed.
- B consumer taxes on flights should be greatly increased.
- C strategies for transport and the environment are incompatible.
- D international cooperation on transport policy is poor.

20 When asked about their own use of air travel, Karen and Ian reveal that they
- A always fly with budget airlines.
- B avoid flying at night.
- C fly less than they used to.
- D have given up flying business class.

Questions 21-30

🔊 **PE04** You will hear five short extracts in which people are talking about a gap year they had between leaving school and starting university.

While you listen you must complete both tasks.

TASK ONE

For questions 21–25, choose from the list (A–H) the reason each speaker gives for taking a gap year.

A to travel the world		
B to gain work experience	Speaker 1	21
C to relax and take it easy	Speaker 2	22
D to help out around the home	Speaker 3	23
E to pursue an interest	Speaker 4	24
F to save up some money	Speaker 5	25
G to be sure of their choice of degree course		
H to develop certain academic skills		

TASK TWO

For questions 26–30, choose from the list (A–H) what effect the gap year has had on each speaker.

A I'm having second thoughts about going to university.		
B I'm more mature than when I left school.	Speaker 1	26
C I've become increasingly ambitious.	Speaker 2	27
D I'll probably set up my own business after university.	Speaker 3	28
E I'll find it very hard to start studying again.	Speaker 4	29
F I've been able to focus on challenging some of my fears.	Speaker 5	30
G Being more mature will be an advantage at university.		
H I appreciate the sacrifices others have made more.		

PE05

> First of all, we'd like to know something about you.
> Where are you from?
> What do you do?

The examiner will ask you a few questions about yourself and what you think about different things. For example, the examiner might ask you:

How long have you been studying English?

What do you enjoy most about learning English?

How interested are you in finding out about the news? (Why? / Why not?)

How important is it to you to spend time with your friends? (Why? / Why not?)

What do you think is the best way to keep in touch with friends? (Why? / Why not?)

Which person do you most admire? (Why?)

What's the most interesting place you've visited recently? (Why?)

What do you remember most about the primary school you went to? (Why?)

What would your ideal job be? (Why?)

Is there anything you'd change about the area where you live? (Why? / Why not?)

 PE06

In this part of the test, I'm going to give each of you three pictures. I'd like you to talk about two of them on your own for about a minute, and also to answer a question briefly about your partner's pictures.

(Candidate A), it's your turn first. Look at the pictures on page 125. They show **people using communication skills in their jobs.**

I'd like you to compare **two** of the pictures, and say **why communication skills might be important in these jobs**, and **how difficult it might be to do these jobs.**

All right?

(Candidate A speaks for 1 minute.) _____

Thank you.

(Candidate B), **which of these jobs do you think would be the most rewarding? (Why?)**

(Candidate B speaks for about 30 seconds.) _____

Thank you.

Now, (Candidate B), look at your pictures on page 126. They show **people learning how to do different things.**

I'd like you to compare **two** of the pictures, and say **what the people might be enjoying about learning how to do these things**, and **which of these things might be most useful to learn.**

All right?

(Candidate B speaks for 1 minute.) _____

Thank you.

(Candidate A), **which of these things do you think would be the most difficult to learn? (Why?)**

(Candidate A speaks for about 30 seconds.) _____

Thank you.

Candidate A

- Why might communication skills be important in these jobs?
- How difficult might it be to do these jobs?

Candidate B

- What might the people be enjoying about learning how to do these things?
- Which of these things might be most useful to learn?

PE07

Now, I'd like you to talk about something together for about two minutes. Look at page 128.

Here are some things people do to help the environment and a question for you to discuss. First you have some time to look at the task.

Now talk to each other about **how useful it is for people to help the environment in these different ways.**

(Candidates talk for 2 minutes.) _____

Thank you.

Now you have about a minute to decide **which two ways of helping the environment are most effective**.

(Candidates talk for 1 minute.) _____

Thank you.

 PE08

Use the following questions, in order, as appropriate.

- Do you think that you do enough to help the environment? (Why? / Why not?)

- What do you think governments should do with companies that cause environmental problems? (Why?)

- Some people say that air travel should be limited for environmental reasons. Do you agree? (Why? / Why not?)

- Do you think children learn enough about environmental problems at school? (Why? / Why not?)

- How important do you think it is for countries to work together to solve environmental problems? (Why?)

- Are you optimistic that people's intelligence and creativity will find solutions to our environmental problems? (Why? / Why not?)

Thank you. That is the end of the test.

> *Select any of the following prompts, as appropriate:*
> - What do you think?
> - Do you agree?
> - How about you?

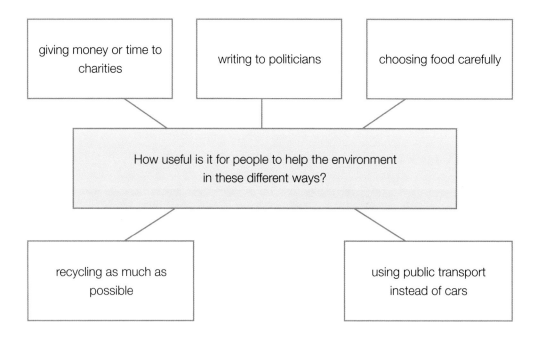

giving money or time to charities

writing to politicians

choosing food carefully

How useful is it for people to help the environment in these different ways?

recycling as much as possible

using public transport instead of cars

LISTENING

Part 1

Practice task | Ex 1

 L01

F: I've just started using rap music in class. I saw a video online showing how it's being used and thought I'd give it a go.

M: That's very brave.

F: My students thought it was a joke at first – the song was called 'April Fools' Day' after all, but they're generally far more up for new methods of learning than teachers, in my experience. So, there was little chance they'd find it a waste of time. It's too early to tell whether it's as good as other ways of developing their understanding, but I want to avoid a mistake I always make, which is to include a new technique I've learnt in every class. The novelty soon wears off and students get as fed up with it as the old ones.

M: I had a class discussion about rap a few weeks ago. What took me aback was the passion it generated throughout the group. I half expected it not to work as a whole-class activity, as I thought the minority who have no interest in it would withdraw from the debate. They had just as much to say as its greatest advocates, though, which suggests it's a powerful vehicle for getting across the things we want to teach.

Strategies and skills: Understanding attitude and opinion | Ex 1

 L02

1   The glossy leaflet describing how great it would be was some distance from the reality, I'm afraid. I was seriously hoping that a course with as many sessions as this one would be able to explore the issue in the kind of detail I enjoy. However, the opposite was the case.

2   In my day, school seemed to reward those who were good at academic theory and didn't address the needs of those who were good at practical applications. I was in the latter group, of course, and although I suppose some staff tried to make the lessons as interesting as they could, I still left with very little to show for it, despite many years of consistent effort.

3   In some ways, the majority of modern movies are extremely clever. They contain both visual and verbal in-jokes that appeal in different ways to different age groups. What's turned me away from going to the cinema so often, though, is that the idea of 'good guy is threatened by a powerful bad guy but eventually wins' has become almost universal. I just really crave something that doesn't use that same tired formula.

Strategies and skills: Understanding attitude and opinion | Ex 2

 L03

1   There was an introductory offer that seemed too good to be true, as they always do, but at least they did tell you what the membership fee would go up to after the initial three months, to avoid any nasty shocks. Some of the machines look as though they've been taken from a futuristic science-fiction film. I initially thought I'd never be able to get my head around how to use them, especially as places like that often employ too few staff to help you out, to save money, I suppose. That's not the case there though so it's been remarkably easy to pick up what to do – you can't keep me off them now.

2   She's proving to be very popular overall, apart from her tendency to arrange two meetings in different places at the same time. She's generally forgiven for that because of how she systematically involves everyone under her in the decision-making process. I think she's actually grateful for their input, given that most of her professional background's been spent in hospitality rather than marketing.

3   I'd like to think that travel companies are getting on the ecotourism bandwagon for altruistic reasons, but I really don't believe that to be the case. I doubt that ecotourism is any more lucrative than traditional travel. But perhaps when large numbers of consumers see the company's name attached to something that's supposedly beneficial for the planet, it'll make them think more kindly of a business whose income comes largely from environmentally harmful activities.

Strategies and skills: Identifying feeling | Ex 4

 L04

1   I know that Jeremy has his faults and that some of his nervous tics and habits drive you mad at times. But I think you should bear in mind his compassion and generosity, rather than solely focussing on rather insignificant behaviours.

2   Sorry to interrupt, and I appreciate that this issue is taking up an enormous amount of your energy at the moment, but much of what you're talking about is of no direct relevance to us and there are fifteen other items on the agenda which we really need to discuss.

3   Any disagreements I had with the theatre director have long since been resolved – I see absolutely no point in holding onto resentments, as this is the best way that I know of losing any sense of inner peace, which I prize above all else these days.

4   The food at the restaurant tasted amazing, but a day later, I was more ill than I've ever been before. I just wanted the stomach pains to stop – it was absolute agony. Once I'd recovered, I contacted the restaurant manager who seemed to suggest that I was lying. He eventually offered me a voucher for a free meal, but why would I want to eat there again?

5   Ever since Martha contacted me about the possible opening within her company, I've hardly been able to sleep. My family have really had enough of me going on and on about how fantastic it would be if it comes off. I honestly can't think of a more perfect opportunity.

6   What unsettles me about Alex is that every time we speak, he makes a real point of saying how amazing he thinks my work is. Don't get me wrong – it's nice to get a bit of praise now and then, but only if it's truly genuine. I can't help wondering what the real reason is behind it.

7   As soon as I've got it clear in my mind that applying to study medicine at university is what I really should be doing, this voice in my head unhelpfully suggests that it'd actually be better to do veterinary science. So then I manage to convince myself that aiming to become a vet's the right course of action. I then repeat the whole process so I end up back where I started!

8 What they're aiming to get from the negotiations with the managers is exactly what we want and need. I can't ever remember a time, though, when we got anywhere near what we were asking for, and I've got no reason to believe things will be different this time round.

EXAM TASK

 L05

Extract 1

You hear a scientist being interviewed about plastic pollution.

F: How serious is plastic pollution?

M: Plastic was and, to some extent, still is seen as a cheap and simple resource to cater for people's needs. However, no one seriously considered what we'd do with it when we needed to throw it away. It takes hundreds of years to biodegrade, so now it's everywhere, and largely in a form that's too microscopic for us to see. We have no idea of the long-term effects on the organisms, including humans, that ingest it. It's no longer a case of how we fix the issue – it's too late for that. The imperative must be to stem the flow of plastic into the environment to minimise the biological cost.

F: Do you think people are responding to the dangers of plastic pollution?

M: A positive public response has already been forthcoming, but my concern is that it's aimed at only the least serious part of the problem. Everyone sees pictures of oceans full of plastic bags and bottles on the news and assumes that this is the biggest issue. While something undoubtedly needs doing about this, it ignores the fact that creatures all the way up the food chain are already eating the plastic micro-fibres from our clothing and the tiny flakes from 50-year-old discarded plastic items, and the results of this could be devastating.

Extract 2

You hear two friends talking about a place where they spent a lot of time as children.

M: So, have you ever thought of going back to Standon?

F: What, where we grew up? A lot, yes, but I've never been able to bring myself to do it. I can't imagine for a second that many, if any, of our old neighbours are still there so I sometimes wonder why I'd bother.

M: Oh?

F: Well, a friend of mine said it's always a mistake to go back somewhere you've really enjoyed being. Not only is it never actually the same as how you recall it, the fact that the reality is so different actually diminishes the affection you remember it with. That, more than anything, is what's stopped me from going.

M: I think I'd have such high expectations going back there that there's no way they could ever be met, so I can really see where your friend's coming from. In some ways, it's not actually the place that you want to visit again, it's the time that you spent there and the things that you did and who you did them with, which you can never recapture anyway. So it's a nice idea, but perhaps one that's never actually ticked off on the 'things I'd like to do' list.

Extract 3

You hear two scientists talking about food hygiene in restaurants.

F: I worry that the system for ensuring food hygiene standards isn't working as well as it could. Many businesses that cause problems only get a caution and a small fine.

M: Even if people end up with food poisoning. The crazy thing is, there's often nothing else judges can do, especially if it's a first offence.

F: And it's not that restaurants aren't being caught when things like this happen but there's always some legal loophole that allows them to get away with it. The proprietors just don't care about keeping their places clean.

M: I think it's ignorance more than a bad attitude myself. They're usually businessmen, not chefs.

F: I guess.

M: Speaking of rules and regulations, how's your government advisory role going?

F: It's certainly been an eye-opener! From the beginning, I've been extremely keen to tell them about all the changes that need to be made in terms of government policy. It's as though I'm speaking another language, as all I get back is a wall of silence, which is really unhelpful. Perhaps it's because I'm a little too forceful in commenting on the deficiencies of the current approach, but that's what they pay me for, after all.

LISTENING
Part 2
Practice task | Ex 1 and Ex 3

 L06 and L07

Darren: Good morning, everyone. Today I'm going to be talking to you about research I've been doing on my geology course into the metal we often associate with winners … gold! So why is gold used as the medal for winners? Well, because it's so precious, of course. In comparison, silver - the metal usually associated with second place - is approximately 19 times more abundant than gold!

We get most of the metals we use in day-to-day life from the ground, often by digging deep underground in a mine to retrieve them. Gold's no exception in this regard, but what sets it apart is the pure form it's in when taken from the ground. Metals such as iron and aluminum are mixed with other minerals which they then have to be separated from.

The earliest evidence we have of humans exploiting gold comes from caves used as dwellings around 40,000 years ago. It would take many more thousands of years before people started working gold into jewellery, and even more for coins to be created from it. But the flakes found on the floor there are the first sign that people valued and worked with this precious metal.

Gold's found in small quantities all around the world, but is present in larger amounts in some countries. I'd never associated China with being a great source of the metal, and assumed that somewhere like the United States was the main producer. It does, however, currently come top of the list, with Australia in the silver medal position behind it, Russia taking the bronze and the USA in fourth place.

A huge majority of the gold found today is used to make what you and I might wear on our fingers or around our necks: jewellery. In the United States, for example, this industry accounts for an amazing 38 percent of the gold produced. The quantity that the electronics sector consumes took me aback, however, as it's not actually far behind at 34 percent. The amount used in dentistry and in the building industry is tiny compared to these two.

Strategies and skills: Identifying cues | Ex 3

 L08

Leila: Hi, everyone! I'm here today to tell you all about a fascinating species I'm involved in researching: the golden tree frog.

The project I'm part of is based on the Caribbean island of Trinidad. Whilst a substantial amount of useful data has been generated there in recent years regarding the golden tree frog's diet, little has been gathered on their reproduction, so we were there to try and provide that.

The species is endemic to Trinidad, meaning it's where it's originally from. Unfortunately, due to many different factors such as the introduction of invasive species from other regions and habitat loss, very few golden tree frogs now remain in the island's forests. In fact, their distribution is now limited to a couple of the highest mountains on the island, El Tucuche and El Cerro del Aripo. This has led to them being reclassified on the International Union for the Conservation of Nature's Red List, the most widely accepted scale of how healthy the populations of different species are. Having been re-categorised from vulnerable to endangered in the past, the golden tree frog has recently been designated as critically endangered – the highest category on the scale.

Losing them in the wild would be a disaster as they're such a beautiful species in so many respects. Their subtle colouration cleverly changes with the frog's temperature. And the elegant way in which they glide through the air from tree to tree is a big contrast to how clumsy they look when crawling around on the leaves and branches of their treetop home.

Strategies and skills: Understanding specific information and stated opinion | Ex 5

 L09

While I was pretty content for quite a while living in the house I was in prior to buying the houseboat, I began to feel restless. It was as though I always thought I should be somewhere else, and was quite the opposite of how well-balanced I am now I'm actually living on the water. I was terribly excited once I'd had the idea, but then got really worried about finding the perfect houseboat!

Strategies and skills: Understanding specific information and stated opinion | Ex 6

 L10

It takes a certain kind of person to take on long solo voyages. Most experienced sailors would identify discipline as an essential. My own take on that is that anyone can learn this, especially if your life depends on it. The same is true for the strength, both of character and physically, that you'll need. Without natural optimism, though, I wouldn't even bother trying it. Things will go wrong, and if your natural tendency is to think negatively about it, you won't last long!

Strategies and skills: Understanding specific information and stated opinion | Ex 7

 L11

The concert was organised almost exclusively by volunteers. In fact, with the exception of the guy who filmed everyone on stage, no one received a penny, not even for travel costs. That's saying something as the woman who booked all the groups and singers came all the way from New Zealand. There was a fantastic person who introduced all the musicians before they came on stage – she was so good, everyone thought she should've been a professional presenter!

Strategies and skills: Understanding specific information and stated opinion | Ex 8

 L12

All the plants and animals in the region are almost totally dependent on a certain amount of rain falling each spring. Rainfall has always been remarkably reliable throughout the area, meaning they have never needed to seek alternative sources further afield. The drastically reduced quantities that have been falling in recent times, therefore, have proved utterly devastating.

Strategies and skills: Identifying and eliminating distractors | Ex 10

 L13

I've been a professional TV weatherman for about eight years now. The novelty of being recognised wore off quite a while ago, so it's actually the variety that still gets me to work every day with a smile on my face. I present from a whole range of places, not just the studio, you see. Studying weather patterns, of course, is always fascinating. I've been doing that for so long now, though, that there isn't much I haven't seen before.

Strategies and skills: Identifying and eliminating distractors | Ex 11

 L14

The problem with my job is that you can never appear on screen looking as though you've arrived at work in a rush – you have to look your best every day. This of course means shaving, which I have to say I would gladly never do again if I didn't have to. I've come to terms with arriving early, as that's quite often necessary. Using make-up was outside of my comfort zone to begin with – it's all just part of the working day now, though.

I do quite a lot of forecasts outside the studio. My producers try their best to ensure I occasionally do it somewhere out of the ordinary. Perhaps the oddest of these was the day they decided we should do it in a zoo. It caused a bit of an argument when they wondered whether I'd like to describe the weather while standing next to a group of giraffes. Thankfully, I won that particular battle, and the penguins waddling around my feet as I spoke to the camera got some great comments from viewers. Many TV weather presenters have a background in journalism, so know little about the subject matter when they start. However, I studied meteorology (or weather) at university, so was already an expert but had never done any broadcasting work before. I was sent on an acting course soon after I got the role, which has helped immensely. Learning about film editing's something I've also been intending to request for a while, just in case I ever get fed up with appearing in front of the camera.

Angkor Mapping Project

Good morning, everyone, my name's Laura Holden. Welcome to my talk about a research project I'm involved with in Cambodia that's mapping the whereabouts of the different parts of the ancient city of Angkor, which has now largely disappeared.

First, let me tell you about how I came to be an archaeologist. Archaeology was seen as a rather boring profession by most people my age, despite some excellent TV documentaries that brought various periods of ancient history back to life. I was already into the subject by the time I saw them, though, thanks to a fascination with the pyramids that dated back to when I was about six and ended up with me studying archaeology at university.

I wasn't sure what to do after completing my degree. I wasn't setting my sights very high and was sure I'd end up working as a museum curator, as many archaeology graduates do. That was until a guy I'd been close to on my course, who'd just got a job as a lecturer at one of the top universities, said I should broaden my horizons, as he had done. I took his advice, and the post for the Angkor project was the first one I saw advertised, so I applied for it immediately.

The project involves taking aerial pictures over where Angkor was believed to be, so a map of it can be created. This means getting our equipment high up over the site. Helicopters provide really precise height and speed when compared to satellites or conventional aeroplanes, so they are ideal. Drones would also have enabled us to do this had the equipment not been too bulky to fit into them.

There are lots of ways of mapping ancient sites. A really interesting method uses cameras which see infrared light rather than light that's visible to us. Ours was the first to use lasers, 16 of them actually, all firing beams of light at each square metre of the area.

A lot of time and resources had already been poured into the project long before we were ready to start our mapping. I knew it had been money well spent the moment a clear impression of a canal appeared on the screen. This was closely followed by an ancient reservoir that had been hidden beneath the jungle for hundreds of years, which was just as amazing.

Everyone involved in the mapping was there for a particular reason. One task was to produce pictures of what life might be like in each part of Angkor using the images we'd taken. I'm not much of an artist but my IT training made me the perfect person to generate 3-D models of them on the computer.

A key finding of the research was the size of Angkor, which took everyone by surprise. No one thought that cities which had roughly the same dimensions as a modern American city existed in the 12th century. It wasn't as big as a giant metropolis like Tokyo, of course, but you have to remember that the world's population was sixteen times smaller back then.

No one knows for sure why Angkor fell into ruin. One theory is that invasion by neighbouring states and a subsequent long war were to blame for it being abandoned. Climate change is the hypothesis that I've actually seen the most convincing evidence for, although many researchers hold disease responsible for its sudden decline.

Does anyone have any questions?

LISTENING
Part 3
Practice task | Ex 1
 L16

Interviewer: On the show today, we have Harriet Brown and Andrew Miller, both of whom have fairly recently set up their own estate agencies. Harriet, how difficult was it to decide to go it alone?

Harriet: Well, I've always felt that the idea of 'home' and having a safe space to relax and unwind, is such an important concept. I guess that's why I got into the profession. I'd already gained lots of experience in selling houses before I even thought about going it alone. Had there been tension with my boss, the decision would have been made for me, of course, but we got on pretty well. Even so, in the few weeks after I'd decided, there was no way I could pick her or my other colleagues' brains for tips on how best to do it – I didn't want anyone there to know what I was planning. Then a few days after I'd received a big bonus at work, some suitable premises became available in the town I'd just moved to, so I thought 'it's now or never!' I was expecting to have to wait ages for everything to fall into place, but I was up and running before I knew it.

Interviewer: Andrew, how did you go about finding somewhere to base your business?

Andrew: I'd already agreed a loan with the bank at a pretty favourable rate, which opened up a much wider range of potential premises. I'm a bit of a perfectionist, so I set about finding somewhere that met absolutely all of my criteria. This didn't exist, of course, and I was faced with this long list of other options, none of which seemed totally suitable. I eventually picked one almost at random, as I was so fed up with trying to decide. There was another similar business just down the road from it. Rather than worrying about whether two could succeed in the same street, I thought 'business is business' and went for it anyway.

Interviewer: What were the initial periods of running your own business like for you both?

Harriet: My expectations were that it'd be a really thrilling time. After all, what could be more exhilarating than running my own estate agency! The reality was somewhat different, though. I was spending as much time as I could at the office, and although the days seemed to fly by I wouldn't be able to tell you now even a fraction of what I did.

Andrew: My lasting impression of that time is of finishing one thing and immediately moving onto the next, without time for serious reflection or to catch my breath, and my memory of it all is a little hazy. I have a young son, so I'd made a promise to myself, and to him, that I'd avoid the trap that many new business owners fall into of being at work all day every day to begin with. I kept my promise, but the first few months seemed to last for years!

Strategies and skills: Identifying agreement and disagreement | Ex 3
 L17

1

M: There needs to be a total re-think on transport in the city, and I mean total! As it stands, the car is king, and there's no culture of looking out for cyclists, which frightens people who would otherwise ride to and from work.

Nonetheless, some cities have managed to transform this almost overnight.

F: Drivers' lack of concern for bike riders is certainly what's kept me and a lot of others off our bikes, but I think you're being incredibly optimistic about how quick it would be to solve the problem.

2

F: I think we've reached the upper limit of how much medical research we can actually afford – I mean, there aren't endless reserves of money available. We'd make significant progress if these resources were targeted much more carefully.

M: The processes for choosing who's entitled to receive financial support are already time-consuming and rigorous enough. We're definitely up to the maximum of the share of budgets that medical research should receive, though.

3

F: The study showed that when upbeat, rousing classical or pop music was played in the factory, output actually rose, whereas the reverse was true for calmer or more sombre music. Interestingly, workers reported feeling more lively and content whatever the music was. That's surely true.

M: It was such a small-scale short-term study that I wouldn't read much into it, certainly when it comes to efficiency on the production line. Having something to break the repetitive nature of that kind of work is bound to lift your spirits, though, even if you don't really like what's being played.

Strategies and skills: Identifying agreement and disagreement | Ex 4

 L18

1

M: I've a theory that people strongly believe it's every citizen's job to fund charities, not the state's, and some even resent it that public money is used on charities rather than hospitals and the like. So increased state help actually leads to the general public becoming less willing to donate money. Cutting state handouts also forces charities to improve the way they're run, so they really make the most of every public donation.

F: I can't say I've ever heard of anyone complaining about the state's level of support for charities, but I can see that it has a direct influence on public donations. I certainly think that being less able to rely on state handouts is a good way of getting charities to think carefully about what they spend every penny on, though.

2

F: The current system of providing students from less well-off families with free food at lunchtimes appears to be working well. What I'd also like to see, now that both schools and the state have actually done something positive about parents' concerns regarding how healthy school meals are, is controlling the amount that students are given.

M: I feel that both education and food are basic human rights. Given that the former is free for everybody in this country, then we should also provide the latter without charge during the school day. It's heartening to see that schools have taken on board advice about providing a balanced lunchtime diet for students, and I think limiting the quantity of food per student could help in the battle to improve students' health.

3

M: Given the amount of money we spent on the course, I'd have expected it to be held somewhere with rather better facilities. That said, the guy who led the course couldn't have done more for the participants. We all had so many questions because everything we covered was so relevant to our needs.

F: If I'd written a list of all the things I wanted to focus on beforehand, I would have been able to tick all of them off, and it was as though he could read our minds as he seemed to know exactly how to handle each of our needs. The amenities at the venue are probably more basic than you're used to, but there was everything there that I could have asked for, and more.

4

F: What would you say is the most important development of the last fifty years?

M: Oh, the internet, of course.

F: Really?

M: Yeah – I mean, what other invention has had such a wide sphere of influence? It's revolutionised education

for starters, and I'm talking about education in its broadest sense. You can now find out pretty much anything you want in a matter of seconds, which also has a negative indirect impact. Everyone now expects instant solutions to things which there's simply no quick fix for. I'm not so enthusiastic about what it's done to our ability to interact with each other face to face, either.

F: I think it's hard to argue with your last point, judging by the declining levels of politeness we're seeing everywhere. I'd go along with what you said about the internet's importance as a learning resource too. I don't think people's expectations of the time it takes to sort out important issues have really altered at all, though – they just have a public platform now to moan about how slow it is!

Strategies and skills: Understanding feeling | Ex 5

 L19

1 At first sight, the opinions presented in the book seem thoroughly convincing. On closer inspection, however, particularly of the data that were used to support the author's arguments, doubts started to creep in about how plausible they actually are.

2 There are, of course, many who are against homeschooling. I wholly go along with their criticisms of the few parents who are found wanting as educators and who are unwilling to do any training. I do, however, object to them using isolated instances of this to give the impression that this is a widespread problem, thereby painting the whole concept of homeschooling in a negative light. Even they must acknowledge that the majority of homeschooled students do just as well as their school-taught peers.

3 Greg McPherson's latest movie *The Yellow Tree* stars Angela Gill as a scientist who's researching the ocean depths for new life forms, a role that's strikingly similar to one she played in her last film. It's an action film, and it certainly lives up to this label, even if the computer-generated sequences are a little uninspired. But even if you're one of the many who are totally fed up with tiresome, formulaic films of this type, there's plenty in *The Yellow Tree* to get excited about.

4 The reputation of professional footballers as a privileged money-grabbing elite hasn't done wonders for the image of professional athletes in general. Despite an overwhelming number of them being incredible examples of discipline and self-sacrifice that we should be encouraging all young people to emulate, the media seem to focus predominantly on the occasional online outburst on social media by otherwise admirable athletes.

5 A friend of mine recounted, at great length, an incident that took place on her commute home from work the other day. A man apparently refused to move from his seat to let an elderly passenger sit down. My friend's story was told in a way that suggested this was now a daily occurrence on our railways. In my forty years' experience of travelling on trains, I can honestly say that just as many rude people existed back then as do now and that the recent golden age that people like to talk about is simply a myth.

6 Having recently completed my first online diploma, I have to say that all the issues I'd had nightmares about prior to starting, about being unable to access virtual learning environments and so on, failed to materialise. It did take me far longer than I'd anticipated, though, largely thanks to there being no fixed deadlines for assignments. If I can put something off, then I will, which my academic supervisor wasn't too happy about, although having access to tutors seven days a week via email was a real plus point.

EXAM TASK

 L20

Interviewer: Today's topic of discussion is technology, and I have with me journalist Yasmin Harvey, who specialises in writing about technology, and research scientist Guy Jameson. How did you end up working in technology, Guy?

Guy: I actually had to resist pressure from my parents and one of my favourite teachers to do what I do today. They knew that academically I was extremely bright, but, funnily enough, what enabled me to fight against their desire to see me do dentistry were films like *Star Wars*. While my friends all wanted to be the action hero, my aim was to be the one in the laboratory inventing these incredible new machines, not for the vast fortunes they would undoubtedly make me, but just for the sake of expanding the boundaries of what we can do.

Interviewer: And what drew you to science and technology, Yasmin?

Yasmin: Um – can I clear something up before I answer that? When you mention technology, the majority of people probably imagine something tangible, like the latest electronic gadget or spaceship, as Guy mentioned. Just so listeners are clear, and I'm sure that you'll both go along with what I say, it can also include more abstract things like innovative ideas or ways of doing things. Anyway, to answer your question, it just seemed to be the area with the most profound impact on all of our lives, I guess.

Interviewer: Has it become more difficult for researchers to secure government funding, Guy?

Guy: In many ways, yes. What's been welcome is the degree to which the complicated steps necessary just to request government money have been simplified. The real issue is that the pot of money that's shared out hasn't got any bigger. Little of the cash that's made from successful technology which emerges from government-funded research is used to fund future projects. Grants appear to get handed out to technology projects that seem thrilling, superficially at least, rather than to those that would be genuinely beneficial to society. That's the case regardless of whether it's in a lowly research institute or one of the country's top universities.

Interviewer: Yasmin, I believe you're soon publishing a book …

Yasmin: That's right. When I was considering ideas for it, I settled on the different ways that eminent people in the field of science and technology work, but then discovered that dozens of titles have been written on this previously. So I decided to answer the question of how variations in research procedures in diverse parts of the world affect the relative success there instead. As part of that, I've looked at regional similarities and differences in creative thinking, and at several inventions that have come about as a result of them.

Interviewer: Many have argued that controls are required to restrict certain new technologies. What are your views on that?

Yasmin: I can understand the reasoning behind this, but if we go down that route, there should be minimal regulation. Deciding which technologies should be subject to any controls and which organisations should be responsible for policing them is close to impossible. I can't see any industry within the tech field wanting to go along with imposing constraints.

Guy: As long as organisations know exactly what's okay and what's not, they're generally happy to do what they're told. Regulatory bodies with clear aims have been put in place many times before and are now successfully monitoring other sectors, so I don't see why that can't happen for research and technology. Whatever's decided, it should be done with a light touch – as little intervention as possible.

Interviewer: How do you both feel about the future of technology?

Guy: Increasing amounts of money are spent by industry as opposed to government on research, which should be welcomed. Without that, technology won't be able to provide the solutions to the ecological crisis we're now facing. The rapid expansion of the green technology sector will help absorb most of the job losses that are inevitable now other industries are turning to robots rather than humans. It's a global problem, so it's time to forget institutional and state differences and tackle it together.

Yasmin: Only by coming together and putting vast effort into cleaning up the planet can we reverse the environmental damage we've done. I worry about leaving this to companies whose principal aim is to make profits, and think an environment tax on industry is the way to fund it. Whichever way it's done, jobs will be created that'll offset the losses caused by automatic production methods.

LISTENING
Part 4
Practice task | Ex 1

 L21

1 It wasn't as though I decided to sail solo across the Atlantic one day and was sailing the next. It took ages to prepare and I needed help from many other people. Thankfully, my employer was sympathetic, probably because they thought doing an immensely dangerous and physical challenge to financially support a good friend who was seriously ill was an acceptable excuse! I'd never done anything like that before and had certainly never spent such a stretch of time on my own. It's given me a taste for it actually, so I wouldn't say no to having a go at something comparable in the near future, just perhaps not in a boat.

2   My friends weren't sure what possessed me to cycle across Australia on my own. I really thought they'd change their tune once I'd done it, but they still think I was mad to take it on. While it's true that there were a few moments that could've turned nasty, things like that always turn out OK. A common theme amongst those who've done something similar is that they're seeking something that's as different to the mundanities of day-to-day existence as possible. My motivation was more personal. I'd always avoided spending time by myself. The longer this went on, the more intimidating a prospect it became. The bike ride seemed like a perfect way to overcome that.

3   I walked from the far north east of North America to the far south west. It all started when the friend who was best man at my wedding poked fun at me for being so unfit. He said I'd never be able to walk more than twenty kilometres, so I just thought up the most ridiculous way imaginable to do it. I actually got a lot from it, so my intention now is to repeat the walk, but across South America instead. It'd be fun if a few of us decided to do it this time, not just me. I'm glad I did it, even though the time it took me was a little outside what I was hoping for.

Strategies and skills: Understanding the main point | Ex 2a

 L22

1   Doing the training in augmented reality was, in hindsight, a mistake. One of my workmates is really into the technical aspects of IT and I'd got a bit fed up of always feeling one step behind her. I really thought that knowing about the topic would make her take my technical skills a bit more seriously. The problem was that I didn't really have enough background knowledge to cope with the content, which was

all new. So, although it enabled me to have a change of scenery for part of the working week, apart from meeting a few interesting people, I can't say it was a success.

2   I make no secret of my desire to do well in my career, so many of the decisions I make at work tend to be based on how quickly I can climb the ladder. Choosing to do a management course was no different in this respect. It's not as though I don't have any management experience, of course, it's just that I'm aware of what criteria the top dogs in the company use when they're deciding who should move up, and your training record is high up on the list.

Strategies and skills: Understanding the main point | Ex 3

 L23

It's been a more complicated process than I was expecting, as moving away from family was tough, but my first impressions of the place are largely positive. I still have the occasional doubt as to whether I should've stayed but I didn't have much choice in the end as my boss said that my skills were needed here. I'm a city girl at heart and this place just feels a little bit small to settle down in in the long term. Don't get me wrong! There's lots going on here and it's a popular place, but the prices of property and the cost of living reflect that. I'm hoping that I'll soon have a bit more say in where I end up once I'm a bit higher up in the company.

Strategies and skills: Understanding the main point | Ex 4a

 L24

I'd spent a long time at more or less the other end of the country to my dad – in my profession, you just have to go where the work is. After I'd had children of my own, though, I thought it was only fair for them to see as much of their grandad as possible. It was only after moving that I realised how tired I'd grown of the tension and stress of city living and it's been a real revelation living in a small town again. It feels like we've lived here for years, even though it's only a few weeks since we moved. Hopefully some opportunities will come up soon to get to know all the neighbours.

Strategies and skills: Interpreting opinions | Ex 8

 L25

1   My original plan was to do some independent study towards my degree subject, so as not to completely lose the habit of being in education, and to earn some money to help pay the university fees and living costs. I foolishly gave myself a couple of months off before doing either, which of course stretched to three. It then took a few weeks to actually find something suitable, but I was then too tired to study. So, at the end of it, I feel like I've lost momentum with education and haven't earned anywhere near as much as I'd hoped either.

2   Taking a gap year is the best thing I could have done. I feel like I've really regained the love of learning and natural curiosity about the world that had slowly faded over thirteen years of full-time study. I hadn't even noticed that it was a problem until I actually stopped! I'd seriously recommend it to anyone going onto university or into work. I have no doubt that I'll do much better in the long term, having recharged my batteries.

3   I was the only one in my peer group who decided to have a gap year. I don't regret it at all as it's enabled me to go off travelling for a few months. However, while they all talk about what life is like on campus wherever they're studying when we meet, I want to tell them about visiting temples in Asia and things like that. It seems that, all of a sudden, we have very little in common with each other.

4   A few of my friends took a year off too and we set up a little business together creating websites for several months, then used the money we made to go to South America for the remaining time. I actually learnt tons of Spanish while we were there and some of the companies we worked with before we went now want us to continue maintaining and updating the sites for them as well. It hasn't put me off the idea of studying at university, but it'll provide some really useful income while I'm there.

5   Having a few months of doing something other than full-time education gave me the space to look objectively at the decisions I'd made about which course to study at

135

university. I think I'd chosen it out of desperation as I simply couldn't think of what better to do. As the year passed, though, it became apparent that I should actually be heading in a different direction, so I contacted the university and arranged to swap to something much more suited to me.

Strategies and skills: Identifying attitude and feelings | Ex 10

 L26

1 When I was nineteen, I decided to give up a university course partway through and go off travelling. My personal tutor begged me to reconsider and suggested seeing the university careers service too, but of course at that age, I thought I knew best. I didn't even tell my parents until it was too late. I hadn't really considered any of the consequences, which I'm sure those who were a bit older and wiser than I was would've pointed out to me, had I taken the trouble to ask.

2 About a year ago, I decided I wanted to live on my own as I'd lived with either family or friends all my life. Finding a flat was easy and I was so excited when I picked the keys up from the estate agents. Walking into the empty flat was one of the most bizarre experiences of my life, though. I'd never felt so alone, and all the fantasies I'd had about how great it'd be to have my own place just collapsed around me, and I wanted nothing more than to be back in the house I shared with friends.

3 Three years ago, I set up my own business as a management consultant. Several former colleagues had done the same thing. What I failed to take into account was that all but one of them had gone back into paid employment within a few months. I'd been in the sector long enough to realise it was entering a bit of a downturn. I honestly thought that I would be different and that my venture into self-employment would succeed where theirs had failed. How wrong could I have been?

4 In hindsight, it wasn't the best decision I've ever made, to say the least. I'd just inherited quite a bit of money and was wondering what I should do with it. One morning, for reasons I still can't really explain, I suddenly decided to go out and buy a sports car. I'd never been that careful with money anyway, and by the end of the day, it was more

or less all gone. I enjoyed the car for a while but then it dawned on me what I'd done. I can laugh about it now, but I've been far more careful with my finances ever since.

5 A few colleagues of mine had planned to go on holiday together, and when one of them fell ill and couldn't go they asked if I wanted to join them instead. They were literally going the next day and would have had just a few hours to find someone else, so I didn't have long to let them know either way. Anyway, the first few days were fine but then the arguments started. I wasn't the cause, I might add, but I couldn't help but become involved. It created a horrible atmosphere and a couple of them still won't talk to me, even at work, which isn't ideal.

Strategies and skills: Correcting mistakes | Ex 11

 L27

1 I got into climbing six months ago. I've always been sporty, and am pretty good at rugby and cricket, but I wouldn't describe many of the skills I developed in those sports as transferable to climbing. I've improved dramatically as a climber, thanks largely to living within a hundred metres of the best climbing centre in the region and two friends who are as keen to go there several times a week as I am. I was aware of the sport's popularity, due to the number of people I saw arriving at the centre, but had little idea that many of them were going there to admire the expert climbers rather than to climb the walls themselves.

2 When you watch any expert doing their sport, they make it look effortless. So when I came to try ice hockey, I had these expectations that you just slide around on the ice without a great deal of exertion. How wrong I was! I ran out of energy far quicker than when I play football or basketball, and still do. I've actually made it onto my local team, which is quite an achievement, given that I've been playing for less than a year. I was encouraged to push myself from the very start, mainly by the other players rather than the trainers funnily enough. It's like being part of an extended sporting family.

3 My first dive after I joined a diving club was a bit of a disaster, because I actually slipped on the diving board and landed on my back! Fortunately,

I've improved a lot since then. My coach has trained hundreds of people over the years. Some of them have to work really hard to become good, whereas others just seem to be able to do it well with a minimum of practice. I'm one of the latter, apparently, which is nice to know. Great divers are very elegant, so they don't look like the kind of people who would do anything just to beat their opponents. They definitely would though!

4 Cricket isn't that popular in my home country, Canada, so when I moved to the UK recently and saw the local club playing a game, I was curious. I went to the next practice session and am already playing for their first team. What I didn't appreciate when I watched that first game was how precise you have to be when you bat. One tiny error and that's game over because you're out. I like that challenge. There's far more to consider than in baseball, which I played in Canada, although the ability that I developed there, to hit a ball in the middle of a bat, has certainly played a large part in my cricketing success.

EXAM TASK

 L28

1 When I saw the advert, I just thought 'this is my dream job'! It's not often that when I think something like that it actually turns out to be true. I've yet to meet anyone here who doesn't focus on the solution to problems, rather than on the problems themselves. It's so refreshing! I do have to spend time during my journey to the office thinking about what the day's likely to bring. Working out which of the day's tasks I need to start off with and which I can leave till later actually takes far more thinking than you'd imagine and, even now, I usually get it wrong.

2 Starting in any new position is tiring and can seem a bit like operating in a fog for the first few weeks, but the new job's gone relatively smoothly. I think I've got my head around what everyone there does, but what I need to do when I'm using some of their company software is still a bit of a mystery to me – I haven't come across anything as complex as that before. Judging by what I've seen so far, company policy is to move people up within the organisation as soon as they're ready for the increased responsibility, so I'm really hoping that I'll be capable of doing that before too long.

3 I've been in my new post for two weeks now and I've yet to actually do any real work, which is quite unusual. Up till now, we've been looking at company policies and procedures, meeting all the staff, visiting the different sites and so on. I already feel like I understand the organisation far more than my previous one, even though I was there for two years – very impressive! One thing I've been asked to do is arrange meetings with my two immediate line reports but they've not responded to any of the emails I've sent. I'm sure someone would have told me if they were away on holiday.

4 I think my introduction to the company consisted of a ten-minute tour and a quick meet-and-greet with a few of the staff, then it was straight down to work. I wasn't really sure I was up to several of the tasks they'd given me to do, and would've preferred more training first, but they seem happy enough with my progress so far. I've certainly enjoyed doing it, even if I don't always know whether what I'm doing is good enough or not. It involves the kind of problem-solving that really gets you thinking. I get so into it that before I know it it's the end of the day.

5 I feel very fortunate to have got a job with the company I work for now. They seem to have a unique approach to everything they do, from the products they create to the way staff are managed, and even how their offices and factory look. There was certainly a lot of competition for jobs there. I was told that over a hundred and fifty people had applied for my job. To be honest, they could've done with employing a couple of other people as well as me. There's certainly more than enough to do and perhaps then I wouldn't have to take stuff home to do in the evening and at weekends.

SPEAKING
Part 1
Practice task | Ex 1
 S01

See page 88.

Strategies and skills: Giving reasons | Ex 8
 S02

1 Yes, the one I've most enjoyed in the last few weeks was called *Seven Weeks*. It tells the story of a man's journey back to civilisation after the small plane he was flying crashed in a rainforest. The reason I liked it so much was that you didn't know until the end if he'd survive or not. It was a really exciting film.

2 Well, my favourite type of holiday is one in which I do lots of different activities. I'm not someone who likes lying on a beach for two weeks. It would therefore be somewhere I could do lots of different things, for example scuba diving, swimming, visiting interesting places, and so on. I like to keep busy, even on holiday.

3 I think it's fairly important, but I don't think it's possible for friends to have exactly the same interests as each other. They may have one or two in common, but not all. I think it helps to keep the friendship growing if you do certain activities you both enjoy together, but it's good to have your own interests too.

4 I'm not sure I'd exactly describe myself as that, but in some respects, I can be quite organised. For example, I like arranging weekend football competitions, so I have to communicate with many different people about when and where it's happening, etc. At home, though, I don't seem to have quite as much discipline!

EXAM TASK
 S03

See page 90.

SPEAKING
Part 2
Practice task | Ex 3a
 S04

Examiner: In this part of the test, I'd like you to talk about these two pictures for about a minute. They show pairs of people performing in different situations. Compare the pictures, and say why the people might have chosen to perform in these situations and how the people might be feeling.

Student A: Um … in the first photo, there's a pair of street musicians performing in the street somewhere. I think the musicians have chosen to play here because they want to make a bit of money from their music. There's a guitar case on the pavement in front of them for people to throw money onto. I also think, though, that they're doing it to bring a bit of pleasure to people who are out and about in the city, just doing everyday things like shopping. My guess is that the two guys are feeling pretty relaxed right at that moment. I imagine that they're pretty skilled musicians and they're not performing in a high-pressure situation, so they won't be too worried about making mistakes. They're just out to have fun and make some money while they're doing it. The pair of actors in the second photo, on the other hand, are being watched by a large audience who have presumably all paid quite a bit of money to watch the play that they're in. The open-air theatre they're in is right by the sea and it looks like the kind of place tourists go to as a treat when they're on holiday, so it'd probably be pretty expensive. They're therefore under a lot of pressure to perform well, unlike the two musicians in the first photo, so could well be feeling quite stressed even though they're almost certainly very experienced actors. I think they've chosen to act there because it's a spectacular place to perform and, on a personal level, it's quite a high-status event to be involved with.

Student B: There are two photos of pairs of people performing in public. The first one looks as though it's in the UK as there are a couple of the famous red telephone boxes behind two street musicians. One of the musicians is standing up playing the drums, special drums that you play with your hands and not with sticks, while the other one is sitting and playing an electric guitar. As I said, they're in front of two red phone boxes, on the street, maybe in a big city like London. They look like they're pretty relaxed and are probably there to make some money. The second photo shows two actors on an outdoor stage. The actors are in what looks like an ancient theatre, and we can see the sea right behind it. There's a large audience watching them, so they're probably feeling fairly nervous. They've chosen to perform there because it's a great place to be in a play.

Strategies and skills: Comparing | Ex 4
 S05

The two pictures show people who are involved in very different kinds of discussion. In the first picture, we can see a group of people who are all having a business discussion, most probably at their workplace. Most of the people are seated around a table and are listening or taking notes. One woman is standing in front of a screen and is perhaps talking the others through some figures or other information that she's presenting. The second picture, however, shows five people, who are probably friends or coursemates. The people are all very relaxed in the second photo, which is in some contrast to the first picture, in which everyone looks more business-like and serious. I imagine that the people in the first picture are discussing important business issues as a means of moving the company forward in some way. This is significantly different to the discussion in the second picture where they are laughing and having a friendly chat. Personally, I think taking part in the business discussion would be far harder than that shown in the other one. You have to know a lot of background information to have a discussion of this kind and perhaps have a strong personality if you want your way of doing things to be accepted. A chat with friends or coursemates, on the other hand, is always much more laid-back and far less stressful to take part in.

Strategies and skills: Speculating | Ex 6

 S06

Student A: I'd guess that if you don't use your teamwork skills when you're working as a chef in a busy kitchen, none of the meals will reach the customers in good time, so they won't recommend the restaurant to people they know. You're also likely to get shouted at by the head chef!

I imagine that it could be incredibly difficult if you don't get on with the other members of the team. If you all work well together, though, I suppose that it would be really enjoyable.

Student B: I'd assume that creating dishes in a restaurant kitchen is quite a complicated process with different people responsible for different parts of the dish, so without good teamwork it would be a disaster!

It could be the case that people who are good at coping with stress will thrive in this kind of work, but if you prefer a quiet life you'll probably find it extremely difficult.

EXAM TASK

 S07

See pages 96 and 97.

SPEAKING
Part 3
Practice task | Ex 1

 S08

See page 98.

Practice task | Ex 2

 S09

Student A: Well, looking at this first prompt, I think choosing a suitable university is incredibly important. You need one that has a good reputation, and I think it's essential that it isn't somewhere that is, like, right round the other side of the world, so you can get home easily for holidays and things. And, of course, it's got to be somewhere that you really want to spend time in. What do you think?

1

Student A: Yes, I agree. And, of course, you have to make sure that you're good enough at the language that the teaching's going to be delivered in. You have to be at a pretty high level before you can study for a degree in another language.

2

Student A: True. How important do you think it is to stay in touch with friends and family while you're studying in another country?

3

Student A: Yes. I think cost's incredibly important too.

Practice task | Ex 3 and Ex 4

 S10 and S11

Examiner: Now, talk to each other about how important these things might be for someone to study successfully in another country.

Student A: Well, looking at this first prompt, I think choosing a suitable university is incredibly important. You need one that has a good reputation, and I think it's essential that it isn't somewhere that is, like, right round the other side of the world, so you can get home easily for holidays and things. And, of course, it's got to be somewhere that you really want to spend time in. What do you think?

Student B: I think what you said is true. It's no use going to study at a university no one's heard of, or to study

at a university that's in a country that you have no real interest in. What's equally important is that it's somewhere that has a respected education system. There's little point in getting a degree that employers or universities in your own country don't really recognise. And, of course, some universities within each country have better reputations than others.

Student A: Yes, I agree. And, of course, you have to make sure that you're good enough at the language that the teaching's going to be delivered in. You have to be at a pretty high level before you can study for a degree in another language.

Student B: I totally agree. It's recognised that the level of language you need for functioning well in an academic environment is much higher than what you need if you're just using the language socially. And the great thing is that you'll be developing your skills in another language as well as getting a qualification. So then, you need to choose a country where they speak a language that's actually going to be useful for you to learn, one that you're going to use in the future or will be an advantage for getting jobs.

Student A: True. How important do you think it is to stay in touch with friends and family while you're studying in another country?

Student B: Oh, it's absolutely essential, without a doubt. You're going to be much happier if you're in regular contact with everyone back home. But the thing is, I don't think that would have any impact whatsoever on where you choose to study, as staying in touch with them will be the same wherever you are in the world. You can't possibly do well at university if you're not happy, and part of that comes from speaking to the people you love regularly.

Student A: Yes. I think cost's incredibly important too. You have to choose somewhere that you can actually afford to study, both in terms of how much the fees are to study there and also the cost of living in the city and country you end up in.

Student B: This is a really important thing to consider because you wouldn't be living at home anymore, so it's going to be expensive. If you're worrying about money all the time, you won't be able to concentrate on studying.

Student A: No, so perhaps getting a part-time job will help, and will also be a good way of meeting people other than those you're studying with.

Student B: Yes, because developing a good social life is really important too.

Student A: I agree. Getting to know lots of people, especially if they're local, is a great way to find out more about the culture of the country you're in and to find out the best places to go and see.

Student B: Yes and, after all, there's nothing worse than being away from home and feeling lonely.

Practice task | Ex 5a and Ex 5b

 S12 and S13

Examiner: Thank you. Now you have about a minute to decide which of these things is most important in order to study successfully at a university in another country.

Student B: It's really hard to decide because they all seem so important. If I were to choose one, though, I think I'd have to go for choosing a suitable university.

Student A: Um, why do you think that?

Student B: Well, I think it's because a lot of the others seem to depend on your choice of university. If you decide on a university that's in a city which has a great nightlife, for example, where it's really part of the culture there, you're very likely to be able to develop a good social life, which means you'll hopefully use and develop your language skills more, and so on.

Student A: I guess that's all true, but having a great social life is only a part of being able to study successfully. You're going to this country to study at university after all, and if you haven't got the language skills to be able to communicate well or learn effectively there, you're never going to be successful. If you can't understand the lectures and teachers, and even the other students, you're going to fail, however busy you are in your free time.

Student B: Hmm, I see what you mean. I hadn't really thought of it like that. I was thinking more of the experience as a whole rather than about how successful the studying would be. In that case, I'll go along with what you said. Yes, there's no way you can succeed academically without being able to communicate well.

Examiner: Thank you.

Strategies and skills: Interacting in a two-way conversation | Ex 3 and Ex 4

 S14 and S15

Examiner: Now talk to each other about the advantages and disadvantages of having a relaxing break in these different ways.

Student A: Well, thinking first about listening to music, my view on this is that it's a perfect way of winding down during breaks because you forget all your stress of work or study and just get lost in what you're listening to.

Student B: I appreciate what you're saying, however listening to music's actually the last thing I'd do during a break because there aren't many types that I find relaxing. It's a far better idea to meet with friends and unwind by having a chat and a coffee together.

Student A: I'm not convinced that's true. As far as I'm concerned, meeting friends during a break isn't a great idea because if you get deeply involved in a conversation, you can really lose track of the time and get behind with whatever it is you've got to do.

Student B: So, what are your thoughts about going for a walk as a way of relaxing?

Student A: From my perspective, it's a great way to relax. For example, I was struggling with something at work last week so I went for a walk to the park and the answer just came into my head as I was walking. It was amazing. How about you?

Student B: Yes, I think it really helps you to relax. The only disadvantage is if there isn't anywhere nice to go for a walk near where you work or where you're studying.

Student A: Wouldn't you agree that having something to eat is good too? For example, I usually have some fruit during my morning break and I feel as though I've got more energy afterwards.

Student B: Well, if you ask me, having something to eat isn't always a good idea because afterwards, you can feel a little bit sleepy and it's actually quite hard to start working again. How do you feel about checking your phone as a way of relaxing during breaks?

Student A: My opinion is that checking your phone definitely isn't the best thing to do because there are often messages that you need to respond to and so on, and it can end up being more stressful than the work or study you're supposed to be escaping from.

Student B: That's a really clear way of explaining it! I feel exactly the same, although that doesn't usually stop me from doing it!

Student A: Me neither!

Strategies and skills: Negotiating towards a decision | Ex 8

 S16

1

Student A: OK, so having discussed all the options, we really need to make a decision. Do you think this one's the most important?

Student B: Yes, I think we're both of the opinion that problem-solving is the most important.

Student A: Great, so that's decided that, then.

2

Student A: OK, well let's rule out this one as being the most important then, shall we?

Student B: Yes, because neither of us thought that was significant. Actually, I don't think we're ever going to agree about which one's most important.

Student A: No, probably not.

3

Student A: OK, so are you telling me that this is the most important one?

Student B: Yes, definitely, and I think you were saying the same thing, weren't you?

Student A: I was! Great! So, we've both decided on problem-solving as being the most important.

4

Student A: So, shall we choose a different one then, if we don't agree on that?

Student B: OK, but I think that we'll just have to agree to disagree about which is the most important.

Student A: Yes, I think we've got very different opinions about it, haven't we?

EXAM TASK

 S17

See page 101.

SPEAKING

Part 4

Practice task | Ex 1

 S18

See page 102.

Practice task | Ex 2–5

 S19-22

1 Do you think that certain people are naturally much better at certain workplace skills than others? Why? Why not?

Student A: I think so, yes. I guess it's probably to do with genetics, so that if one or both of your parents is really good at being organised, for example, then you probably will be naturally good at it too. But I don't think that stops anyone else becoming good at being organised too.

Student B: I was just going to say something similar to your last point, actually. I think anyone can become good at a certain skill if they practise enough. The difference is in just how good they become, so someone who's naturally better at giving workplace presentations, for instance, will be better than someone who isn't after the same amount of practice.

2 Do you think work experience programmes would be beneficial for students who are still at school? Why? Why not?

Student B: I think so, yes. School is so different to working life, so a work experience programme would be a great way to introduce school students to employment. I think it should happen towards the end of their school careers, so they don't lose study time when they really need it, but I think it's a good idea.

Student A: I agree with you, as I think schools have a much more academic focus than a vocational one. They do provide some of the basic skills you need for many different jobs, such as reading, writing and working closely with other people, but using these skills in the classroom and knowing how to put them into practice in the workplace are two different things. There's nothing better for preparing students for the world of work than direct experience with employers.

Student B: I can't think of any jobs I was ready to start when I left school.

Student A: Me neither!

3 Which do you think is more important for being successful in the workplace, knowledge and qualifications or experience? Why?

Student A: I think you need all of these things to be a really good employee, but if I had to say which one was more important, I'd go for the experience. What about you?

Student B: Yeah, I agree with you, but I don't think it's as simple as choosing one or the other. For example, if you're studying, you're developing your knowledge but you might also get quite a lot of experience of some tasks and skills while you're working towards your qualification.

Student A: True, but someone who has a lot of experience at doing a job is always going to be better at it than someone who doesn't.

4 Who do you think should pay for workers to develop new skills in their jobs, the employer or the employee? Why?

Student B: Oh, the employer, definitely. They're the ones who will benefit the most from the employee developing the new skills, so I think it's only fair that they should pay for the training.

Student A: I'm not so sure, you know … I mean, suppose an employer spends thousands of pounds or dollars or whatever training an employee on how to use a particular piece of software. Then after a few weeks, the employee uses the new skills they've gained to get a better-paid job with another company. The first employer has basically lost all of the money they've invested in that employee.

Student B: Well, I'd go along with you in that it's not fair on the employer, but maybe they should have paid the employee more and it wouldn't have happened … No, seriously though, companies can put it in employees' contracts that if they leave within a certain time after they've received some training, they have to pay the money back.

Student A: That's a really good idea, actually.

Strategies and skills: Justifying your opinions | Ex 5

 S23

1 Do you think people should learn more than one foreign language at school?

Student A: If they want to, yes – but they shouldn't be forced into it. To give you an example from my own experience, I've been learning three languages at school – English, French and Russian – and I think that learning more than one has actually helped me to get better at all of them.

2 Why do you think some people find it harder to make decisions than others?

Student B: I guess it's because of their personality. I have a friend who finds decision-making almost impossible. They're quite an anxious person, which is probably why. I'm a bit more confident than they are so I don't find it so difficult.

3 How do you think young people can be encouraged to take on more responsibilities?

Student C: I think the best way is for adults to push them a bit more. What really helped me to do this was when my teacher started asking me to do things that I found challenging, like leading a debate on plastic pollution. I was naturally a bit shy so wouldn't have normally put my hand up to take on something like that.

Strategies and skills: Developing a discussion | Ex 10 and Ex 11

 S24 and S25

1 Do you agree that banning all motor vehicles from city centres is a good idea?

Student A: Yes, I do – definitely. They did this in a city in my country that's not far from my home town. The difference it made was amazing. If they did the same thing in all cities, it would certainly make them more pleasant places to live, work and visit. I mean, the pollution in them is terrible.

Student B: I hear what you're saying but I'm not sure I totally agree with you. It would reduce pollution for sure, but it would also stop lorries and vans delivering to all of the shops there. Many of the customers in those shops drive to the city and park there, maybe because they live in an area where the public transport isn't so good.

2 Do you think people worry about the environment too much these days?

Student B: No, not at all. In fact, it's such a big problem that they should be anxious about it, actually, because the changes we need to make aren't happening quickly enough. If anyone is even a little bit anxious about it, hopefully their concerns will push them to do more to help.

Student A: I agree with you. What I'd also say is that it's something we all need to address. It's not just something the government should sort out – it's up to all of us to help.

3 How do you think people can be encouraged to save energy and water?

Student A: I think the best way is if they could be made cheaper for anyone who uses very little of them. That would be a really good way of reducing how much people use.

Student B: Is it OK if I make a point about that too?

Student A: Of course.

Student B: Well, I think part of the problem is that people just don't know how to do it so they need to be shown what to do. Perhaps there could be adverts on TV showing ways of doing this.

Student A: Good idea!

4 Some people think that the environment is already too badly damaged to fix. Do you agree?

Student B: No, I don't agree at all. Any problem can be solved if we put in enough time, money and effort.

Student A: If I could, I'd really like to add something to what you've said. If we think this is true, then we might as well just give up now, but in fact the technology already exists to reverse the problems – we just need to do it.

5 Do you think that all countries need to work closely together to solve environmental problems?

Student A: I couldn't agree more. It's called global warming, not national warming, so it's everyone's problem. And if it's everyone's problem, then it's up to all of us to solve it. I know lots of countries don't get on, but they need to forget their political differences because it's such a big issue.

Student B: If they don't, it will make the whole problem much more difficult to deal with. And in addition to the ideas you mentioned, I'd also say that many scientists from many different countries are already working closely together, but at government level this needs to be happening much more.

Student A: I totally agree.

EXAM TASK

🎧 S26

See page 105.

Practice Exam

LISTENING
Part 1
🎧 PE01

Extract 1
You hear two friends discussing the topic of advertising.

F: I'm researching an essay on advertising at the moment.

M: Oh yeah? I'd swear that the time between commercials somehow gets shorter every time I switch the television on.

F: That's the impression I get too. They're frustrating, but at least there's the occasional one that's just as, if not more, enjoyable than the actual programme.

M: I've yet to see one that's made me think that way, but maybe one day … I suppose the fact that there's advertising everywhere these days must mean it works incredibly well.

F: Companies wouldn't do it otherwise – I mean, it costs them millions.

M: There's lots of pressure at the moment to stop any adverts appearing on websites and during TV shows aimed at kids …

F: Ah … yes, I'm not sure the government would go along with it, as it generates business, but my guess is that plenty of parents would. I can't help feeling that it puts toy manufacturers at a bit of a disadvantage, though, as no other sector's prevented from showing adverts to its target market. I don't suppose a few toy companies going out of business would bring the whole country to its knees economically, but it would certainly have a big impact on the people working for them.

Extract 2
You hear part of a discussion programme in which two journalists are talking about the theatre.

M: Whilst we're on the subject of theatre attendance, it seems to me as though many theatres are overly obsessed with having a full house. Limiting the cost of a certain number of seats for each performance is no guarantee of bringing this about, of course, so instead they've gone down the route of exclusively staging pieces created by someone audiences will have heard of. It's their name that then appears centre stage, so to speak, in any advertising material the theatre produces. I'm not doubting the quality of the work, but it does lead to up-and-coming talent being excluded from the majority of theatres nationwide.

F: I'm sure listeners are all too aware of why some theatres are being forced to adopt such a strategy, so I don't think we need to dwell on this. What I object to, though, is that this approach is anywhere near as widespread as you're claiming. Sure, a small number of the biggest and most high-profile theatres may be doing this, but that leaves an awful lot of other establishments throughout the capital and the country as a whole which are doing the exact opposite.

Extract 3
You hear a woman telling a friend about living on a houseboat.

M: You've been living on your houseboat for a couple of years now. How's it going?

F: Pretty good, although it could do with a few repairs.

M: Oh? Is it turning out to need more doing to it than you originally thought?

F: It takes time to sort out, but it's just general maintenance stuff, which all houseboats need. Having made it through my second winter, I'm not completely sure how many more I can stand. The owners of the boats around mine just laugh when they hear me moaning about how cold it is, and ask me what I was expecting. I guess I should have known.

M: Well, you can never tell. My brother bought an old cottage in the countryside a few years ago. He phoned me up after he'd first looked round it, telling me how great it was. Then a few weeks after he moved in, he suddenly realised it wasn't for him after all. The reasons he gave were all things you could have predicted beforehand, like the lack of facilities, but sometimes you just don't know until you actually go and experience it for yourself. It might seem like a mistake, but I don't see it that way at all.

LISTENING
Part 2

 PE02

Hi, everyone. My name's Sandra Ibbotson, and I'm a marine biology student. I was lucky enough to be part of a recent research expedition studying Greenland sharks in their cold native waters.

I was really excited as we set sail from Bergen in Norway with a variety of students and research scientists on board. There were seven of us from the UK, including the head of my university department, six from Denmark, one of whom sorted out the team, the financing and the boat, and several from Sweden. One of the Swedish scientists is probably the world's foremost expert on Greenland sharks.

Over a hundred students applied for the expedition, many of whom had been studying marine predators for several years. The organisers were keen to take someone who'd done plenty of filming underwater before, though, which is why I ended up going. The students were there primarily to help out with practical stuff like that.

One thing I really wasn't prepared for was how rough the sea could get at times. I think the closest I can get to explaining what it's like on the boat during a storm is for you to imagine how your clothes must feel inside your washing machine. That's probably a more accurate description than a colleague's comparison of being on a rollercoaster in a fairground.

As for the research itself, well, the research scientists all worked for an international research programme. It's recently been discovered that Greenland sharks have the longest lifespan of any vertebrate, so they hoped to investigate that further. Over and above this, however, was the need to discover more about their migration, which was a complete mystery.

During the expedition, the scientists shared their knowledge about Greenland sharks. I'd already heard about their amazingly poor eyesight – which is seldom a hindrance, as they generally stay in the dark ocean depths – but one scientist informed us about their extraordinarily slow heart rate, which helps them cope with the extreme cold by beating only six times a minute.

Until recently, it was assumed that Greenland sharks' diet consisted of dead animals they find on the ocean floor, such as whales. It's become apparent, though, that they actively hunt their prey too. I'd never have considered polar bears to be something they'd target, but remains of them, as well as of seals, have been found in Greenland sharks' stomachs.

I was fortunate enough to dive with Greenland sharks we encountered. I'd heard they could appear as though they'd run out of energy due to their slow movements. The ones I saw were quite purposeful, but unlike many of the other species I'd dived with, they never showed any aggression, which was curious for such large sharks.

The scientists explained that their research into Greenland sharks might have a wider application beyond marine biology. A project analysing whale behaviour that one of them had previously been involved with, for instance, also ended up helping climate change research. Perhaps surprisingly, they're hoping that studies of certain human illnesses could well be informed by some of the discoveries related to why Greenland sharks live so long.

LISTENING
Part 3

 PE03

Interviewer: On today's programme we have two journalists who specialise in writing about the environment, Karen Brearley and Ian Gill. Karen, you recently published an article about limiting flights to all but essential ones, with immediate effect. It's caused quite a bit of controversy …

Karen: Yes, and it would've got under even more people's skins if my boss hadn't toned it down. I can understand why she wanted to do that, even if I didn't really go along with how she did it. I was a bit taken aback by a few of my colleagues' comments, though, as they appeared to suggest that my central argument was flawed, which I refute totally, of course. According to the online comments, it seems to have outraged more general readers than environmental researchers, who largely agree with me. I'm not holding my breath for any great change in the national mood about the issue, though.

Interviewer: What's your take on Karen's proposals for limiting flights, Ian?

Ian: I can understand the idea behind it, as air travel has an undoubted effect on global warming, but so does something like playing sport, if you think about it. Each sport requires the use of manufactured goods and sometimes special places to do it, from balls and bats up to swimming pools and stadiums. All of these take energy to produce, thereby harming the environment. Yet no one would propose an overnight ban on sport – this would be seen as too drastic a measure. I'm in total agreement that something needs to be done, it's just the pace of the implementation I'd question. Alternative employment would need to be developed for the workforce, for instance.

Interviewer: But the statistics relating to the aviation industry's impact on the environment make for quite alarming reading …

Ian: I agree, and the figures in the press only actually tell us one small part of the overall picture. I'm not suggesting that what we're told by the airlines is in any way inaccurate, but it generally relates to how much carbon dioxide aeroplanes produce. Even the most recent statistics fail to take account of the emissions that result from refining the fuel for the aircraft, or in the running of airports or even the production of the aircraft themselves.

Interviewer: Surely technological improvements in design will result in less environmentally damaging aircraft …

Karen: Er, they will, but I suspect it won't be enough. While there have been incredibly rapid leaps forward with automobiles and trains, for example, these have centred on converting them from fossil fuel-burning engines to electric motors. There's a general consensus that, however much time and effort you put into attempting the same thing with aircraft, motors will never be sufficiently powerful to lift something as heavy as an airliner off the ground. So developers are defeated before they've even begun.

Interviewer: A question to you both, now. Do governments do enough to help on this issue?

Ian: Very few nations argue against policies that are aimed at allowing a greater number of flights. Those in power want to allow massive growth in travel and tourism yet, at the same time promise huge cuts in emissions. Modest increases in taxes on both aviation fuel and tickets have made little, if any, difference.

Karen: I think that introducing tighter emissions tests on aeroplanes, like we have on many cars, is a way forward, but it's certainly hard to reconcile many governments' conflicting aims on supporting green issues, whilst at the same time promoting ways of getting people and goods around the country and around the world that are ecologically harmful.

Interviewer: And what can you and other individuals do to help?

Ian: I guess flying less is the obvious answer!

Karen: Yes, or giving it up altogether, which is practically impossible. I've taken to travelling only during daylight hours, as the vapour trails that planes produce reflect the sun's rays back into space, counteracting the effect of harmful emissions somewhat. My biggest concession is using only the carriers that offer the cheapest tickets. They tend to pack their planes with people, so are more ecological in terms of passenger miles. Business class was never something I indulged in, so my conscience is clear on that one.

Ian: Mine too! I'd like to say I'm a less frequent flyer these days, but I'm afraid the reverse is actually true. I always choose the cheapest flights, as the airlines offering these usually operate newer, more efficient aircraft. I'm not sure I'd ever have guessed that the time of day made such a difference environmentally, so I'll add that to my list of strategies too.

Interviewer: Thank you both very much.

LISTENING
Part 4
 PE04

1

One of my friends decided to have a gap year too. Our motivations for doing so couldn't have been more different. Whilst I was not exactly wholeheartedly discovering whether I'd be able to turn a lifelong love of music into a professional career, she went off to see how many stamps from different countries she could get in her passport. Oddly enough, learning that I was probably never going to be a good enough musician helped me to focus my energies on the academic alternative, and my career beyond this. I guess I figured that if I couldn't make it in one vocation, I'd stop at absolutely nothing to succeed in the other.

2

There have been some unforeseen yet welcome consequences of having a gap year. I was deeply concerned that going back into education afterwards would feel incredibly daunting. I seem to have unexpectedly regained my enthusiasm for studying, though, so my worries proved unfounded. I feel as though my decisions are now being made from an adult perspective, rather than from that of a school student. In my final year at school, I was torn between studying medicine or veterinary science at university. The answer to this seemingly impossible dilemma was pretty easy to arrive at, once I wasn't devoting all my energies to schoolwork, so the aim of the year out has definitely been met.

3

The sports science course I've wanted to do for some time is far more practical in nature than something like nutrition. I've played sport for as long as I can remember, but have always been coached rather than coaching others. I decided to use the time the gap year afforded me to put this right, which has also allowed me to make additions to my CV that prospective employers might find attractive. Coaching full-time is hard, and the respect I have for my mum and dad, who've held down jobs as teachers for however many years to support me and my sisters, has grown as a result.

4

I was expecting that the break from studying would allow me to recharge my batteries so I'd be ready to go full speed into a degree. Funnily enough, it's had completely the opposite effect, leaving me pondering whether higher education's for me after all. My family isn't that well-off, so I'd decided to find work wherever I could so I'd have enough for the tuition fees and living costs. An uncle who has his own construction company heard what I wanted to do and, knowing that I wanted to study architecture, found me a job. I'm enjoying it so much, and I can pay rent to my parents too, so I may end up staying.

5

I've always admired people who finish school then go off to broaden their knowledge of other countries and cultures, and I really wanted to follow their example. My teachers knew that my heart was set on a career in journalism, but as I neared the end of my final school year, they kept warning me that I'd have to improve my spelling and grammar if I wanted to make it in that profession. I decided to do just that for a year, before I started the journalism course. I've changed a lot during the year and have become far more sensible and responsible, which I think will serve me well when I start college.

SPEAKING
Part 1
 PE05

See page 124.

SPEAKING
Part 2
 PE06

See page 124.

SPEAKING
Part 3
 PE07

See page 127.

SPEAKING
Part 4
 PE08

See page 127.

READING AND USE OF ENGLISH
Part 1 Multiple-choice cloze
Practice task

2

0 C **1** A **2** B **3** D **4** A

3

1 4 ('made up of' has a similar meaning to 'consists of')

2 0 (All the words have similar meanings but 'exist', 'reside' and 'dwell' are all followed by 'in', so 'inhabit' is the only word which fits here.)

3 3 ('for the most part' means 'usually' or 'mainly')

4 1 (All four options have similar meanings but 'vast' is the only which collocates with 'majority'.)

5 2 (All four options have similar meanings, but only 'solitary' is correct.)

4

1 (Each of the words is used because they collocate most naturally with the following word in the sentence: 'vast majority', 'enormous number', 'immense amount', 'gigantic statue'.)

2 (Each of the words has a slightly different meaning, which the four sentences in this set help to illustrate.)

3 (Each sentence contains a word from question 3 of the Practice task used in a fixed phrase.)

4 (Each sentence contains a phrasal verb with 'up' using verbs from the options for question 4.)

Strategies and skills
Fixed phrases

1

1 things ('all things considered' means that you take the whole situation into account)

2 notice ('at short notice' means that something happens with very little warning)

3 balance ('strike a balance' means you have the right amount of two or more things)

4 desire ('a burning desire' means a very strong need or urge to do something)

5 power ('doing everything in your power' means you do all you can do to achieve something)

6 room ('room for improvement' means something needs to get better)

7 hesitation ('have no hesitation' means that a decision or choice is very easy to make)

8 horizons ('expand your horizons' means to try new things or approaches)

2

1 grasp ('grasp the complexities' means you understand the deeper meaning of something)

2 took ('take their toll' means to affect something, usually in a negative way)

3 cracked ('crack a joke' means to tell a joke)

4 drove ('drive someone to do something' means to force someone)

5 held ('hold an opinion' means you have an opinion about something)

6 caught ('catch someone's attention' means to interest them)

7 present (if something 'presents difficulties', it creates problems)

8 pose ('pose a threat/danger' means to potentially cause a problem)

Collocations

3

1 B ('make a wish' means to think of something you'd really like to happen)

2 A ('take note of' means to remember or pay attention to something)

3 A ('leave someone doing something' means they continue doing something while you do something else)

4 D ('come naturally' means you're good at something right from the beginning)

5 C ('tell the difference' means you know which one is which)

6 A ('fulfil an ambition' means to achieve it)

4

1 location ('on location' means it's being filmed in a particular place and not in a studio)

2 labour ('the labour market' is the jobs that are available in an area or country. 'Job market' is an acceptable alternative, but is more informal.)

3 near ('nowhere near' means it's a long way from something or somewhere)

4 industry (a 'growth industry' is a sector that's becoming very popular)

5 word ('keep your word' means you do what you say you'll do)

6 broken ('broken English', or any other language, means you don't speak it very well)

Phrasal verbs

5

1 C ('bump into' means to meet by accident)

2 A ('cut out' means to stop having something in your diet or doing something in your routine)

3 D ('get at' means to show what something really means)

4 B ('kick in' means to start to be effective or to happen)

5 A ('put forward' means to suggest something or ask for opinions about it)

6 D ('stem from' means where something comes from)

Easily confused words

6

1 aggression (an 'act of aggression' is angry or violent behaviour towards someone or something)

2 acclaimed (someone who is 'acclaimed' is praised by a lot of people)

3 comprehensively (if a team is beaten 'comprehensively', it means they were easily beaten)

4 withdrawn (to 'withdraw' means to take money out of an account)

5 speculation ('speculation' is when people guess, often with others, without knowing for sure)

6 plunged (to 'plunge' means to fall suddenly and dramatically, often in relation to temperature)

Prepositions

7

1 C ('comparable' is usually followed by the preposition 'to'; 'consistent' + 'with'; 'matching' + 'with', or no preposition; 'alike' + no preposition)

2 A ('Contrary' is usually followed by the preposition 'to'. None of the other words usually take prepositions.)

3 B ('accordance' is usually preceded by the preposition 'in' and followed by 'with'; 'contract' + 'with' (but the wrong word in this context); 'duty' + 'to'; 'assurance' + no preposition')

4 D (you can use 'in respect of' or 'with respect to'; 'concern' + 'with' or 'about'; 'regard' + 'to'; 'connection' + 'with')

5 B ('intended' is usually followed by the preposition 'for', 'aimed' + 'at'; 'directed' + 'at'; 'focused' + 'on')

6 D ('concerned' is usually followed by the preposition 'with; 'disturbed' + 'by'; 'troubled' + 'by'; 'worried' + 'about')

8

1 on (you are 'dependent on' somebody or something)

2 to (you 'dedicate something to' somebody or something)

3 of (you use 'in the event' with the preposition 'of')

4 in (you use the phrase 'no harm in +' verb + -ing to mean that it's a good idea to do something)

5 about (if you are 'in two minds about' doing something, you can't decide whether to do it or not)

6 with (if you 'keep pace with' someone, it means you run, walk or drive at the same speed)

Verb patterns

9

1 that prices will rise ('anticipate' is usually followed by a 'that' clause)

2 of spending ('beware' is usually followed by 'of +' verb + -ing)

3 matters further ('complicate' is usually followed by a noun)
4 making ('envision' is often followed by verb + -ing or a noun)
5 to avoid ('instructed' is always followed by an infinite or negative infinitive, e.g. 'not to talk to')
6 to give ('invited' is usually followed by an infinitive)

Linking words

10

1 interestingly (this linking word is used to add interesting information)
2 whereas ('whereas' is used to contrast two pieces of information in two clauses)
3 or ('or' is used here to give a reason why something must be the case)
4 consequently ('consequently' is used to show a result of something)
5 owing to ('owing to' is used to explain a reason for something happening)
6 nonetheless ('nonetheless' is used to show how one thing happened despite something else)

EXAM TASK

0 D (a 'widely held belief' is something that most people assume is true)
1 A (if someone is 'disciplined' they have a lot of self-control)
2 B (a 'principle' is an idea or rule, often one which explains how something works)
3 D (the phrase 'in question' refers you to a particular example of what is being discussed)
4 C (if something 'meets a requirement', it is good enough for a particular need)
5 A (if something 'points to' a conclusion, it shows that something it likely to be true)
6 B (if you 'reveal' something, you show it, perhaps for the first time)
7 B ('accounts for' has a similar meaning to 'is responsible for')
8 D (if something is 'arguably' true, you think it is but others may disagree)

READING AND USE OF ENGLISH
Part 2 Open cloze
Practice task

2

1 it **2** to **3** with **4** which **5** as

3

a 3 **b** 4 **c** 1 **d** 2 **e** 5

4

1 c **2** a **3** d **4** e **5** b

Strategies and skills

Perfect and continuous tenses

1

1 been (present perfect continuous)
2 are (present simple passive)
3 have (present perfect passive)

4 do, did (present simple interrogative or past simple interrogative)
5 being (-ing form is used following 'after' and 'before')
6 has (present perfect passive)

Conjunctions

2

a 1, 2, 4
b 3
c 5, 7
d 6

3

1 Although **2** Far **3** addition **4** despite
5 provided **6** whilst **7** considering

Conditional forms

4

1 C (This is a 'mixed' conditional, a mix of second and third conditionals.)
2 C (This is an example of a third conditional.)
3 A (This is an example of a third conditional with an inversion.)
4 B (This is an example of a third conditional.)
5 C (This is an example of a first conditional with 'unless'.)
6 A (This is an example of a second conditional.)
7 C (This is an example of a first conditional with 'if.')
8 B (This is an example of a third conditional with 'have' as both the main verb and the auxiliary verb in the 'if' clause.)

Future tenses

5

1 will be sailing **2** will have to
3 will have been travelling **4** will be able
5 will be witnessed **6** will have started

6

1 be (future simple passive)
2 being (passive with the -ing form used following 'after' and 'before')
3 have (future perfect)
4 be (future continuous)
5 have (future form of 'have to')
6 been (future perfect continuous)

Relative clauses

7

In most cases the word before each gap is a noun or pronoun, and after the gap there is another clause: a relative clause.

8

1 which (because 'The city' is a thing)
2 whose (because the boat belonged to the captain)
3 whom (because the object of the first clause are people)
4 who (because the instructor is a person)
5 which (because 'my glasses' are a thing)
6 where (because 'the school' is a place)

Comparative forms

9

1 e ('at the very least' means a minimum requirement)
2 a ('comparatively little' + uncountable noun means 'not much')
3 d ('a great deal more' + noun means 'a lot more')
4 b ('such a long time' means 'a very long time')
5 f ('nowhere near' + 'as … as' + subject and verb)
6 c ('one of the (world's/country's/etc.)' + 'most' + (adverb) + adjective)

10

1 more ('more likely' + verb)
2 rather ('rather than' + -ing form)
3 far ('by far' + superlative)
4 neither (X couldn't do something + and neither could Y means that Y also couldn't do the thing.)
5 except ('except for' + noun or pronoun)
6 so ('and so is X' means 'X is too')
7 no ('without a doubt' means 'definitely')
8 to ('comparable' + 'to')

Reference words and impersonal structures

11

1 what (impersonal structure)
2 There (impersonal subject pronoun)
3 It (impersonal structure)
4 that (impersonal structure)
5 it (impersonal structure)
6 there (impersonal subject pronoun)

Phrasal verbs, prepositions and fixed phrases

12

1 into **2** out **3** against **4** of **5** back **6** on
7 off **8** together

13

a 3 ('to come up against something' means to have to deal with a problem or difficulty)
b 8 ('to put something together' means to prepare a plan or document)
c 5 ('to get back to someone' means to contact them at some point in the future)
d 2 ('to check something out' means to examine it carefully to get more information)
e 7 ('to lay someone off' means to sack them so they lose their job.)
f 1 ('to bump into someone' means to meet them by accident)
g 6 ('to insist on something' means to make sure that something happens, even if others are against the idea)
h 4 (to 'dispose of' something means to throw it away)

14

1 to ('all down to' means the same as 'because of')
2 once ('once and for all' means the same as 'permanently')
3 After ('After all' is used to add evidence that shows what you just said is true)
4 whether ('whether or not 'is used to show that something will happen regardless of what you do)
5 put (if you 'put yourself in someone's shoes', it means to see an issue from their point of view)
6 without ('without a doubt' means something is definitely true)
7 no ('to come as no surprise' means that something is what you would expect)
8 but ('no other choice but to' means there's only one possible course of action)

EXAM TASK

0 of ('in excess of' means the same as 'more than')
1 no ('no easy task' is a fixed expression meaning that something is difficult or time-consuming)
2 with ('equipped' takes the dependent preposition 'with')
3 a ('as a rule' means that something is generally true)
4 within/in (the expression 'within sight' or 'in sight' means you can see it)
5 in (the phrasal verb 'settle in' means to become comfortable in a place where you're staying or working)
6 on ('on offer' means the same as 'available')
7 which ('of which' is a relative pronoun that refers back to the plural noun 'ingredients')
8 been (part of a present perfect passive construction)

READING AND USE OF ENGLISH
Part 3 Word formation
Practice task

2

0 straightforward (This has a similar meaning to 'simple' or 'easy' in this context.)
1 significant (This adjective has a similar meaning to 'important'.)
2 extraordinary (This adjective has a similar meaning to 'amazing'.)
3 findings (This plural noun has a similar meaning to 'results' or 'conclusions'.)
4 conversion (This noun means to change from one form to another.)

3

a 2 **b** 0 **c** 1 **d** 3, 4

Strategies and skills
Prefixes

1

1 normality **2** abnormal **3** logical **4** illogical **5** satisfaction **6** dissatisfied/unsatisfied **7** maturity/maturation **8** immature **9** relevance **10** irrelevant

2

1 consequence (The prefix 'con-' changes the meaning but not to an opposite.)
2 misbehave (The prefix 'mis-' changes the meaning to something done badly or incorrectly.)
3 overconfident (The prefix 'over-' changes the meaning to *too* + adjective.)
4 autobiographical (The prefix 'auto-' means it relates to yourself.)
5 interactive (The prefix 'inter-' means 'between'.)
6 reconsider (The prefix 're-' means 'do something again'.)

Suffixes

3

1 -ity: capability, sensitivity
2 -ship: leadership
3 -ce: competence, innocence
4 -y: jealousy
5 -al: disapproval
6 -ness: nervousness, rudeness, selfishness, willingness
7 -tion: cancellation, consumption, reception
8 -ance: allowance, annoyance
9 -ment: assignment
10 -cy: deficiency, competency

4

1 archaeologist **2** adviser/advisor **3** professional **4** technician **5** ambassador **6** consultant **7** fisherman/woman **8** novelist **9** civil servant **10** surgeon

5

1 reputable (This collocates well with 'company'.)
2 administrative (This collocates well with 'error'.)
3 changeable (This means that something changes a lot in a short time.)
4 diplomatic (This means that you are careful not to offend anyone or hurt their feelings.)
5 edible (This means that you can eat it safely.)
6 exhaustive (This means it's very complete and includes everything.)
7 idealistic (This means that you have very clear ideas about how to achieve things you believe in.)
8 persuasive (This means that you are good at persuading people to agree with you or do what you want.)

6

-ive: aggressive, constructive, responsive, substantive
-ous: courageous, spacious
-ing: convincing, refreshing
-tial: confidential, spatial, substantial
-worthy: newsworthy, trustworthy
-able: comparable, variable
-al: occasional, statistical
-ible: responsible, terrible

7

Students' own answers

8

1 satisfactorily (The adverb is needed here because it describes the verb 'explain'.)
2 uncomfortable (The adjective is needed here as it's describing the noun 'silence'.)
3 dishonestly (The adverb is needed here because it describes the verb 'obtain'.)
4 jointly (The adverb is needed here because it describes the verb 'award'.)
5 realistic (The adjective is needed here as it's describing the noun 'models'.)
6 noticeably (The adverb is needed here because it describes an adjective 'quieter'.)
7 officially (The adverb is needed here because it describes the verb 'open'.)
8 technologically (The adverb is needed here because it describes an adjective 'advanced'.)

9

1 acknowledging (You have to use the -*ing* form in this sentence.)
2 differentiate (This means to tell the difference between things.)
3 evaluate (This means to comment on the good and bad things about something.)
4 imprisoned (This means to put in prison, and it's a passive so you need the past participle.)
5 lengthening (This means to get longer.)
6 simplified (This means to make something simpler.)

Internal word changes

10

1 adjective (suggested by use of 'It is not …' before the gap.)
2 adjective (suggested by 'more' before the gap.)
3 verb (because of 'to' before the gap.)
4 adjective (because of 'wasn't very' before the gap.)
5 noun (suggested by the adjective 'conventional' just before the gap.)
6 adjective (suggested by the noun 'changes' after the gap.)

11

1 advisable (The 'c' changes to 's' and the 'e' disappears when you add the suffix -*able*.)
2 destructive (This is the adjective.)
3 clarify (This is the verb.)
4 decisive (This is the adjective of the verb 'decide'.)

5 wisdom (This is the noun.)
6 minimal (This is the adjective from the noun 'minimum'.)

12

1 believable (The final 'e' disappears when adding a suffix which begins with a vowel.)
2 controlling (The final 'l' doubles when adding '-ing'.)
3 luxurious (The final 'y' changes to i when adding 'ous'.)
4 pleasurable (The final 'e' disappears when adding a suffix which begins with a vowel.)
5 disastrous ('-er' at the end of the noun changes to just '-r'.)
6 repetitive (The final 'a' of repeat disappears when forming the adjective.)

Compounding

13

1 e
2 c
3 a
4 f
5 b
6 d

14

1 widespread
2 eye-catching
3 waterproof
4 background
5 supernatural
6 alongside

15

1 groundbreaking
2 setbacks
3 time-saving
4 undergo
5 meantime
6 whatsoever

EXAM TASK

0 length (This is the noun of the adjective 'long'.)
1 insignificant (This is the adjective formed from the verb' signify', and it needs to be negative in this sentence.)
2 organisms (This noun has a similar meaning to 'creatures'.)
3 worldwide (This adverb means 'all around the world'.)
4 intriguingly (This adverb has a similar meaning to 'interestingly' here.)
5 visible (This adjective means it's possible to see something.)
6 critical (This adjective means 'vital' or 'extremely important'.)
7 dramatically (This adverb means 'a lot'.)
8 dependent (If something is 'dependent on' something else, it needs it to survive.)

READING AND USE OF ENGLISH
Part 4 Key word transformation
Practice task

2

1 was (finally) talked into joining (If you 'talk someone' into doing something, it has a similar meaning to 'persuade'.)
2 warning about the risks of cycling (The noun of 'warn' is 'warning' and the noun of 'risky' is 'risk.')
3 gave a clear explanation about/of (The noun of 'explain' is 'explanation' which collocates with the verb 'give'.)
4 hadn't/had not been for Hannah's (This structure is commonly tested in Part 4.)

3

a 3
b 1
c 1, 4
d 2
e 1 (to create a passive form)
f 2, 3 (The noun of the verb 'warn' is 'warning'; the noun of the verb 'explain' is 'explanation')
g 1 ('to join' becomes 'joining')
h 2 (The plural noun of the adjective 'risky' is 'risks')

Strategies and skills
Passive forms

1

1 is being repaired (the present continuous passive)
2 had (all) been finished (the past perfect passive)
3 has been cleaned (the present perfect passive)
4 being taught (verbs which are normally followed by gerunds take the -ing form of 'to be')
5 had to be rescued (this is an infinitive passive form)
6 may be lowered (modal verbs take the bare infinitive (without 'to') to form a passive)
7 would have been fed (this is a third conditional passive form)
8 he was being ignored (the past continuous passive)

Reported speech

2

1 had been having his lunch (The past continuous changes to past perfect continuous.)
2 hadn't/had not meant to be (The past simple changes to the past perfect.)
3 I was going to finish writing (The present continuous changes to the past continuous.)

4 would be more straightforward than we (Future with 'will' changes to 'would'.)
5 when it would be possible to ('can' here changes to 'it would be possible')
6 have been better if I had/to have included

Comparative forms

3

1 A **2** C **3** C **4** A

4

1 'wasn't anywhere near as long' (because the person expected it to last much longer)
2 'such a small amount of' (because 'such a' emphasises the amount of something)
3 'as good as' (because people imagine the past was better that it was in reality)
4 'more speedily than' (because it was faster than ever before)

Verb and noun phrases

5

1 a hand **2** get in **3** raise **4** quite
5 faith in **6** hang of **7** go into **8** take a

6

1 give a clear description (the noun of 'describe')
2 take into consideration (the noun of 'consider')
3 a common assumption (the noun of 'assume')
4 very little acceptance (the noun of 'accept')
5 virtually no affordable/cheap (the adjective of 'afford')
6 highly imaginative (the adjective of 'imagination')

Clause patterns

7

1 could **2** If/When **3** Should **4** Pay

8

1 the best you/one can hope / all you/one can hope / all that can be hoped
2 should there be
3 if listened to / if you listen to it
4 and they will tell you / and you will know

Collocations and fixed phrases

9

1 any difference ('it doesn't make any difference to me' means you're not bothered if something happens.)
2 accustomed to ('become accustomed to' has a similar meaning to 'get used to'.)
3 behind the times ('behind the times' has a similar meaning to 'old-fashioned.')
4 felt compelled (If you 'feel compelled' to do something it means you feel like you have to do it.)
5 dedicated himself (If you 'dedicate yourself to something', it means you put all your energy into it.)

6 dependent upon (If something is 'dependent upon' something else, it means it is related directly to it. If a person is dependent on someone else, it means they rely on them totally.)

7 no harm in (If there's 'no harm in doing something', it means there are no disadvantages in doing it.)

8 in two minds (If someone is 'in two minds' about something, it means they can't decide whether they should do it or not.)

EXAM TASK
(You receive one mark for each correct part, so two marks for a completely correct response.)

0 has been reopened | in the light (You need to use a present perfect passive and the fixed phrase 'in the light of'.)

1 regardless of | the objections ('regardless of' has a similar meaning to 'despite' and you need to change the verb 'object' to the plural noun 'objections'.)

2 haven't/have not (got) / don't have/do not have | a clue how (If you 'don't have a clue', it means you really don't know something.)

3 came (completely) | out of the blue (If something 'comes out of the blue', it is a complete surprise.)

4 inclined to believe/think (that) there would (If you are 'inclined to believe something', it means you have an opinion about it, but not a strong opinion.)

5 took the liberty | of booking (If you 'take the liberty of doing something', it means you do it without asking for the permission or approval of anyone else involved.)

6 mind at rest | by phoning (her) (If you 'put someone's mind at rest', it means you say or do something to stop them worrying.)

READING AND USE OF ENGLISH
Part 5 Multiple choice
Practice task

2

1 C **2** A

3

1 There doesn't appear to be any comparison or ranking of how seriously each group is affected.
2 The writer lists them.
3 to show that noise pollution affects all living things
4 No.

4

a 1 D **2** C **3** A **4** B

b Option A matches 3 exactly (the writer asks this rhetorical question to suggest that people feel powerless over noise pollution because it's such a huge problem.)

c Option D does not match 1 exactly (because the writer suggests that denial would be one explanation for people not talking about noise pollution, but that this is unlikely.)
Option C does not match 2 exactly (because the writer says that everyone causes it, not just business and industry.)
Option B does not match 4 exactly (because the writer says that everyone from government to individuals is responsible for noise pollution, and doesn't state that governments do little to make people aware of it.)

Strategies and skills
Understanding inference and implication

1

1 C is correct: Phil is normally overly talkative in meetings but goes quiet when the subject of budget overspending is raised, thereby suggesting that Phil has something to do with it.
A There's no indication of this.
B The writer is not suggesting this.
D There's no suggestion that Phil's team do all the work.
2 A is correct: There's no chance of the writer having a picnic on the sun so this is also true of the likelihood of a sequel to *The First Kick* appearing.
B A sequel hasn't yet been written.
C Heywood is not currently writing a sequel.
D The writer is not suggesting this.
3 B is correct: the writer says she could never imagine going for a coffee, as friends do, with the tour guide.
A There's no suggestion of this in the paragraph.
C There's no suggestion of this in the paragraph.
D The tour guide directed interesting information to a few of them, but there's no reference to a shared interest.
4 D is correct: the writer suggests that lack of action (doing nothing to bring about equality) gives a clearer picture of what the president really thinks than what he says.
A There's no suggestion that lack of time is the problem.
B The focus is on what the president failed to do, not his staff.
C There's no suggestion of this in the paragraph.

Understanding purpose and attitude

2

1 By Madison's anecdotes; the reviewer says that the book isn't 'short of fascinating anecdotes' but is 'thin on the ground' (there aren't enough) in discussing drawbacks.
2 No; the writer finds the ruins fascinating while his fellow travellers seem to be using it as a photo opportunity to impress friends back home.
3 A dismissive way; the writer says that all the methods that came before the current one and all those to come in the future give the same benefits so are therefore not 'revolutionary' at all.
4 The writer is surprised by the richness that human voices give a composition; the writer uses the phrase 'What I could never have been prepared for …' to signify surprise.

3

1 C – The reviewer became exasperated (irritated or annoyed) with the author's style after reading fewer than two pages.
2 A – The writer says that the team members felt they could follow the team leader anywhere without any problem 'coming to pass' (happening), so they trust her.
3 C – The writer's choice of vocabulary ('unique') and the fact that he/she seems impressed by the organisation's approach tell us that he/she admires them.
4 A – The writer's use of the quote and the phrase 'must have taken great comfort' shows understanding of how the research team must have felt.

Matching meaning

4

1

A False; There is no indication of this in the text.
B True; The rhetorical question shows the writer's surprise.
C False; The writer is describing being in bed in a cabin, and doesn't mention the landscape.
D True; The writer suggests this in the description of their reaction to the cold and in the rhetorical question which follows.

2

A False; There's no indication that Great-Aunt Caroline is rude to the writer.
B False; The writer isn't taken into Caroline's office.
C True; She radiates authority yet doesn't say a word.
D True; The writer feels like they did when in trouble with the headteacher at school.

3

A False; This could have happened if a plan had been in place, but it wasn't.
B False; Not everywhere in the country was the centre of the steel industry.
C True; Had a plan been worked out, the negative consequences might have been avoided ('it might have been a very different story').
D False; The steel industry 'never recovered' to what it had been previously, but we don't know that there's none left.

4

A True; The paragraph says that the idea of living underground is 'developing quite a following': people who like them or are interested in them.
B False; No disagreement is mentioned, only that different architects have different approaches.
C False; Some architects design the buildings using modern architecture as a starting point, but no mention is made of the facilities in the homes.
D False; There probably are many different reasons, but these are not mentioned in the text.

5

1 It is responsible for collecting data about boats hitting whales, and it has recently released some of this data.
2 A breakdown of the types of vessels most often involved in a collision with whales.
3 We don't know which vessels, because they are not identified. However, whale-watching vessels was involved in the most collisions where the vessel was identified.
4 Because they are there to allow people to admire the whales and inadvertently end up hurting them.

6 B

A The accuracy of the numbers is not questioned, just the interpretation of these statistics.
B is correct: In the final two sentences, the writer suggests that the whale-watching industry may have interpreted the data in such a way as to lessen the blame attached to whale-watching boats.
C There is no indication whether the figures are close to what was expected or not.
D This may be the case, but it is not stated or suggested in the paragraph.

Using context to guess the meanings of unknown words

7

1 weak; he's likely to feel weak after an illness and he goes on to get his strength back, showing he must have felt weak.
2 unpleasant; Alicia knew she was 'in trouble' from the way the guards treated her.

3 quickly; if he's looking through it in an anxious way because of the turbulent flight, he's likely to be doing so quickly and not really reading any of the articles.
4 a long time; as the festival the writer is witnessing is unlike the short-lived ones in his or her own country, it's likely the celebrations he or she's describing go on for a long time.
5 less; the players are more exhausted than the coach expected, he's likely to give them less training for a few days.
6 negative; it's given at the end of a list of things that were wrong with the hotel.

Understanding text organisation features

8

1 B ('this image' refers to all of the negative behaviours that are used to stereotype teenagers. A is not correct as the image in question is a negative one, whereas 'loving' is positive. C is not correct as 'this image' refers to teenagers, not parents. D is not correct as 'this image' refers to teenagers, not neighbours.)
2 C (This refers to the time after the advisor had seen the photos, and was still refusing to accept their mistake. A is not correct as it refers to a time long after the writer received the laptop. B is not correct as there's a refusal to admit responsibility at the beginning of the call, but 'Even then' does not refer to this. D is not correct as it refers to one time during the call, not the whole call.)

9

a 1 A
b 1 C **2** B **3** D **4** A
c A (because *Amelia* is part of a current trend for style over substance.)
d B is incorrect as the production quality is 'faultless'. C is incorrect as it looks different 'on the surface' but the story is 'worryingly familiar'. D is incorrect as the cast are all experienced ('seasoned') actors.
e 2 C is correct: A once socially unacceptable song is now played at supermarkets and no one notices, so public acceptance has broadened. The final sentence of the paragraph rules out Option A. Option B is incorrect because no comment is made in the paragraph of how music affects people's state of mind. Option D is incorrect because the writer makes no comment about how the song sounded to him.

10

a 1 D (Reading enjoys a similar social status to classical music, yet fewer teenagers perhaps want to do it than the other activities listed.)

b A is incorrect as there is no comparison drawn between classical music and typical teenage activities in general. B is incorrect as playing computer games is seen to hold a much lower status than classical music. C is incorrect as using social media is seen to hold a much lower status than classical music.
c B is correct (Chlöe says that Venus proves global warming happens in reality, which climate change sceptics cannot deny. A is incorrect as Chlöe doesn't believe that Earth will follow the worst-case scenario of Venus. C is incorrect as Chlöe is not using the comparison with Venus to list any characteristics – only one (very high temperature) is actually mentioned. D is incorrect as there's no indication that Chlöe is using the comparison to show gratitude.)

EXAM TASK

1 B (The irony is that we can hold phones in our hands but it's the phones that are actually holding us in their grasp, metaphorically. A is incorrect as the mobile phones are not mentioned in relation to efficiency. C is incorrect as the phones are not used to show how relationships between people have changed. D is incorrect as phones are not used to make a comparison between humans and machines.)
2 D (The writer says that always doing things is something that people should aspire to and those that do have the 'moral high ground', so this is the motivation. A is incorrect as people's commitment to family and friends is mentioned as a symptom of busyness, not a motivation for it. B is implied as being necessary but is not mentioned as the motivation. C may be a reason why people are so busy but is not the motivation for it.)
3 C (The writer describes how he came to realise the true nature of pauses by speaking to lots of people over a period of time. A is incorrect as there are no ways in which he benefits in daily life mentioned. B is incorrect as the other people are exemplifying their use of pauses, not defining them. D is incorrect as the views of other people seem to agree rather than contrast.)
4 A (His visitors appear to solve their problems because of being able to pause more at his home than in their normal daily lives. B is mentioned, but it's not what the sentence emphasises. C is incorrect as it's not people's perception of time that changes but having more opportunities to pause. D is incorrect as the paragraph suggests that it's having more opportunities to pause which strengthens the effect.)

5 D (The writer suggests in the final sentence that most people have opted to go down the 'time is money' route rather than for the spiritual benefits that pausing brings. A is incorrect as the writer suggests there's a tension between doing and pausing, but doesn't mention any drawbacks to pausing. B is incorrect as the writer doesn't suggest the need to pause is misunderstood, but that people choose not to. C is incorrect as the writer suggests that people who pause more will benefit more but not that some get more from pausing than others.)

6 A (The writer suggests throughout the paragraph that it's people's perception of time that needs to be changed ('Letting go of the idea …'; 'Instead of setting life …'). B is incorrect as the writer says that how enjoyable an activity is alters our relative experience of time, but doesn't suggest we should do more fun things. C is incorrect as there is a lot of analysis of people's experience of time in the paragraph but the writer doesn't make this suggestion. D is incorrect as the writer is arguing that we shouldn't do this – we should rather change the way we think about time.)

READING AND USE OF ENGLISH
Part 6 Cross-text multiple matching
Practice task

2

1 A (Reviewer D says that the author of the book avoids writing about the complexity of the situations in different regions, so it lacks depth; reviewer A says that the author's treatment of the situations borders on the superficial, so it also lacks depth.)

2 C (Reviewers A, B and D all say they were surprised by some of the choices of region; reviewer C says that they didn't find any regions they weren't expecting to read about.)

3

1

A 'the treatment of the current situation in each region, and the influence that global superpowers have or are seeking to have there, borders on the superficial at times'
B 'Not only that, I discovered revelation after revelation in her detailed exploration of each of the regions, and the decisions that led up to their current state of unrest.'
C 'The blurb on the back of Campbell's book makes the rather extravagant promise that never before has a book of this type examined global geopolitics so comprehensively. The majority of

books that make such claims often then spectacularly fail to live up to them, but this is definitely not the case with *The Global Game*.'
D 'it wasn't always possible to come away from many, if any, of the chapters with a good understanding of the actual circumstances there. Campbell appears to have avoided tackling much of the complexity that one needs to fully comprehend any region.'

2 Negative (Reviewer D says that Campbell has 'avoided tackling' the complexity needed to understand what's going on in a region.)

3 A (because reviewer A says that the author's treatment of the situations 'borders on the superficial', so it lacks depth.)

4

1

A 'There's everywhere you'd expect to be included in such a book and plenty of surprises too'
B 'Had I been asked to name the twelve most significant areas of political tension around the globe, my list would have included perhaps six of those selected by Campbell. I would never have predicted the others she's included'
C 'I can't help wondering whether Campbell was adventurous enough when making the decisions about where to write about. It would have upped the interest levels considerably had I come across at least a few chapters on somewhere I wasn't expecting to read about'
D 'What I was pleasantly taken aback by, however, was the inclusion of sections dealing with the situations in parts of the world where I didn't even know tensions existed'

2
Reviewer A ('everywhere you'd expect plus plenty of surprises')
Reviewer B ('would never have predicted many of those that Campbell chose', therefore they are surprised)
Reviewer C ('would have been more interesting if there were chapters about unexpected places' – therefore they are not surprised)
Reviewer D (they were 'taken aback (surprised) by sections about places that reviewer didn't even know had tensions')
3 Reviewers A, B and D are all surprised by some of the places chosen for the book.
4 Reviewer C has a different opinion to the others.

Strategies and skills
Identifying contrasting opinion

1

1 C (The writer thinks the opposite to most people, who believe there should be less.)
2 B (The writer thinks those who told him Kinsella was original haven't read many other books.)
3 A (The writer doesn't go along (agree) with the opinion that art should be universal.)
4 C (The writer says that replacement materials may even be more harmful than plastic.)
5 A (The writer questions the evidence that's provided to say standards are falling.)
6 B (The writer says that the effects of the policy are not what the government had in mind.)

2

1 'I'm of the opposite opinion entirely.'
2 'I'm not sure how many other authors those who told me this had read, but it can't have been many.'
3 'I've never gone along with the opinion'
4 'but may ultimately end up being counterproductive'
5 'yet the majority of evidence … is subjective'
6 'which are perhaps not what the government had in mind'

Identifying similar opinions

3

1 similar (both say that people who want to be writers mistakenly think they have a natural talent)
2 different (A thinks archaeology is a waste of time; B thinks it's a useful field of study)
3 similar (both say that business must consider climate change when making decisions)
4 different (A thinks it's better to avoid big events and spend the money directly on public amenities; B thinks events leave a good legacy of facilities for the public.)
5 similar (both think that school inspections should be as rigorous as ever)

4

1 False (She says the people who want to ban them are in a minority.)
2 False (She says she understands people's motivations for wanting them banned.)
3 True (She gives the example of tennis causing more deaths and injuries than extreme sports.)
4 False (She says she has warmed to them after trying one of them out.)
5 True (She says that the progress would be reversed if extreme sports are banned.)
6 True (He says that they are pointless.)

7 False (He says that given the right incentives, people could be persuaded.)
8 True (He says that they already exist or are in the latter (later) stages of development.)
9 False (He uses this as an example of a safe extreme sport that's real, not virtual.)
10 True (He says that the computing power available today will make them possible.)

5

1 Calcedo: disagree (She thinks that actual, safer or virtual versions are fine.)
Tenby: disagree (He thinks that safer and virtual versions are OK.)
2 Calcedo: agree (She thinks that they make the sports as safe as they can be.)
Tenby: disagree (He thinks whether they exist or not, too many people will be killed.)
3 Calcedo: agree (She has changed her opinion of them since trying one out.)
Tenby: agree (He thinks people should use them rather than doing the real thing.)
4 Calcedo: disagree (She opposes a ban on extreme sports, so would also oppose one on other sports.)
Tenby: disagree (He appears to have an issue with extreme sports, not conventional ones.)

Identifying paraphrases and synonyms

6

1 e (to 'abolish' means to 'prevent people from doing something')
2 h (a 'regulation' means the same as a 'standard' in the context of these texts)
3 a (a 'prototype' is an early version of something)
4 f (a 'governing body' is synonymous with an 'official organisation' in these texts)
5 c ('sustain injuries' is synonymous with 'end up hurt')
6 g ('electronic equivalent' is synonymous with 'virtual reality simulation' in these texts)
7 b ('supervise' means the same as 'oversee'.)
8 d ('implement' means the same as 'put into place'.)

7
Possible answers:

1 organisation, corporation, company, multinational, enterprise, establishment
2 green, ecological, eco-friendly
3 effects, consequences, results, upshot, outcomes
4 decreasing, lessening, cutting, lowering, bringing down
5 massively, immensely, hugely, a great deal, very much, enormously, greatly
6 negligible, insignificant, very little, almost no
7 difficult, testing, taxing, tough, trying, demanding
8 development, growth, improvement, advancement

1 D (Reviewers A, B and C all think that Grahame discusses the media in a confident way. Reviewer D says Grahame doesn't seem to believe his own arguments in most of the book.)
2 C (Reviewer B says that Grahame provides some fresh insights into the topic. Reviewer C says that Grahame comments perceptively on the topic.)
3 B (Reviewer D says that it's frightening how much control newspapers have. Reviewer B says that their power has dangerous consequences.)
4 D (Reviewer B says that Grahame doesn't back up his comments on this issue with convincing evidence. Reviewer D says that his conclusions about the issue are hard to have faith in.)

READING AND USE OF ENGLISH
Part 7 Gapped text
Practice task
2
1 C **2** A
3
a 'this basic courtesy' at the beginning of paragraph C refers back to customers phoning restaurants to cancel bookings at the end of the paragraph before.
b 'The need for one' refers back to Helen's comment about creating 'a clear, honest and open system' for tipping, mentioned in the paragraph before.

4
a 'having to ask' refers back to 'demanding credit card details' in missing paragraph C.
b 'the machinations of a business' refers back to whether businesses and waiters are being honest about what happens to tips in missing paragraph A.

Strategies and skills
Using content clues

1
1 'I undoubtedly will' refers back to 'come on an expedition again.'
2 'This careful consideration' refers back to the writer's attempts to not step on the crabs.
3 'Many of them' refers back to 'the surrounding villages'
4 'manipulates a dustpan and brush to clean up a broken plate' refers back to 'domestic tasks'
5 'the points of the compass' refers back to 'north, south, east or west'
6 'the style no longer lives up to its name' refers back to 'modernist architecture'.

2
a 6 ('modernist architecture')
b 3 ('surrounding villages')
c 5 ('north, south, east or west')
d 2 ('careful consideration')
e 1, 4 ('going on an expedition'; 'domestic tasks')

3
1 A; the text has a cynical attitude to businesses' reasons for appearing to be environmentally friendly. Also, B does not mirror this cynical tone.
2 B; 'one' and 'the next' refer to Kinsella's novels.
3 A; 'It' refers to the routine, and the content matches the content of the preceding sentence, both giving the idea of a very flexible routine.
4 A; The point made in A refers back to the behaviour of the animal described in the previous sentence.

Understanding the structure of a text

4
1 D (This option refers back by saying state education provides access to art subjects for poorer children. The following sentence also refers back to drama and music in D with 'them'.)
2 A (The argument mentioned in A refers back to the debate in the previous paragraph. The sentence following A refers back to things that are of great concern, mentioned in A, and adds another concern with 'As is'.)
3 F ('As a result of this' refers back to it being difficult to becoming a professional artist. The paragraph after F refers back to teaching in F as 'this profession.')
4 B (This is an example of what is stated in the sentence before the gap. The sentence after the gap refers back to the film industry example.)
5 C (This expands on and explains why some of the prices paid for art are ridiculous.)
6 E (This gives one example of a source of creativity, and the text following the gap gives another.)

5
1 C (It explains why some of the prices paid for art are ridiculous.)
2 B (This gives an example of public interest in a form of art growing as funding is reduced.)
3 D (This reaches a conclusion based on an opinion about access to the performing arts in the previous paragraph.) F (This reaches a conclusion based on information about becoming a professional artist in the previous paragraph.)
4 A (This states one of the author's worries about art lessons disappearing before a second is mentioned in the following paragraph.; E (This gives an example of a source of creativity mentioned in the previous paragraph.)

6

1 D (Both are similar ideas about doing just one job.)

2 A (A is a contrasting idea about automation.)

3 F (F is a contrasting idea about relationships between employers and employees.)

4 C (This is a similar idea supporting the information given in 4.)

5 E (This gives a similar supportive idea for working from home mentioned in 5.)

6 B (This gives a contrasting idea about the need to raise the retirement age.)

7

1 Although this may be true (The following idea contrasts with the preceding one.)

2 This explains why (What follows is an example of the body clock changes that happen in adolescence.)

3 Doing so (What follows is a result of what is mentioned in the first sentence.)

4 A perhaps unexpected result of this is (What follows is a result, not an example.)

5 What's already become obvious (What follows in an observation of dolphin behaviour, not a reason for why the research is in its early stages.)

6 I would therefore propose that (What follows is a proposal not an explanation.)

EXAM TASK

1 E ('This record-breaking development' refers back to the world's biggest bike park in the previous paragraph.)

2 A ('Her sentiments' refer back to what Stientje Van Veldhoven hopes about making better use of cycling to combat congestion, poor air quality, etc. in the previous paragraph.)

3 G (The 'however' refers back to, and contrasts with, the statistics for the Netherlands as a whole in the previous paragraph.)

4 C ('this strategy' refers back to investment in public transport, etc. in the previous paragraph.)

5 F ('These days' contrasts with the final sentence of the previous sentence, which is a historical example.)

6 B ('This bold claim' described in B refers back to the statement about the developing cycling infrastructure being one of the most impactful things a city can do, at the end of the previous paragraph.)

READING AND USE OF ENGLISH
Part 8 Multiple matching
Practice task

2

a B ('Ideal conditions at Mavericks include light winds from the north')

b A ('these variations in weather patterns are bad news' for almost everyone else)

c B ('As when practising their sport in any location, surfers at Mavericks should proceed with caution')

d A ('El Niño is a naturally occurring weather cycle which can affect climactic conditions on both a local and a global scale')

e B ('the rapid alteration which brings about these perfect conditions for surfing can suddenly vary just as swiftly in the opposite sense')

3

1 d (Because the cause is El Niño, and it can affect conditions globally.)

2 b (Because the changes in weather pattern are the effects of climate change and are bad news for almost everyone else apart from surfers in California, who are a small minority.)

4

1 don't use

2 a larger chunk

3 the context

5

a: 'Ideal conditions at Mavericks include light winds from the north, …'

c: 'As when practising their sport in any location, surfers at Mavericks should proceed with caution …'

e: '… the rapid alteration which brings about these perfect conditions for surfing can suddenly vary equally swiftly in the opposite sense.'

6

1 No

2 The writer advises that surfers should proceed with caution wherever they go surfing, suggesting it's a risky activity everywhere.

3 'rapid alteration'; 'suddenly vary as swiftly'; 'opposite sense'

Strategies and skills
Identifying paraphrase

1

1 f ('makes a comparison' matches with 'bears a vague resemblance to', and 'other work' matches with 'previous titles'.)

2 d ('he appears to have spent little time finding factual support for the claims he makes' is critical of how much research the author has done.)

3 a ('I found little I could argue against' demonstrates agreement.)

4 h (The reviewer says that he can't understand why Tierney included chapters on sport and television, suggesting that they are strange choices.)

5 b ('chosen contexts from around the globe' illustrates the book's wide geographical scope.)

6 g ('influenced by the work of other people' matches with 'owes a particular debt to two of the twentieth century's most perceptive political commentators'.)

7 e ('equally good at' matches with 'skills might be put to just as effective use' and 'other topics' matches with 'social justice or capitalism'.)

8 c ('sequence of the chapters' matches with 'the order in which the sections appear'.)

2

A I found little I could argue against when it came to Tierney's contentions regarding political bias in the media.

B It's admirable that Tierney has chosen contexts from around the globe to illustrate his points, rather than sticking close to home.

C There's little apparent logic to the order in which the sections appear. I can only assume he chose this by drawing them out of a hat.

D While Tierney undoubtedly writes beautifully, he appears to have spent little time finding factual support for the claims he makes.

E Perhaps Tierney's authorial skills might be put to just as effective use in creating works on social justice or capitalism.

F Although it bears a vague resemblance to Tierney's previous titles, he has made great progress as a writer, stylistically.

G I feel that Tierney's book owes a particular debt to two of the twentieth century's most perceptive political commentators.

H I'm sure that Tierney had a motive for choosing to write chapters on sport and television. What this was is quite beyond me.

3

1 A: 'There's a lot to be said for following your own instincts when you're doing this.' This relates to choosing the right employees at interview. B: 'You'll soon know which road you're on if you trust your instincts.' This relates to knowing whether your business is going to succeed or fail.

2 B (it's about knowing whether a business is succeeding or not)

3

a A: 'Had I followed my own advice, my first business venture would never have failed.'

b B: 'Build in time for other out-of-work activities too.'

c A: 'If I'm not convinced that it's written by someone who has actually done it and succeeded, I tend to ignore it.'

d A: 'I would estimate that I've employed four staff I'd rather have not bothered with for every one that really knew what they were doing.'

e B: 'The biggest mistake people make at the beginning is assuming that their business will be flourishing within a few weeks of opening.'

4

1 A: doing something really eye-catching; doing something that involved risk.
B: Doing something that involved endurance.
2 A ('I also thought people would be liable to give more if they felt there was an element of risk')
3 a B b A c B d B e A
4
a ('I work in sales, so I'm used to persuading people to part with their money')
b ('I'm an introvert so the prospect of pressuring people for money was quite alarming, but I soon developed what was almost like a script, which somehow gave me more confidence')
c ('a climate change charity campaign')
d ('I'm also a very keen cyclist and had wanted to undertake something like that for years but could never really justify taking that much time out')
e ('It's a bit of a paradox in a way, as I'm absolutely over the moon that it's done, yet I have this nagging desire to go and do it all over again.')

Avoiding distraction

5

1 'The chair of the panel commended me on how I'd done …'
2 Possible answer: The writer wasn't sure if the praise was genuine or not.
3 'I guess that's the downside of setting yourself such high expectations …'
4 Possible answer: The writer says that their high expectations led to them feeling disappointed about their performance in the interview.

6

1 'More senior researchers then set about piecing together the fragments into more complete items, both electronically and in reality.'
2 Possible answer: Senior researchers put the objects back together in real life and also on a computer.
3 'The size of the building and the nature of what we were finding in it meant it was unlikely to be anything other than a home to the wealthiest and most important residents of the city.'
4 Possible answer: What the researchers found in the building and how big it was showed that it belonged to someone very rich and important.

7

1 C ('Our parents used to joke that there was an invisible piece of string joining us together.')
2 B ('Crossing that field had felt like a major expedition when I was eight.')
3 A ('I've reached that point in my own life when I find myself reflecting on my childhood a great deal. Perhaps the birth of my first child acted as a trigger for my thinking back.')

4 B ('… escaping the attention of the farmer, usually unsuccessfully …')
5 C ('They had a model railway that I had spent hours admiring.')
6 A ('I wondered if any of them still lived there, and whether I'd have the courage to knock on the doors to find out.')

Understanding implication

8

1 C (They are smiling a lot because warmer weather has arrived.)
2 A (The writer thought it was close to land because it looks as though it is on a map. A six-day journey there changed her mind about this.)
3 B (The writer was willing the video to go viral, so was disappointed when it didn't.)
4 C (The writer suddenly realises that their decision has made them financially insecure.)
5 C (If someone goes red, they could be angry. If someone counts slowly to ten, they are likely trying to calm themselves down.)
6 A (The writer suggests that human survival is as dependent on colour as that of animals.)

EXAM TASK

1 C (Writer C says that they'd heard that one of the main reasons publishers turn books down is that things move too slowly.)
2 A (Writer A says that being rejected is an inevitable part of the process of finding a publisher for everyone.)
3 E (Writer E says that the central figure in the novel has to create their own destiny and not be someone who just goes along with events and things that happen to them.)
4 D (Writer D says that they thought about self-publishing but not knowing anyone whose novel had become successful by doing so was what put them off.)
5 B (Writer B says different publishing houses focus on particular genres so writers should carefully research who is most likely to publish the type of book they've written.)
6 C (Writer C says that they met a literary agent at a party, who pointed out the necessity of including a covering letter with the manuscript, after which they got a publishing deal.)
7 D (Writer D says that it's important for writers to be true to their own way of writing rather than adapting it to appear like someone else's simply to get into print.)
8 B (Writer B says that at least one aspect of a novel – plot, characters, context, style – must provide something totally original.)
9 E (Writer E says that having someone they weren't particularly close to who would read and critically appraise their work as they wrote it was key.)

10 A (Writer A says that publishers who haven't got a best-selling author contracted to them are more careful with risk as they have little spare cash to play with.)

WRITING
Part 1 Essay
Practice task
1–3 Students' own answers

Strategies and skills
Structuring an essay
1
C (It gives a general introduction to the topic and sets the scene for the discussion which follows. Introduction A does not really address the topic in the task, and doesn't give an overall introduction to what the essay will be about. It gives reasons, which should really be in the following paragraphs. Introduction B includes opinions, which should really be in the following paragraphs or conclusion.)

2
Students' own answers

3

1 As … ; so; Therefore; First of all; In contrast; While; As; especially; In summary, therefore; However; even if
2 should be given; if funding were increased; should be targeted
3 many countries move away from manufacturing and towards more service-based industries; The proportion of national income related to business has increased considerably; art and other cultural activities have failed to develop in terms of what they offer to the country; the sector has grown little
4 it would be ideal if funding were increased for every course currently on offer at universities around the country; any additional financial support should be targeted towards thriving vocational sectors; The programmes of study that obtain more funding should be the ones which best meet the country's needs.

4

1: to create a sense of flow throughout the text and to give it structure so that it's easy for the reader to follow
2: to add to the formality and the impersonal tone of the essay
3: this is asked for in the task and they are essential for supporting any argument
4: this is asked for in the task and is essential in an argument essay, especially in the conclusion

5

1 formal (for example, 'let us consider'; 'would appear to be a sensible strategy')
2 no (for example, 'let us', 'that is')

3 serious (for example, 'In summary, therefore')

4 an academic (The essay is to be written as part of your course and its purpose is to discuss the statement in a balanced and formal way)

6

1 Although (This is used to introduce a contrasting idea or ideas.)

2 in addition to (This is used to add information. If it's followed by a verb, use the -ing form.)

3 Therefore (This is used to introduce a consequence of what you have said previously.)

4 even though (This is used to link an idea and an unexpected result.)

5 Despite (This is used to introduce an idea that will be contrasted in the following clause.)

6 Furthermore (This is used to add another point to one you've already made.)

7

a 5, 6, 12
b 1, 3, 10, 11 ,13
c 4, 8, 9
d 2, 7, 14

Complex sentences

8

1 since it **2** due to them not **3** rather than (it) **4** despite the fact that they are **5** because of having **6** without extensive investment

Using formal language

9

1 e **2** b **3** h **4** d **5** f **6** a **7** g **8** c

Impersonal sentences

10

1 the majority of people **2** considered to be **3** is one proposal **4** others have been **5** is a fairly widespread phenomenon

EXAM TASK

Example answer:

The topic of health and fitness is one that is never far from people's minds. Even if they are not actively seeking to improve their own health, they are often considering ways of becoming healthier. Despite this, national levels of health and fitness remain relatively poor.

Habits are formed at an early age, and living healthily is no exception. It is therefore essential that children are exposed to good examples of healthy living from an early age. While many argue that it should be parents who educate their offspring on this subject, too often both parents have busy jobs and little time in which to ensure healthy food and plenty of exercise for their children. Allowing schools to take on this role, therefore,

would be a productive step. Regular sessions on the theoretical aspects of healthy living plus compulsory physical education classes would go a long way to improving the nation's health.

The creation of more sports centres and gyms has also regularly been proposed as a solution. All too often, people join a gym or sports centre with the best of intentions, meaning to go regularly in the long term. However, people find it difficult to maintain their motivation; soon their attendance becomes less regular and they often stop completely soon after.

In conclusion, a national education strategy targeted at school children of all ages which seeks to promote healthy living in all its forms would be the most effective means of changing people's ingrained unhealthy habits, thereby improving the health of the whole nation.

WRITING
Part 2 Proposal
Practice task

2

Students' own answers

3

1 'The event will benefit not only local people …'

2 'The proposal will include …'

3 'I am convinced that this would be the best possible …'

4 '… united against the dangers faced by our beautiful world'

5 '… which would be done via social media and a poster campaign …'

6 'I would therefore like to propose organising …'

7 'The proposed activity'

8 The aim of this proposal is …'

9 'I would urge you to consider this proposal favourably …'

10 'A concert or similar idea, whilst a good idea in principle, …'

4

Students' own answers

Strategies and skills
Using persuasive language

1

Although this <u>unique</u> building requires a substantial amount of work, it is my <u>sincere</u> belief that investing in it will be <u>immensely beneficial</u> to the town. Even in its current state of disrepair, it is a <u>much-loved</u> landmark that will <u>undoubtedly</u> be transformed into a <u>potentially lucrative</u> centre of attraction if it were restored.

2

Possible answers:

1 beautiful/delightful/charming
2 highly/extremely

3 positive/beneficial
4 attractive/eye-catching/appealing
5 very/enormously/tremendously
6 important/helpful/valuable
7 crucial/essential/vital

3

1 advise (This is a polite way of pushing someone to do something.)

2 benefit (A persuasive way of saying how good something is.)

3 grateful (This helps to show how much the decision means to you.)

4 certain (You can also use 'convinced' or 'sure' instead of 'certain'.)

5 doubt (This tells the reader you really believe in your proposal.)

6 agree (Inviting the reader to agree with you is a good way of persuading them.)

7 advantages (Having many advantages makes the ideas sound very impressive!)

8 evidence (Supporting your proposal with evidence is a good way of persuading people.)

4

Possible answers:

1 I am sure that you will be able to see the many benefits that my ideas will bring.

2 Many thanks for taking the time to consider my detailed proposals.

3 Nothing would benefit the town more than new and improved sports facilities.

4 An interesting idea that would have many potential benefits is organising an exchange with students from another country.

5 What could be more engaging and entertaining for young people than having a sports day?

6 The obvious place for international students to visit is the museum, which will give them a much greater understanding of the city.

5

1 c, f (Both use numbers or amounts that are greater than in reality.)

2 a, g (Both use rhetorical questions to help the reader arrive at a conclusion.)

3 d, j (Both use repetition to force a point home.)

4 b, i (Both use emotive language)

5 e, h (Both use inclusive language which encourages the reader to agree.)

Writing effective introductions

6

1 True (This is the point of an introduction.)

2 False (It generally needs to be longer than this.)

3 False (The details come in the main body of the proposal.)

4 True (The opinions should come in the main body of the proposal.)

5 False (It may give one brief reason for submitting a proposal but never several.)

7

Suggested answers:
1 **A** too informal **B** opinion
2 **A** short **B** task/instructions
3 **A** letter **B** detail

Writing effective conclusions

8

1 strongly (This collocates well with 'recommend.')
2 Doing ('Doing so' is used to avoid the repetition of 'accept my proposals'.)
3 therefore (Because what follows is a consequence of what came before.)
4 wholeheartedly (This has a similar meaning to 'passionately' or' completely' but collocates with' recommend.')
5 appreciate (This has a similar meaning to 'like' and 'value'.)
6 to come ('for years to come' means a long time into the future.)
7 reason (A 'reason to believe' means some sort of evidence to arrive at a conclusion or belief.)
8 course (a 'course of action' is a series of things that someone can do.)
9 to lead to (If one thing 'leads to' something else, the second thing is a consequence of the first.)

EXAM TASK

Example answer:
Introduction
The aim of this proposal is to recommend an event that will attract as many new members to our cycling club as possible. It will outline the details of the event and explain why it would be likely to encourage new members to join.
Details of the event
To me, the best way of attracting someone to participate in a sport is to see people doing that sport and enjoying themselves as a result. With this in mind, I would strongly suggest that the club holds a fancy-dress cycle ride through the town centre during the busiest period of the weekend. After riding around a set route for half an hour or so, we could then stop and explain to people there why we are doing it, taking details of anyone looking to join the club as we did so.
Why it would attract new members
Most people join cycling clubs not to take part in races, but to go on interesting and enjoyable rides with other members. I think, therefore, that a race would not be the best approach but a fun event such as a fancy-dress ride would really grab people's attention. Seeing a hundred cyclists going past wearing silly costumes is sure to distract even the most serious shopper and would appeal as much to children as it would to adults.

Conclusion
I would urge you to seriously consider this highly original proposal, as I am confident that this will provide the best possible means for attracting new members to our wonderful club.

WRITING
Part 2 Email or letter
Practice task

2
Students' own answers

3

1 'Even if sport isn't really your thing …'
2 'It's great to hear from you.'
3 'I'd say the best sporting event you could take them to …'
4 'It's best to see the race in the mountains.'
5 'The cyclists pass more slowly going uphill …'
6 'Hi Rick,' 'All the best'
7 'There really isn't any sporting event that's more French!'
8 'I hope that's helpful. Would it be OK if I came with you?'
9 'How are you and your family?'

4
Students' own answers

Strategies and skills
Using correct register

1

informal: I couldn't believe it!; I'm really sorry ☹; Good to see you.; Look on the bright side.
semi-formal: It was hard to believe.; I would really like to apologise; It was very nice to see you.; There's positive as well as negative.
formal: I found it somewhat difficult to believe.; I can only apologise for the mistake.; It was a great pleasure to meet you.; There is every reason to be optimistic.

2
Possible answers:
1 I'm really sorry but I can't come ☹
2 Can we meet and have a chat about the problem?
3 I've got lots of experience of managing people.
4 Can I come to your school soon to watch a class?
5 Can you please send a price list as soon as possible?
6 Thanks for coming to the sports centre opening.

3
Possible answers:
1 I would be grateful if you could repair the broken computer as promptly as possible.

2 It has been some time since I was fortunate enough to visit your city.
3 I am writing to complain about this morning's 8.20 service to London, which was delayed by an hour.
4 I was extremely sorry to hear that you have been unwell and wish you a rapid and full recovery.
5 It has come to my attention that you are regularly late for work. Would it be possible for you to provide an explanation for this?
6 It is with great regret that I must inform you that I am unable to attend your wedding.

Using formal language

4
Students' own answers

5
Students' own answers

6
The writer has failed to:
1 start the email with a formal greeting.
4 write a short final paragraph to conclude the email.
5 use an appropriate way of ending a formal email.
6 use formal language throughout the email.

7
Hi Angela,
I've done lots of outdoor stuff, like climbing, hiking, mountain biking, canoeing and running.
I'd be brilliant at this …
All the best,
Marek

8
Possible answers:
Dear Ms Holmes,
I have a lot of experience of many different outdoor pastimes, including climbing, hiking, mountain biking, canoeing and running.
I think I would be the perfect person to take this role at your summer camp …
Yours sincerely,
Marek Balinski

9

1 hearing ('I look forward to hearing from you' is a common phrase in the final paragraph of a letter in which you're expecting a response.)
2 convenience (Be careful to avoid any expression meaning 'soon' (unless it's a complaint) as this sounds like you're rushing or putting pressure on the recipient.)
3 Should ('Should' is used in the same way as 'if' here, but sounds a little more formal.)
4 respect ('in respect of' is a formal way of saying 'about'.)

5 hesitate ('Should you require any further information, please do not hesitate to contact me' is a useful, formal way to end letters of application.)

Common expressions used in formal language

10

1 e (Use 'Yours faithfully' if you don't know the name of the person (when your letter begins with 'Dear Sir/Madam'). Use 'Yours sincerely' when you do know their name.)
2 g (The first paragraph usually explains why you are writing.)
3 a (This is a useful expression to learn for letters/emails of application.)
4 c (This is a useful expression to use if you are replying to an email or letter, if you replace 'email' with 'letter'.)
5 b (A useful expression if you have to apologise formally.)
6 d (A useful expression if you have to arrange to meet someone.)
7 f (This is a useful phrase in letters/emails of application to refer somebody to your CV.)

EXAM TASK

Example answer:

Dear Ms Jarvis,

I am writing to you to apply for the position of volunteer on the Amazon rainforest expedition, advertised recently on the Research4U website.

I am a nineteen-year-old student currently on a gap year between school and university. I wish to make the most of this time, and going on such an expedition would be an excellent way of achieving this. I will be studying biology and ecology at university, so this expedition matches my academic interests perfectly. My ultimate aim is to become a professional ecologist, working in areas such as the Amazon rainforest to help to preserve the delicate ecosystems there.

I am someone who thrives on being in isolated places, surrounded by nature in its purest form. I regularly spend time in forests in my own country, so know I can cope well with being in this environment. Another of my strengths is the ability to work effectively in a team. I am keen to do whatever is necessary in order to meet the objectives of the group. I am also patient, an essential quality for anyone involved in observing and researching the natural world.

The main benefit I would gain on the expedition is experience in a field that I have wanted to be part of for several years. I would also hope to develop an increased understanding of how ecosystems in such an environment function, and lasting professional relationships with other team members.

I look forward to hearing from you at your earliest convenience.

Yours sincerely,
Yasmin Underhill

WRITING
Part 2 Review
Practice task

2

Students' own answers

3

1 'I would highly recommend *Village Life* to …'
2 'What's especially enjoyable about the series …'
3 '… as it always keeps the viewer (and Rachel!) guessing as to what will happen next.'
4 '*Village Life*'
5 'Who can resist a good TV drama?'
6 'However,'
7 'The central character is a policewoman called …'
8 'My favourite is …'

4

Students' own answers

Strategies and skills

Using descriptive and dramatic language

1

1 B (a more descriptive way to say 'funny')
2 C (a more descriptive way to say 'scary')
3 A (a more descriptive way to say 'interested in')
4 A (a more descriptive adverb to use)
5 C (a more descriptive way to say 'moved into')
6 B (a more descriptive way to say 'emotional')
7 A (a more descriptive way to say 'not much')
8 C (a more descriptive way to say 'a bit boring')

2

1 f **2** d **3** a **4** h **5** c **6** g **7** b **8** e

3

1 'thought-provoking' (this means it makes people think deeply about something)
2 'sun-baked' (this means hot and dry)
3 'record-breaker' (this means better at something than anyone or anything else)
4 'absent-minded' (this means 'forgetful' and perhaps not very conscious of your surroundings)
5 tear-jerker (something that's very sad)
6 time-saver (something that saves you time)
7 kind-hearted (Someone who is 'kind-hearted' is a good person.)
8 mean-spirited (If you are 'mean-spirited', it means you are hard and uncaring.)

4

Possible answers:

1 All things considered, this is a must-have app that I'd recommend every single reader get hold of.
2 So unless you're unfortunate enough to have no other available entertainment, I'd seriously avoid seeing this film.
3 I must have attended at least a hundred concerts in my life, some of which were exceptional, but this one was superior to even the best of them.
4 The town seems to have forgotten that holiday resorts are supposed to provide exciting activities and entertainment for visitors.
5 I had very high expectations of the acting in the play but these were exceeded by every single member of the cast.
6 No other restaurant in the area comes close to matching the outstanding quality of its food.

Engaging the reader

5

1 b (uses personalisation and a rhetorical question)
2 e (near the beginning of the review)
3 a (where the play is set)
4 d (of one of the central character's 'adventures')
5 c (one reason why it's funny)
6 c (the writer's opinion)
7 f (why the writer chose the script as the best feature of the play)
8 a/f (about the writer of the play and her work)
9 g (who should go and see the play)
10 f (about how much readers might enjoy the play)

6

1 would ('I would recommend' is often used in recommendations)
2 strongly ('strongly advise' is a common collocation in recommendations)
3 undoubtedly ('should undoubtedly' is a common collocation in recommendations)
4 wholeheartedly ('wholeheartedly recommend' is a common collocation in strong recommendations)
5 Unless ('Unless' means the same as 'except if')
6 regret ('regret' means to feel bad about doing or not doing something)

Structuring a review

7

1 A (The reviewer uses 'in-depth' and 'backs up all of the arguments … with detailed, reliable data' to say this.)
2 B (The reviewer is commenting on how believable the characters are, not on the quality of the acting.)

3 A (The reviewer is writing about the colour in the café, not how it was built.)
4 A (The reviewer is critical of the narrow range of paintings in the exhibition.)
5 B (The reviewer praises how large an area can be explored in the game.)
6 B (The reviewer is critical of how dull most biographies are but thinks *Inside Billy Frost* is not like this.)

8
1 Sound ('Sound' is used here to mean 'seem'.)
2 However (This links two contrasting ideas.)
3 As well as (This is used to link additions to a list.)
4 could (This is used to say that it's possible.)
5 issue (A useful general word with a similar meaning to 'problem'.)
6 occasionally (To show it doesn't happen often.)
7 literally (A fashionable word used to emphasise a point or idea.)
8 If (This is a conditional sentence with 'if'.)

9
Suggested answers:
A
Summary of content: Amusing, exaggerated description of friend. Reason for buying the item.
Purpose: Engage the reader; introduce the item.
B
Summary of content: Basic description of what the item is. Explain initial attitude towards the item.
Purpose: Give an outline of what the item is and what it does.
C
Summary of content: Detailed description of some of the functions of the item that the writer uses it for.
Purpose: Give more detail of why the item is useful (question 1).
D
Summary of content: Give description and supporting details of a problem with the item
Purpose: Identify an issue (question 2).
E
Summary of content: Say who would find the item useful and support this with reasons.
Purpose: Recommend who might like the item (question 3).

10
Paragraph A: 'I have a friend who buys the most up-to-date electronic devices and then somehow turns any conversation around to the subject of how great her latest gadget is.'
Paragraph B: 'For those who don't know, a digital assistant is the electronic box that sits in your home and does things for you when it's told to.'

Paragraph C: 'However, the longer I've had it, the more uses I've actually found.'
Paragraph D: 'The only issue with my new electronic buddy is that it occasionally misunderstands my accent.'
Paragraph E: 'I'd recommend this device to literally anyone.'
In each case the whole sentence introduces the topic.

Using adjectives that indicate opinion

11
Strongly positive: fabulous, luxurious, sparkling, splendid, terrific
Positive: pleasurable
Neutral: average
Negative: inadequate, inferior, mundane, repetitive, shabby, tedious
Strongly negative: disastrous, appalling

12
1 certainly **2** vastly **3** perfectly **4** actually
5 slightly **6** definitely **7** over **8** terribly

EXAM TASK
Example answer
The world's best museum
Long gone are the days when a visit to a museum meant a tedious few hours looking at tired exhibits in dusty glass cases. Many now have interactive displays that take your breath away. My vote for the best of these goes to the Smithsonian in Washington, USA.
If you're planning to see everything in a single day, forget it! The Smithsonian is actually made up of nineteen (yes, nineteen!) different museums, plus a zoo. Unlike most false claims you read on museum websites, there genuinely is something for everyone there.
The most impressive place to begin is the Museum of Natural History. It would be easy to spend a whole day just in this one location. On my visit, I found the exhibition on sharks the most educational. There was a huge quantity of fascinating information, videos and displays about how essential these incredible creatures are for marine ecosystems. I also found out about the absolutely appalling damage being inflicted on shark populations by human activities and greed.
If marine biology isn't your thing, however, there are countless other galleries and buildings dedicated to outer space, American history, and even postal services, amongst many others.
It's probably easier to say who the Smithsonian would not appeal to than making a long list of those that it would. I think the only individuals who would not enjoy the delights of this amazing place are those who have genuinely lost interest in the world around them. I can't think of many people who fit this description!

WRITING
Part 2 Report
Practice task
2
Students' own answers
3
1 'The current facilities are clearly inadequate …'
2 'However, …'
3 'which remains virtually empty …'
4 'users can play badminton, table tennis …'
5 'Should the above recommendations be implemented …'
6 'The aim of this report is to …'
7 'There is a relatively narrow range of sports facilities …'
8 'Additionally, I would advise the creation of …'
9 'the sports centre will not only become more popular …'
10 'somewhat'
4
Students' own answers

Strategies and skills
Structuring a report
1
1 d (The paragraph describes the main parts of the tour.)
2 f (This paragraph mentions the negative aspects of the tour.)
3 b (The paragraph is about whether the writer would recommend it for other classes.)

2
1 No; it would be too long and very repetitive. It would not leave enough words to complete the rest of the task.
2 the visitor centre; the highest part of the stadium; the changing rooms (they saw the pitch from the stadium but we don't know if they visited it).
3 The tour moved too quickly so they didn't have time to enjoy each stage.
4 Wherever they had gone, someone in the group would say they weren't interested in the subject.
5 C (It sums up all of the aims, as identified in the task. A is well-written, but the areas mentioned in the introduction do not match those in the task. B also includes information which is not in the task outline.)

3
1 terms **2** highly **3** so **4** most **5** Perhaps
6 case **7** subsequent

4

Suggested answer:

Conclusion

In summary, the football stadium trip was a success with most students enjoying it. Extending the length and duration of the tour would be an effective way of improving it should other groups be taken there.

5

1 aim of: I
2 summarise: C
3 intends: I
4 general: C
5 conclusion: C
6 identifies: I

Referring to research

6

1 b   2 e   3 c   4 a   5 d

7

1 number/proportion/minority   2 fifths
3 none   4 Eighty   5 majority   6 half

Using formal language

8

1 cause of dissatisfaction   2 has proved
3 seriously concerned that   4 insufficient funds   5 fortunate enough   6 in favour of

9

1 were given   2 was mentioned
3 is considered   4 are expected
5 has been suggested/was suggested
6 was/is not thought

Making recommendations

10

1 offering (You use the -ing form after 'advise.')
2 that we organise (You can also use the -ing form after 'suggest': 'organising.')
3 putting (You use the -ing form after 'recommend.')
4 be given (You need a passive form here.)
5 should be made (You need a passive form here.)
6 I would propose (You are proposing, so you need the active form here. Note that the -ing form is used after 'propose.')

EXAM TASK

Example answer:

Introduction

The purpose of this report is to evaluate the recent English-language study programme undertaken in Miami, USA, comment on the accommodation provided for students during the stay, and to make recommendations for any changes for future trips.

The study programme

Central to the programme organised by International English, Miami, were 20 hours of English language tuition per week. The classes took place in well-equipped, modern classrooms in a spacious school. The teaching was excellent, using a range of methods and making the most of the available technology. The study programme also offered a range of exciting extra-curricular activities. These included sports, cinema and theatre trips and social events such as parties.

The accommodation

Students were housed in a residential block close to the school. Each bedroom had its own bathroom and there was a shared kitchen for every 15 students. The rooms were small but comfortable. However, the kitchens had insufficient cooking equipment for the number of students.

Recommendations for future trips

There is little I would suggest changing about the programme of study. It was well-run by highly experienced teachers and it exceeded my expectations. I would strongly advise requesting alternative accommodation, however. The kitchen facilities were inadequate and being housed with other students from the same country meant we often used our first language rather than English. I would recommend placing students with American host families on future trips.

Conclusion

This was a highly enjoyable and profitable trip that I would recommend to other students, especially if the changes suggested regarding the accommodation are implemented.

LISTENING
Part 1 Multiple choice
Practice task

2

1 B (She says that she often uses new techniques too much so students get bored, but she's keen to avoid doing that this time.)
2 A (He says that even those who have no interest in it had just as much to say as those who like it.)

3

1 C (she thinks students are generally positive about new teaching techniques)
2 A (she isn't sure about its value yet as she's only just started using it)
3 B (she says she wants to avoid using it too much)

4a

1 A   2 C   3 B   4 A

4b

Section 4 gives you the answer.
1 No, he says that the whole group was passionate about the discussion.
2 No, he says that everyone engaged with the discussion

A is the correct answer. He makes the point that the topic of rap music generates a passionate response from all learners, and it's therefore a powerful vehicle for teaching.

Strategies and skills
Understanding attitude and opinion

1

1 B ('I was seriously hoping that a course with as many sessions as this one would be able to explore the issue in the kind of detail I enjoy. However, the opposite was the case.')
2 C ('… school … didn't address the needs of those who were good at practical applications. I was in the latter group … I still left with very little to show for it, despite many years of consistent effort.')
3 A ('… the idea of "good guy is threatened by a powerful bad guy but eventually wins" has become almost universal.')

2

1 A (She says, 'Some of the machines look as though they've been taken from a futuristic science-fiction film. I initially thought I'd never be able to get my head around how to use them … it's been remarkably easy to pick up what to do – you can't keep me off them now.')
2 B (He says, 'she systematically involves everyone under her in the decision-making process. I think she's actually grateful for their input …')
3 A (She says, 'perhaps when large numbers of consumers see the company's name attached to something that's supposedly beneficial for the planet, it'll make them think more kindly of a business …')

Identifying purpose and function

3

1 B (the speaker is defending why some people didn't have a ticket)
2 A (the speaker is suggesting a course of action)
3 C (the speaker is complaining about the management's work practices)
4 B (the speaker is persuading someone to go to a concert)
5 A (the speaker is justifying why the work will be late)
6 A (the speaker is summarising the plot of the play.)
7 B (the speaker is warning the listener about a course of action)
8 A (the speaker is politely refusing an invitation)

Identifying feeling

4

1 C (the speaker is defending Jeremy so feels protective towards him)
2 B (the speaker is impatient and interrupts to move onto other agenda items)

3 A (the speaker prizes inner peace and has let go of her resentments, so is content)
4 C (the speaker is dissatisfied with the restaurant manager's reaction to his illness)
5 A (the speaker is eager to work with Martha's company)
6 C (the speaker is suspicious of Alex's motives for praising him all the time)
7 B (the speaker is unsure of which subject she wants to study at university)
8 A (the speaker is doubtful about the success of the negotiations)

Identifying agreement

5

1 Disagree (Speaker A thinks the system is a good idea, but speaker B suggests it's only effective for part of the year.)
2 Agree (They agree that gyms often hide limitations within their terms and conditions.)
3 Agree (The speakers agree that the content of the course is relevant to their work.)
4 Disagree (Speaker B thinks that the book steers clear of doing what speaker A suggests.)
5 Disagree (Speaker A wants all school students to study philosophy, but speaker A thinks that goes too far.)
6 Agree (Both speakers agree that people don't notice changes to cities because they happen gradually.)

EXAM TASK

1 C (The man says that it's imperative we prevent more plastic pollution entering the environment.)
2 B (The man uses bottles and bags to highlight the misconception that these are the most immediate problem, when he thinks micro-plastics are more serious.)
3 A (The woman says she agrees with a friend who thinks going back somewhere always negatively affects the affection you remember the place with.)
4 C (The man says that his expectations would never be met and that going back is more about revisiting the time you spent there, which is impossible.)
5 A (The man says judges can't punish restaurants appropriately and the woman says that there's always a legal loophole they can use to escape serious punishment.)
6 B (The woman says that it's as though she's talking another language when she gives the government advice and she says all she gets is 'a wall of silence', so she's frustrated by their response.)

LISTENING
Part 2 Sentence completion
Practice task

2

1 pure form ('what sets it [gold] apart is the pure form it's in when taken from the ground.')

2 flakes ('the flakes found on the floor there [in the caves] are the first sign that people valued and worked with this precious metal.')
3 China ('I'd never associated China with being a great source of the metal … It does, however, currently come top of the list …')
4 electronics ('The quantity that the electronics sector consumes took me aback')

3

1 The key is that it has to be something that doesn't apply to most metals. The student thought no other metals come from mines, which isn't true.
2 The student thought the coins were made 40,000 years ago, like the flakes.
3 The student has chosen one of the countries that Darren used to think was the biggest producer until he realised that China was.
4 The student has written one of the answers mentioned that Darren was not surprised about, which uses a relatively small amount of gold.

Strategies and skills
Identifying cues

1

Leila's <u>research focuses</u> on the
(1) _____ of the golden tree frog. Leila says that golden tree frogs are now <u>largely confined to two</u>
(2) _____ in Trinidad.
Leila says golden tree frogs are now <u>listed as</u> **(4)** _____ <u>on international conservation scales</u>.
Leila uses the word **(3)** _____ <u>to describe the golden tree frog's flight</u>.

2

a 4 (This is a description of their flight.)
b 2 (This relates to the two places where the frogs still live.)
c 1 (This is about why Leila's research team were in Trinidad.)
e 3 (This relates to where they are on the international conservation scale.)
(**d** is not used)

3

1 reproduction (lots of research has been done about diet, so Leila's team are studying reproduction)
2 (of the highest) mountains (the frogs live only on the two highest mountains in Trinidad)
3 critically endangered (they were listed as vulnerable, then endangered and are now critically endangered)
4 elegant (their flight is 'elegant', although she describes their movement on the trees as 'clumsy')

Understanding specific information and stated opinion

4

1 adjective (it's describing how she feels)
2 noun (personal qualities are nouns)
3 verb (the person was paid to do something)
4 adverb (the word in the gap describes the adjective so must be an adverb)

5

well-balanced (This is how Helen feels now she's living on the water in the houseboat.)
content (how she felt about living in her house for some time)
restless (how she began to feel when she was in her house)
excited (how she felt after deciding to buy a houseboat)
worried (how she felt about not being able to find the perfect houseboat)

6

Jim mentions 1, 2, 5 and 6. The adjective 'experienced' is used and not the noun form.
Jim says that 'optimism' is the most important quality (as many of the others can be learned, and you need to stay positive when things go wrong).

7

Maddy uses 'organised', 'booked' and 'introduced' to describe what the volunteers did.
She uses the verb 'filmed' to describe what the person who was paid did ('with the exception of the guy who filmed everyone on stage'.)

8

Neil uses 'totally', 'remarkably', 'drastically' and 'utterly'.
'Totally' is used to describe the dependence plants and animals have on the rain
'Remarkably' is used to describe how reliable the rains used to be
'Drastically' is used to describe the recent reduction in rainfall
'Utterly' is used to describe the effects of the lack of rain
The answer is therefore 'drastically'.

Identifying and eliminating distractors

9

1 a noun about his job
2 a verb related directly or indirectly to his work
3 a noun possibly a person's job title, an animal or something else that's unusual
4 a noun relating to what he had to train in

10

1 'variety' (it still gets him to work with a smile on his face.)
Distractors: 'being recognised' (the novelty has worn off, so he doesn't enjoy it so much anymore); 'studying weather patterns' (he's seen them all before)

11

2 shaving (he'd never do it again if that were possible)
Distractors: 'arriving early' (he's come to terms with it now); 'using make-up' (he didn't like it at first but has got used to it now)
3 penguins (he ended up presenting with them around his feet)
Distractor: 'giraffes' (he argued against this and won)
4 acting (he did this soon after getting the role)
Distractors: 'meteorology' (he studied this before he started his job); 'film editing' (he wants to do this in the future)

EXAM TASK

1 the pyramids (this was the first archaeological thing that Laura was interested in, and not the TV documentaries)
2 (university) lecturer (he encouraged Laura to be more adventurous in her aims which led to her seeing the job on the research project)
3 helicopters (these can fly at a precise height and speed unlike satellites and aeroplanes; drones can't carry the heavy equipment)
4 lasers (Laura's project used 16 lasers; a previous project used infrared cameras)
5 canal (she knew the money had been well spent when she saw an image of a canal)
6 (3-D) models (Laura is good at IT and created 3-D models on the computer)
7 modern American city (Angkor was the same size as a modern American city but smaller than a huge metropolis like Tokyo)
8 climate change (Laura thinks the evidence for climate change causing the decline of Angkor is the most convincing; others think disease, invasion or war were to blame)

LISTENING
Part 3 Multiple choice
Practice task

2

1 D (Harriet says that after she had moved, some premises became available in the town where she'd moved to, and she also got a bonus at work, so she thought 'it's now or never!'.)
2 C (Andrew says that he was faced with a long list of options and became fed up trying to decide which location would be best.)

3 A (Harriet says she couldn't now tell us a fraction of what she did; Andrew says his memory of the period is a bit hazy.)

3a
C
The question tests understanding of what helped Harriet make the decision.

3b

1 B **2** A **3** D **4** C

3c
D is correct because Harriet says that after she had moved, some premises became available in the town where she'd moved to, and she also got a bonus at work, so she thought 'It's now or never!'.
A is incorrect because Harriet says she couldn't ask her boss or colleagues as she wanted to keep her plans secret.
B is incorrect because when Harriet is talking about tension between her and her boss, it's hypothetical as they get on pretty well.
C is incorrect because she was expecting to wait for ages but didn't have to in the end.

4a
A (It's testing understanding of Andrew's uncertainty.)

4b
A: already agreed loan with bank at favourable rate, opened up wider range of potential premises
Incorrect: It gave Andrew more choice, not less.
B: perfectionist, set about finding somewhere that met his criteria
Incorrect: His ideas were *too* clear.
C: faced with a long list of options, none seemed totally suitable, eventually picked one almost at random, fed up of trying to decide
Correct: He got upset at having such a long list of places, none of which were ideal.
D: Rather than worrying about whether two could succeed in the same street, I thought 'business is business', went for it anyway
Incorrect: He didn't worry about this at all, thinking 'business is business'.

Strategies and skills
Identifying agreement and disagreement

1

1 c (both are about memory)
2 a (both are about perceptions of time)
3 d (both give the impression of excitement)
4 b (both are about working hours)

2

1 c (Their opinions about memory are more or less the same.)

3

1 a (Both speakers say that drivers don't really care about cyclists.)

2 a (Both speakers say that spending on medical research is already at a maximum.)
3 b (Both speakers think that listening to music makes you feel better at work.)

4

1 C (The man says that people resent the government spending money on charities that could be spent on hospitals and other things. The woman says that she's never heard of anyone complaining about government support for charities.)
2 B (The woman says that the current system in which only students from less well-off families get free school meals is working well. The man says that everyone should have free school meals as it's a basic human right.)
3 A (The man says he thinks the facilities were poor, given what they'd paid for the course. The woman says that there was everything at the centre that she needed, and more.)
4 C (The man says people now unrealistically expect instant solutions. The woman says people were always impatient, but moan about it more now on the internet.)

Understanding feeling

5

1 B (The speaker says that the arguments only look convincing until you look at the data used to support them.)
2 A (The speaker says that critics use a few isolated examples of bad teaching to give the impression that homeschooling as a whole is ineffective.)
3 C (The speaker says that even if you're bored of action films, there's plenty to get excited about in the film.)
4 B (The speaker says that most sportsmen and sportswomen are 'incredible examples of discipline and self-sacrifice that we should be encouraging all young people to emulate.')
5 A (The speaker says that 'just as many rude people existed back then as do now.')
6 C (The speaker says that if he can put something off, he does, which his academic supervisor wasn't happy about, but 'access to tutors seven days a week via email was a real plus point.')

Dealing with paraphrase

6

1 c (If there aren't 'anywhere near as many as', it means it's a much lower number.)
2 e (If a balance is 'struck', then a sensible compromise between two things is reached.)
3 b (If something 'goes against conventional wisdom', it goes against what the majority of people believe.)

4 a ('Nothing could be further from the truth' has a similar meaning to something being a lie or definitely not true.)
5 d (If 'criteria need to be met', then certain qualities are required.)

7

1 hold (If something 'holds your attention', you are interested in it.)
2 hope (Doing an activity 'in the hope that something happens' means you want it to happen and believe that it might.)
3 moderation (Doing things 'in moderation' means to do them in a sensible way.)
4 room (If there's 'room for improvement' in something you do, it means it needs to be better.)
5 matter (If something is 'only a matter of time', it's certain to happen; we just don't know when.)
6 mind (If you 'put someone's mind at rest', you reassure them about something.)

EXAM TASK

1 C (Guy uses the *Star Wars* films to make the point that he wanted to create incredible new machines that push the boundaries of what we do.)
2 B (Yasmin suggests that most listeners have a limited understanding of what technology actually is, so gives a broader definition.)
3 A (Guy says that funding goes to projects that seem superficially thrilling but that are not necessarily beneficial.)
4 C (Yasmin says that her book will focus on where research takes place to see if it influences how successful it is.)
5 D (Yasmin and Guy both say that any restrictions should be minimal, with as little intervention as possible.)
6 B (Guy says that funding from the private sector is to be welcomed whereas Yasmin expresses concern that so much money should come from organisations whose main aim is to make profits.)

LISTENING
Part 4 Multiple matching
Practice task

2

1 C (The speaker says she was doing it to financially support a good friend who was seriously ill.)
2 B (The speaker says she'd always avoided spending time by herself and the longer this went on, the more intimidating a prospect it became, but doing the bike ride helped her face the fear.)
3 D (The speakers says the best man at his wedding said he'd never be able to walk more than 20 km, so he just thought up the most ridiculous way imaginable to do it.)

4 A (The speaker says she 'wouldn't say no to having a go at something comparable in the near future, just perhaps not in a boat.')
5 D (The speaker says her friends still think she was mad to take it on, which she wasn't expecting.)
6 C (The speakers says it'd be fun if a few people decided to do it this time, not just him.)

3a

1 A ('employer' suggests work and a boring routine)
2 E ('immensely dangerous and physical challenge' relates to 'test the limits of physical ability')
3 C ('financially support' relates to 'money' in option C.)

3b

Phrase 3, because it matches the option exactly: it's about raising money to support a friend financially.

4a

A: 'I wouldn't say no to having a go at something comparable in the near future, just perhaps not in a boat.'
C: 'I needed help from many other people'
D: '… they thought … was an acceptable excuse!'

4b

'I wouldn't say no to having a go at something comparable in the near future, just perhaps not in a boat': this matches option A exactly as it's about trying a different kind of solo voyage in the future.

5a

1: Task Two option C ('others' matches with the friends in this section of text)
2: Task Two option D (the speaker is surprised the friends didn't change their opinion about the trip)
3: Task One option B (moments being 'nasty' matches with the 'fear'); Task Two option E ('things like that always turn out OK' matches with 'grateful to have survived')
4: Task One option A ('the mundanities of day-to-day existence' matches with 'escape from a boring routine')
5: Task One option B (the speaker is talking about a fear of spending time alone)

5b

Section 5 gives the answer for Task One (option B: it relates to facing a fear the speaker has had for a long time).
Section 2 gives the answer for Task Two (option D: it's about his friends' reaction after the event).

6a

I walked from the far north east of North America to the far south west. It all started when the friend who was best man at my wedding poked fun at me for being so unfit. He said I'd never be able to walk more than 20 km, so I just thought up the most ridiculous way imaginable to do it. I actually got a lot from it, so my intention now is to repeat the walk, but across South America instead. It'd be fun if a few of us decided to do it this time, not just me. I'm glad I did it, even though the time it took me was a little outside what I was hoping for.

6b

Task One: D; his friend joked about him being so unfit
Task Two: C; he wants to do another walk across South America with friends

Strategies and skills
Understanding the main point

1a

F (The speaker says that it allowed him to get out of the office for a day a week, which was why he signed up for it.)

1b

Options A and D are also mentioned but neither of these are the reason why the speaker attended the training course.

2a

Speaker 1: E (Speaker 1 says he did it so that a workmate would take his technical skills more seriously.)
Speaker 2: A (Speaker 2 says that many of her decisions are made to improve her chances of climbing the career ladder, including doing management training courses.)

2b

Speaker 1 also mentions options B, C and F, but none of these are the main reason why the speaker chose to do the training. Speaker 2 also mentions options B, D and E. None of these are the main reason why the speaker chose to do the training. In addition, management is not new to the speaker (option D) and she wants to impress the top *dogs*, not just one of them.

3

Task One: A (The speaker says she didn't have much choice in the move and that her boss asked her to move there.)
Task Two: B (The speaker says that it's not the sort of place she wants to settle in long term and hopes her employer will give her more choice in where she moves in future.)

4a

Task One: C (The speaker says that after having children, he wanted them to be close to their grandad.)
Task Two: D (The speaker says that it seems like he's been living there for years when they only moved there a few weeks ago.)

4b

Task One: Options A and E are mentioned. The speaker did move a long time ago for work, but not this time. He realised how stressful city living really was only after he moved, so it wasn't the reason for moving.
Task Two: Options C and E are mentioned. He hasn't had the opportunity to meet many of the neighbours yet. He suggests he's enjoying the atmosphere in the small town, not disappointed by it.

Understanding gist

5

1 B **2** C **3** A **4** C

6

1 d **2** a **3** e **4** b **5** c

Interpreting opinions

7

1 d (The speaker says they needed to predict how customers think, so they needed to understand people well.)
2 b (The speaker says they've never met anyone at the top level who is shy, which suggests they had to have self-confidence to succeed.)
3 a (The speaker says they have learned a lot from their own failures.)
4 f (The speaker says that academic excellence was the only way to achieve success.)
5 c (The speaker describes an inner need to constantly be at the next level up.)
6 e (The speaker describes learning about how other people have succeeded.)

8

1 F (The speaker says she didn't really achieve either of her aims, because she wasted time.)
2 B (The speaker says he's got his energy and love of learning back thanks to a gap year.)
3 H (The speaker says she feels like she has little in common with her old school friends now.)
4 A (The speaker says his travelling allowed him to learn Spanish and his work on websites will bring in some income while he's studying.)
5 D (The speaker says she realised that she should be going in a different direction in her career, so changed the course she was going to study at university.)

Identifying attitude and feelings

9

1 A (If someone is 'taken aback', it means they are surprised by something.)
2 B (The speaker says they felt as though they needed a law degree to complete the necessary paperwork.)

3 B (The speaker says there were no weak links in the chain, so everyone did their job well.)
4 A (The speaker says that everyone involved was responsible, not just them.)

10

1 C (The speaker says that if he'd taken time to speak to people older and wiser than him, they would have told him about the consequences of giving up his course.)
2 F (The speaker says that she wanted to be back in her old house as soon as she walked into her new flat.)
3 D (The speaker knew about ex-colleagues' businesses failing and that the sector was entering a downturn, but decided to set up his own business anyway.)
4 A (The speaker says she can laugh about it now and it has taught her to be far more careful with money.)
5 H (The speaker says he didn't have much time to consider his colleagues' offer of going on holiday with them.)

Correcting mistakes

11

1 The candidate has put A, but the correct answer is E. The candidate probably thought the information about cricket and rugby made option A the answer.
2 The candidate has got this answer correct.
3 The candidate has put F instead of the correct answer D. This is probably because Speaker 3 mentions their coach.
4 The candidate has put C instead of the correct answer, A. The candidate has already incorrectly used option A in Question 1, so then possibly didn't think it was the answer for Question 4. Speaker 4 also mentions seeing a cricket match but this is what started his interest, not what improved his ability.
5 The candidate has got this answer correct.
6 The candidate has got this answer correct.
7 The candidate has got this answer correct.
8 The candidate has got this answer correct.
Correct answers:
1 E (The speaker says she lives near a climbing centre and has friends who are keen to go there several times a week with her.)
2 B (The speaker says that the other players in his team encouraged him to push himself, and it's like being in an extended sporting family.)
3 D (The speaker says that she just seems to be able to dive well with a minimum of practice, so has natural talent.)

4 A (The speaker says the skills he developed playing baseball have helped him succeed at cricket.)
5 D (The speaker says she had no idea that many of the people going to the climbing centre go there to watch the experts climb, and not climb themselves.)
6 A (The speaker says he was wrong to think that ice hockey didn't require much energy.)
7 E (The speaker says that divers don't look like they'd do anything to win, but appearances are deceptive, so it is therefore not true.)
8 F (The speaker says that he didn't know how much precision is required to bat successfully when playing cricket.)

EXAM TASK

1 E (The speaker says that everyone focuses on solutions, not problems.)
2 C (The speaker says that it's the company's policy to move people up in the organisation as soon as they're ready for more responsibility.)
3 G (The speaker says she's spent two weeks learning all about the organisation.)
4 A (The speaker says the work really makes him think. He says he's enjoying it and loses track of time, suggesting he finds it interesting.)
5 H (The speaker says that the company has a unique approach to everything, from products to offices to the way in which they manage their staff.)
6 A (The speaker says that working out what to do first and what to leave until later is more difficult than it seems.)
7 E (The speaker says that some of the software his new company uses is a mystery to him.)
8 C (The speaker says she needs to arrange meetings with line reports but they're not responding to emails.)
9 F (The speaker says he's not sure if he's doing the work right or not.)
10 B (The speaker says she wishes more people had been employed so she wouldn't have to take so much work home to do in the evening and at weekends.)

SPEAKING
Part 1 Interview
Practice task

2

1 B **2** C **3** A **4** A **5** C **6** B **7** A **8** A

3

1: A is too short and lacks detail.
C includes too much detail. It sounds more like written English than spoken English. Perhaps the candidate has prepared the answer before the test and rehearsed it.

2: A answers the wrong question. The response should be about their main activity e.g. work or study.
B doesn't include enough detail.
3: B answers the question 'How much time do you spend studying English?'
C doesn't include enough detail.
4: B relates to why they are learning English, not what they enjoy about it.
C is very negative, and lacks detail.
5: A is just an opinion and does not answer the question.
B gives a list of what the candidate likes, but does not go into detail or give reasons.
6: A talks about people in general when the question asks for a personal opinion.
C lacks detail (Which field? What role within this? How much?).
7: B doesn't answer the question and is quite negative in tone.
C lacks detail.
8: B lacks detail (e.g. Where? Why?).
C might be an attempt to be funny, but it doesn't answer the question and is actually a little rude.

Strategies and skills

Extending your answers

1

1 hard ('It's hard to … but if I had to, I'd …' is a way of choosing a favourite (or least favourite!) out of all your ideas or experiences)
2 other ('on the one hand … on the other hand' allows you to make a positive and a negative point in a single sentence)
3 addition ('in addition to' is used to add extra information)
4 opportunity ('Given the opportunity, I'd …' is a good way of hypothesising about something you'd like to do in the future)
5 plan ('If everything goes to plan, …' is a good way of introducing what you want to do in the future)
6 fact ('due to the fact that …' is a good way of giving a reason for something)

2

Suggested answers:
1 If you could visit anywhere in the world, where would you go?
2 How would you describe the area where you grew up?
3 How do you usually find out about the news?
4 What new skill or sport would you like to learn in the future?
5 What sort of work would you like to do in the future?
6 Which person do you most admire?

3

1 The speaker gives reasons for their choice and examples of what's interesting.
2 The speaker explains why both the negative and positive factors were true.

3 The speaker gives a reason (why they watch the news on TV).
4 The speaker explains in detail why they would choose a particular activity.
5 The speaker adds detail about their university course, the type of company and where they'd like to work.
6 The speaker gives a detailed reason and compares his dad to the general population.

Adding examples

4

1 For instance ('For instance' is used to add an example; 'As well as that' is used to add an example after a previous example.)
2 such as ('such as' is used to add an example; 'then again' is used to add contrasting information.)
3 like ('like' is used to add an example; 'as' is used to show a similarity with something.)
4 say ('say' is used here to add examples of activities he already does; 'perhaps' can be used to give examples of things you might do or try.)

Giving reasons

5

1 due/owing (either can be followed by *to* + gerund (*-ing* form))
2 reason ('for the reason that' is used to add a reason)
3 due/owing (either can be followed by *to* + noun)
4 view ('in view of' is a more formal way of adding a reason)
5 result ('as a result of' explains why something happened)
6 grounds ('on the grounds that' is often used to explain why you did or didn't do something)
7 seeing ('seeing as' is used to add a reason for something)
8 start ('for a start' is used to add the first of several reasons for something)

6

Students' own answers

7

Students' own answers

8

Students' own answers

Using a range of language

9

1 affordable (something that is 'affordable' is 'cheap')
2 exceptionally ('exceptionally' is a slightly stronger way of saying 'extremely')
3 accomplish ('accomplish' has a similar meaning to 'achieve')
4 imaginative ('imaginative' has a similar meaning to 'creative')

5 substantially ('substantially' has a similar meaning to 'a lot')
6 illustrate ('illustrate' has a similar meaning to 'explain', especially if it's with an example)
7 hysterical ('hysterical' means very funny and is often used with 'absolutely'); in this case, only the second instance of 'funny' can be replaced.
8 immediately ('immediately after' means the same as 'just after')

Asking for repetition

10

1 b ('would you mind' is followed by the *-ing* form of the verb)
2 d ('could you' is followed by the bare infinitive (infinitive without 'to') of the verb)
3 f (Use the past tense here because the examiner asked the question in the past)
4 e (Use the past tense here because you 'didn't hear' the question in the past)
5 a (Use the full infinitive (with 'to') after 'is it possible')
6 c (this is a very polite and formal way of asking someone to repeat something)

EXAM TASK

Example answers:
Where are you from?
I'm from a city in the north of Colombia called Cartagena. It's on the Caribbean coast of Colombia and it's a really nice place to live.

What do you do there?
Well, I actually completed my degree in engineering last year, but I thought I'd almost certainly get a better job if I spent some time improving my English. So at the moment, I'm actually learning English full-time. I also have a part-time weekend job as a waiter in a restaurant, to earn a little money while I'm studying.

How long have you been studying English?
For about eight years now. I started when I was still at primary school and continued it throughout high school and college.

What do you most enjoy about learning English?
Well, there's so much on the internet that's in English – more than in any other language. The best thing for me, though, is being able to communicate with other online gamers around the world, even though English isn't necessarily our first language.

Do you prefer spending time with a large group of friends, or just one or two?
Lots of people prefer to be with a big group of friends, but I'm actually much more comfortable being with only one or two. The reason is that I'm quite a quiet person, and large groups tend to get dominated by the louder, more confident people, which I find quite frustrating. I much prefer to be in the company of a smaller number of people.

What's the best thing about the town or city you live in?
I think the best thing about it is that there's so much to do there, and I don't just mean for people my age. For instance, if you're young like me, there are lots of nightclubs and places like that, but there are also cinemas, theatres, museums and shops that people of all ages and backgrounds will love.

Who was the biggest influence on you when you were a child?
My grandparents, I guess. I used to stay with them a lot, for example after school each day, because both of my parents work full-time. I loved the way they gently guided me in the right direction in life, and actually still do.

Would you prefer to have a job you really enjoy or one which pays very well?
Preferably one which I enjoy and which also pays very well! But seriously, if I had to choose, without a doubt I'd go for the one I really enjoy. The quality of my life is what's most important, and while it's true that money buys a certain amount of freedom and contentment, I wouldn't want to spend eight, nine hours a day feeling miserable just to have lots of it.

Do you think you spend too much time on the internet?
Sometimes I do, I guess, but most of the time I don't feel that way at all. What I use it for most is keeping in touch with my friends. While I'd much prefer to do this face to face, I don't always have time to meet them, and they don't either, so I see it as a more efficient use of my time, actually.

How do you hope to use your skills in English in the future?
I use them a lot already, of course, because I have a lot of friends from other countries and we all use English to communicate. My aim is to work for a large multinational business, say a big tech company such as Apple or Microsoft. To get to the top in companies like that, you have to know how to speak English really well, so I hope that's where my skills will take me.

Is there a festival or celebration you particularly enjoy?
The one I enjoy the most is a local celebration that only happens in my town, not nationally. It originated when the main industry there was fishing and has continued since then. On 21st March each year, they build a wooden model of a fish and carry it through the streets. It's then set alight and thrown into the sea. It's meant to bring good luck to the fishermen. I don't know if it works, but it's great fun.

What's the most interesting aspect of trying new things?
I'm someone who gets bored quite easily, so I love that feeling I get when I'm trying out a new sport, for example, or a different kind of food. It really helps to keep me entertained. It causes problems too, since I rarely practise anything for long enough to get really good at it, but that's just the way I am.

SPEAKING
Part 2 Individual long turn
Practice task

2
Students' own answers

3a
1 Student A compares the pictures. Student B only describes each one.
2 Yes, both students do this, and both speak for about a minute.
3 Both students talk mainly about the people but also about other things in the pictures.

3b
Student A, because he provided more detail and compared the pictures as well as answering the questions.

4
Students' own answers

Strategies and skills
Comparing

1
Students' own answers

2
Suggested answers:
1 The main similarity between the pictures is that in each one there is a group of people who are having a discussion.
2 What the two pictures have in common is that the people who are having the discussion are gathered around a table.
3 In the first picture, it appears as though the people are taking part in a formal business discussion, whereas in the second one, a group of friends or classmates have met in a café and are having an informal and relaxed chat.
4 A significant difference between the pictures is that in the first picture, the people are in a work-based situation. This is not the case in the second picture, which seems to be a café.
5 The people having the discussion in the first picture appear to be quite serious, suggesting it's a formal discussion, whereas the people seem more relaxed and smiling in the second picture as it's a rather informal gathering.

3
First picture:
It's likely that they're taking part in a business discussion, therefore they're probably discussing issues to try and convince members of the team that their viewpoint is the correct one.
They are perhaps discussing business issues with a view to moving the business forward in some way.
I'm of the opinion that this type of discussion is quite hard to be a part of, because you have to know lots of detail about what you're discussing and respond carefully to points that other people have made.
I think certain types of people are extremely good at this type of discussion and therefore find it quite easy to take part in, whereas others perhaps are less capable of putting their point of view forward confidently, so will find it difficult.
Second picture:
The people in the picture are likely to be friends and/or classmates, so probably know each other well. There's no apparent pressure on them.
They could be catching up on news or just taking a relaxed break from studying.
This looks like it would be a very easy discussion to be part of, as everyone is so relaxed and they're not debating challenging business issues.
I think the time would fly in this kind of discussion because it would be fun and not difficult at all to be involved in.

4
Students' own answers

Speculating

5
Possible answers:
They might be good at coping with stress because they look quite relaxed.
I would guess that they've had a lot of training to be able to work in a busy kitchen like that.
It's possible that they sometimes make mistakes and get told off by the head chef.
It could be the case that they've worked together for a long time, which would make it easier and quicker.
I'd imagine that they are incredibly busy at certain times of day and less busy at others.
I suppose that they're all used to working really quickly and carefully.
I'd assume that they've either been told exactly what to do, or just know because they're so experienced.

6
Students' own answers

Structuring a long turn

7

1 First of all (this phrase is a common way to introduce a long turn)

2 In contrast (this phrase highlights the difference or differences between things)

3 whereas (this word is used to compare differences between two things or ideas)

4 on the other hand (this phrase is used to highlight a difference between two things or ideas)

5 However (this word has a similar meaning to 'but', so contrasts things or ideas)

6 as is the case (this phrase means that something is true; 'as you'd expect' doesn't apply here as it used to describe something you believe is likely, not something that you know)

7 when compared to (this phrase is used to compare two things or ideas)

Answering the follow-up question to your partner's long turn

8

1 B (it is impersonal and gives a general opinion supported by an example)

2 A (it extends the answer with a reason)

3 A (it extends the answer with a reason. B gives a reason but doesn't really answer the question.)

4 B (A answers the question from the wrong perspective.)

Dealing with unfamiliar vocabulary

9

1 give me a moment (this phrase is used to ask for thinking time)

2 gone blank (this phrase is used to say that you can't think of what to say)

3 come back to me (this phrase indicates you're trying to remember something)

4 not totally sure (this phrase is used to show you don't know something is definitely correct or true)

5 should know (this phrase is used to show you can't remember or don't know a word or how to say something)

6 think of what it is (this phrase indicates that you can't remember how to say something)

EXAM TASK

Suggested answer:

Examiner: Candidate A, it's your turn first. Here are your pictures. They show people helping others in different situations. I'd like you to compare two of the pictures, and say how difficult you think it might be to help someone in these situations and how you think the people who are helping might be feeling.

Candidate A: First of all, I'd like to talk about the similarities and differences between the two pictures. The first one shows a nurse who is helping a female patient to walk. The nurse is gently holding her arm to support her. In contrast to the other photo, which shows a man giving directions to two people who are possibly tourists, the picture is taken indoors, in a hospital ward. The second photo is taken on a small road with houses. It's maybe spring or autumn as the tourists are wearing warm clothes.

I'd imagine that it's relatively easy for the nurse to help the patient, as she will have received lots of training in how to do this, and probably has lots of experience of doing this too. Similarly, I'd guess that the man knows the city he presumably lives in very well, so will have little difficulty directing the tourists to where they want to go. It's my belief that the man likes helping visitors to his city and is feeling pleased to be able to help out in this small way. The nurse, on the other hand, is assisting the patient in a far more significant way as she is helping her regain her health, perhaps after having an operation of some sort. I therefore think that the sense of satisfaction she gets from helping is much deeper than that of the man.

Examiner: Thank you. Candidate B, which of these ways of helping do you think people would be most grateful for?

Candidate B: I think it would probably be the patient in the hospital. She's clearly not feeling that great, and that tends to make anyone is in this situation more grateful for help than they would normally be. I'm sure the tourists are very grateful for the help they're getting too, but I suspect it won't be to the same degree as the patient.

Examiner: Thank you. Now Candidate B, here are your pictures. They show people attending important events. I'd like you to compare two of the pictures, and say what the people might find enjoyable about attending these events, and how difficult you think the events might be to arrange.

Candidate B: The two pictures I've chosen show very different kinds of important event. The first shows a wedding. It looks as though the actual ceremony has finished and now everyone's come out of the venue and is standing around the bride and groom to watch them doing something important to do with the event – I think they're cutting the wedding cake, actually. The second event couldn't be more different as it shows a stage at a huge music festival or concert. There are thousands of people watching whoever's performing, but we can't actually see the band in the photo because of the bright lights that are shining out from the stage. The people there are probably very informally dressed and generally relaxed, but excited to see the band. In contrast, the wedding guests all look very smart and relatively formal. Perhaps some of them don't know the others particularly well, so are probably feeling quite tense and on show. However, going to a wedding is always an interesting experience. It's always a privilege to see two people getting married, and it also provides a great opportunity for guests to meet new people or catch up with those that they haven't seen for a long time. The music festival is interesting in a different way as it must be incredibly exciting, for the audience of course, but especially for the musicians that play there. I think the wedding would be far easier to organise than the festival. There's still an enormous amount to arrange, such as invitations, venues, food and so on, but it's on a much smaller scale than a music festival attended by tens of thousands of people.

Examiner: Thank you. Candidate A, which of these events do you think would be the most expensive to organise?

Candidate A: The music festival, without a doubt. For the wedding, you might have one band playing and food for perhaps a couple of hundred people to arrange, but for a festival of that size, you'd need to pay for a huge security team and fencing to go around the site, and book and pay for all the bands. I have no idea how much all the stages and sound systems would cost, but it can't be cheap.

SPEAKING
Part 3 Collaborative task
Practice task

1

Students' own answers

2

Students' own answers

3

Students' own answers

The following should be ticked:

The value of a qualification depends on where it comes from. (Student B says both the country and the university within a country changes the value of the qualification.)

Being unhappy will affect your ability to study. (Student B says you can't possibly do well at university if you're not happy. Having money worries will affect your education. (Student B says if you're worrying about money all the time, you won't be able to concentrate on studying.) A good social life can help you learn about a country's culture. (Student A says that getting to know lots of people, especially locals, is a great way to find out more about the culture of the country.)

Not ticked:

It's better to go to an English-speaking country. (Student B says that the language must be one that you'll be able to use in the future but doesn't specify it should be English.)

Working at the same time as studying is a bad idea. (Student A says that perhaps getting a part-time job will help with living costs.)

4

1 Yes (e.g. 'What do you think?')
2 Yes (e.g. 'There's little point getting a degree that employers or universities in your own country don't really recognise.')
3 Yes (e.g.' You can't possibly do well at university if you're not happy, and part of that comes from speaking to the people you love regularly.')

5a

Yes. The students agree in the end that language skills are the most important.

5b

The following should be ticked:
I see what you mean; I hadn't really thought of it like that; I'll go along with what you said

6

Students' own answers

Strategies and skills

Interacting in a two-way conversation

1

Asking for opinions: How do you feel about …; So, what are your thoughts about …; Wouldn't you agree that …;

Giving opinions: From my perspective …; My view on this is …; Well, if you ask me …

Referring to your partner's points: I appreciate what you're saying. However …; I'm not convinced that's true …; That's a really clear way of explaining …;

2

Possible answers:

1 As far as I'm concerned, meeting friends during a break isn't a great idea because if you get deeply involved in a conversation you can really lose track of the time.
2 If you ask me, going for a short walk during a break is a great way to relax. For example, I was struggling with something at work last week so I went for a walk to the park, and the answer just came into my head as I was walking.
3 I'm not convinced that having something to eat is always a good idea because afterwards, you can feel a little bit sleepy and it's actually quite hard to start working again.
4 My thinking is that listening to music is a perfect way of winding down during breaks, because you forget all your stress and just get lost in what you're listening to.

5 It seems to me that a light snack is a great idea during a break. For example, I usually have some fruit during my morning break and I feel as though I've got more energy afterwards.
6 My opinion is that checking your phone isn't always the best thing to do, because often there are messages that you need to respond to and so on, and it's more stressful than the work or study.

3

1 Yes, both students seek the opinions of their partner. All of the phrases from Ex 1 are used during the conversation.
2 Yes, they do this throughout the conversation.

4

Students' own answers

Evaluating, referring, reassessing

5

1 correctly ('if I understand you correctly' is used to check your understanding of the other speaker)
2 saying ('Are you saying…' is used to check your understanding of the other speaker)
3 understood ('Just to make sure I've fully understood what you've said' is used to check your understanding of the other speaker)
4 by ('So by saying that, do you mean…' is used to check your understanding of the other speaker)
5 thinking ('And thinking about what you said about…' is used to check your understanding of the other speaker or add information to their point)
6 trying ('Are you trying to say that you agree with …' is used to check your understanding of the other speaker)
7 said ('When you said that you think …' is used to check your understanding of the other speaker, add information or agree/disagree with the other speaker)
8 clarifying ('Would you mind just clarifying the point you made about …' is used to ask the other speaker to clarify what they meant)

Agreeing and disagreeing

6

1 A: weak disagreement but with an acknowledgement of importance; B: strong disagreement; C: weak disagreement
1: B, 2: A, 3: C
2 A: strong agreement; B: weak agreement C: moderate agreement;
1: A, 2: C, 3: B
3 A: neutral; B: moderate disagreement; C: strong disagreement
1: C, 2: B, 3: A

4 A: strong agreement; B: moderate agreement; C: weak agreement
1: A, 2: B, 3: C
5 A: moderate disagreement; B: strong disagreement; C: weak disagreement
1: B, 2: A, 3: C

Negotiating towards a decision

7

Negotiating towards a decision:
1 c **2** f **3** d **4** a **5** e **6** b
Reaching agreement on a decision:
1 f **2** a **3** e **4** b **5** d **6** c
Expressing inability to reach a decision:
1 e **2** d **3** a **4** b **5** f **6** c

8

1 you think this one's the most important; both of the opinion that
2 rule out this one as being; think we're ever going to agree about
3 you telling me that this is the most important one; decided on problem-solving as being
4 we choose a different one then, if we don't agree on; just have to agree to disagree about

EXAM TASK

Example answer

Examiner: Now, talk to each other about how much these events might affect people's lives.
A: OK, well I'd say that all of the events might have a big effect, but let's start with becoming famous, shall we?
B: Sounds good to me … Well, I've heard people say that you have no idea how much being famous changes your life until it actually happens.
A: Yes, I've heard that too.
B: I guess it has an impact on your whole life. You can't do lots of the normal, everyday things that people do, like going shopping or going out for a meal.
A: Yes, I definitely go along with what you say. It must be so difficult when people come up to you all the time when you're just out and about. It'd be quite nice to begin with, but it must become annoying really quickly – you'd have no private life at all unless you just stayed at home. So how do you feel about passing your driving test?
B: I think that has a big effect, but maybe not as much as some of the others. It gives you more freedom if you can get your own car and just go off in it when you want.
A: I hear what you're saying, and I agree that it's definitely not as significant as becoming famous, but I think most people love the independence that being able to drive gives them.
B: Hmm, I guess so. What about receiving a lot of money, then? What are your thoughts about that?

A: I think it must have quite a big effect, but how much probably depends on the amount of money you receive. It it's a few thousand pounds, then it's quite a lot of money but it won't have a huge long-term effect.

B: That's really true, but if it was millions, then you'd be able to pretty much do what you want. You could buy what you wanted, go where you wanted. The freedom it would give you would be incredible. You wouldn't have to work or anything.

A: Absolutely! So what are your opinions about starting your first job then?

B: I think it's a big event in anyone's life. It's the first time you're earning and really being part of the adult world, in a way.

A: Are you saying that you think it'll have a bigger effect that something like being famous then?

B: I wouldn't say that, but you're only ever going to start your first job once so it's still really important. Being famous will bring lots of negative changes as well as the positive, but I can't think of many negative ones for starting your first job.

A: I suppose you lose the freedom to do what you want when you want, which you have much more of when you're not working.

B: True. What about moving abroad, then?

A: I suppose it has a massive effect if you go somewhere really different. Wouldn't you agree that if the country you move to is pretty similar to your own country, then it's probably not going to feel that important?

B: Yes, totally. But if it's like nothing you've experienced before, then it will have a big effect on you. I suppose you get less of an effect the longer you stay there, too. It probably has more impact when you first go abroad.

Examiner: Thank you. Now you have about a minute to decide which of these things has the most significant effect on people's lives.

A: I think I'd definitely rule out passing your driving test.

B: I'd go along with that. I'd also argue that, unless your first job happens to be as something like a professional footballer, starting your first job isn't the most significant either.

A: Whereas becoming famous probably is. In fact, what you said might be the best way for us to consider each one.

B: I'm not sure exactly what you mean …

A: Well, it's not just the immediate effects that we have to think about, but how long-term they are too. Starting your first job, for example, might have a really big effect at the time, but that doesn't last for ever.

B: No; maybe a few months, but then you get used to it.

A: Exactly! So, I'm definitely of the opinion that becoming famous would have the biggest impact. It'd affect every area of your life, some positively, some negatively, and it's not as though people suddenly stop being famous, is it?

B: And a lot of the changes are very profound, like not being able to do a lot of the things that we take for granted because you'd be recognised.

A: There are some positive aspects too, of course, like having your talent or work recognised, whatever that is, and possibly having lots of money. Yes, it's got to be becoming famous.

SPEAKING
Part 4 Discussion
Practice task

2
Students' own answers

3
1 Yes (e.g., Student A gives the example of someone being naturally good at being organised if both their parents are. Student B gives the example of someone who's naturally better at workplace presentations.)
2 They agree with each other. Student B says that he was going to say something similar to Student A, and adds an example to support his agreement.

4
1 is made (Student A mentions this: 'I think schools have a much more academic focus than a vocational one')
2 is not made (Student B says she can't think of any jobs she was ready to start when she left school.)
3 is made (Student A says schools provide skills needed for many jobs, such as reading, writing and working closely with other people.)

5
1 Yes (Student A says 'What about you?')
2 Yes (Both students give their opinions about whether knowledge and qualifications or experience are more important.)
3 Yes (For example, Student A says 'someone who has a lot of experience at doing a job is always going to be better at it than someone who doesn't'; Student B says 'if you're studying, you're developing your knowledge but you might also get quite a lot of experience of some tasks and skills')

6
1 'That's a really good idea, actually.'
2 'I'd go along with you'
3 'I'm not so sure, you know'

7
1 The employer benefits most so they should pay.
2 She disagrees.
3 An employer spends a lot on training and the employee then gets another job.
4 The employee has to pay the cost of their training back if they leave within a certain time.
5 She thinks it's a good idea.

Strategies and skills
Justifying your opinions

1
1 e (The list of benefits can all be linked to tourism in a city.)
2 h (The reason matches with individuals and the environment.)
3 a (The reason matches with whose responsibility it is and skills people need in the home.)
4 b (The reason gives a disadvantage of working from home.)
5 g (The reason matches the topic of asking people for advice before making a big decision.)
6 d (The reason matches with communicating face to face.)
7 f (The reason matches with how a room is decorated.)
8 c (The reason matches with friendship and honesty.)

2
1 A ('on top of that' is another way of saying 'also'.)
2 C ('as well as this' allows you to add another reason.)
3 B ('plus' allows you to add a second reason.)
4 C ('In addition to that' is used to add an extra reason.)

3
1 instance ('For instance' is used in the same way as 'for example'.)
2 an example ('To give you an example' is used as a way of introducing an example.)
3 common knowledge ('It's common knowledge' is used to introduce an example that's generally thought to be true.)
4 only have to ('You only have to …' is used to introduce an example that supports an opinion.)
5 Doing so ('Doing so' allows you to introduce an example of a previously mentioned action.)
6 Amongst other things ('Amongst other things' tells the listener that this is just one example out of many.)

4

Possible answers:

1 Amongst other things, they read an awful lot of information on social media, for example posts by friends, news feeds, and so on.

2 It's common knowledge that each newspaper has a different political point of view, so they will write stories which match with that.

3 You only have to go to any large town or city to see how many shops there still are there and how many people there are using them. Business might be more difficult with the internet, but it's not impossible.

4 Doing so will improve employees' motivation at work and their loyalty to the organisation.

5 For instance, there could be more serious documentaries and discussion programmes and maybe fewer shows about cooking, which are all very similar.

6 To give you an example, people generally feel good about themselves if they help an older person carry something, so it improves your self-esteem.

5

The following should be ticked:
I have a friend who …; To give you an example from my own experience …; What really helped me to do this was …

6

Possible answers:

1 I don't agree with that at all. Speaking for myself, I spent four years after school studying hard to get an accountancy qualification, so I don't think it'd be fair if I was then paid the same as someone who has gone straight into a job that doesn't require specialist training and skills.

2 I think it's very important indeed. On one occasion, I remember not doing this at all. It was just before I had several important exams. I assumed I had enough time to study for them all but didn't really plan anything, and realised at the last minute that I didn't have enough time to properly prepare. I've never made the same mistake since.

3 I think so, yes. In fact, I have some experience of that myself, actually. When I left university, I got a job with a small local firm but there wasn't really much chance to progress. I soon left and started working for a big IT company which has loads of opportunities for promotion and specialisation in certain areas.

Developing a discussion

7

1 add something to
2 make a point
3 interesting argument
4 hear what you're saying

5 also say is
6 in addition to
7 one point you mentioned
8 apart from what you
9 the complete opposite
10 you a question about

8

Students' own answers

9

a 3 (Showing adverts is a way of encouraging people to do something.)
b 5 ('Forgetting their political differences' relates to countries working closely together.)
c 1 ('Pollution' relates to vehicles; 'them' refers back to 'city centres'.)
d 4 ('Technology already exists' relates to whether the environment can be fixed.)
e 2 ('anxious' connects to whether people should worry.)
f 4 ('any problem can be solved' links to whether the environment can be fixed.)
g 3 (Making something cheaper is a way of encouraging people to do it.)
h 1 (This relates to city centres.)
i 2 ('their concerns' connects to whether people should worry.)
j 5 ('If they don't' refers back to countries working closely together.)
Students' own answers

10

1 h, c **2** e, i **3** g, a **4** f, d **5** b, j

11

1 I hear what you're saying but I'm not sure I totally agree with you.
2 What I'd also say is that
3 Is it OK if I make a point about that too?
4 If I could, I'd really like to add something to what you've said.
5 And in addition to the ideas you mentioned, I'd also say that

EXAM TASK

Examiner: Given the choice of living anywhere in the world, which country or region would attract you the most?
A: I think I'd choose a big city in an English-speaking country – somewhere like Melbourne in Australia. I've heard that it's a really cosmopolitan place, so there's lots going on there and it'd be relatively easy to find work. The climate in that part of Australia's pretty good too, I believe. What about you? Where would you choose?
B: I'm not a big city person like you, but I'd definitely want to spend time in a place where English is the first language. I've often wondered about California in the USA. I have a friend who went there and loved it, not to the big cities like Los Angeles and San Francisco, but to the north of the state. There aren't many people there so I think I'd really like it.

Examiner: Some people choose to live in many different places throughout their lives. Do you think this is a good idea?
B: In some ways I suppose it is. I mean, it's a great idea to go somewhere new every couple of years as it'd stop life from getting boring, but more often than that and I think it'd be really disruptive. As soon as you'd settled in somewhere, it'd be time to move somewhere new.
A: What I'd also say is that it really depends on the type of person you are. Some people like nothing better than living in the same place all their lives, but others never feel settled anywhere so move from place to place very often – it just comes naturally to them.
B: I agree, and if I could just add something to what you've said: it's not that one is necessarily better than the other. It's just that each one suits different people.
Examiner: Which has a greater influence on someone's life, the home that they live in or the town or city where they live?
A: I think the home probably has more of an influence. You spend so much more time there than you do out and about in town, so if you've got an apartment or house that's really spacious and comfortable, that'll have much more of an influence on your life than how nice the city you live in is.
B: I'd go along with the point you made and also say that when I went to college, I lived with some friends in this horrible house and I just wasn't happy there. I loved the people I lived with, I really liked the city, but it wasn't enough. As soon as I'd moved to a different house, I was happy again, so I think that's a really clear example of the point we're both making.
A: Exactly!
Examiner: Some people say that the weather in an area influences the character of the people living there. What's your opinion on this?
B: I think it definitely has an influence but it's not the only thing that does. In my opinion, the weather changes the way you live your life so, for example, if you live somewhere that's really cold and dark in winter, you're perhaps going to spend a lot of time in your own home and have fewer chances to socialise. But I think personality is more powerful than this – if you're a sociable person, you're going to find chances to meet and be with people wherever you live.
A: I think you're right, and in addition to what you said, I'd say that people are naturally social, perhaps to a greater or lesser extent depending on the individual, so they'll find opportunities to be sociable regardless of the climate. The context might change – indoors or outdoors – but people the world over love spending time with others.

Examiner: Some people say that almost everyone will live in cities in the future. Do you agree?

A: I'm not sure I do, actually. I think there'll be more and more migration to cities, but I still think a significant proportion of the population will live in rural areas. Lots of people prefer living in these quieter regions, and even if a greater percentage of jobs are based in the city, it's totally possible to commute from a town or village into a city to work.

B: I agree, and what I'd add to that is that I predict that working from home will become increasingly common, so should the vast majority of jobs be based in cities in the future, because they're the natural places for many companies to be, thanks to modern technology many workers won't actually have to be physically present at the company buildings in order to carry out their duties.

Examiner: Some people say that living in the countryside is better suited to older people. What's your view on this?

B: No, I don't agree with this at all. I think it depends on your character far more than how old you are. Speaking for myself, although I live in a city now because I'm studying here, I'd much rather be out in the countryside, away from the crowds of people.

A: I'm sorry, but my opinion is more or less the opposite of what you said. I find spending any time at all in the countryside really boring and can't wait to get back to the city when I'm there.

B: But what I was saying is that that's because of the kind of person you are, not because of your age. I'm more or less as old as you are, but there's nothing I like more than spending a weekend or a whole holiday in the countryside.

A: Hmm, I guess you're right – it's more to do with personality than age.

PRACTICE EXAM

Reading and Use of English

Part 1

0 C ('predominantly' has a similar meaning here to 'mainly')

1 B (If you can find a large amount of something in a place, you can say there is a 'concentration' of that thing.)

2 D ('constitute' has a similar meaning here to 'make up')

3 A (If something is 'resident' in a place, it means it lives there.)

4 D ('bear a resemblance' has a similar meaning to 'look like')

5 C ('in the form of' is used here to specify what kind of nutrients the algae provide.)

6 A (We use 'in return' to say what one thing or person gives back to another after receiving something.)

7 B (If something is 'under threat', it means it is in danger.)

8 A (To 'meet a requirement' means to provide something that is needed.)

Part 2

0 to (The phrasal verb 'amount to' is used to compare two things that are the same.)

9 use (The phrasal verb 'make use of' means to use something for a particular purpose.)

10 far ('far' is used here to give the impression of 1997 being a long time ago.)

11 which ('which' is being used as a relative pronoun to refer back to the materials.)

12 a (You need the indefinite article, 'a', before 'thrill' here.)

13 how ('how' is used here to express the degree to which something happens.)

14 on (The verb 'thrive' is usually followed by the preposition 'on'.)

15 but (The phrase 'not only … but' also is used to give two facts, reasons, etc.)

16 Whether ('whether or not' is used to express a choice between two possibilities.)

Part 3

0 typically (We use 'typically' to say that this is what usually happens.)

17 combination (A 'combination' is a mixture of two or more things.)

18 considerably (We use the adverb 'considerably' to mean a 'lot'.)

19 exposure ('exposure' is the noun of the verb 'expose', meaning that something comes into contact with something else.)

20 impossibility ('impossibility' is the negative noun formed from the adjective 'possible'.)

21 exceedingly (We use the adverb 'exceedingly' to mean 'very' or 'extremely'.)

22 consequence (A 'consequence' is something that happens as a result of something else.)

23 pressure (If something is 'under pressure', it is pressed or squashed by something.)

24 harden ('harden' is the verb made from the adjective 'hard'; it means to become hard.)

Part 4

0 makes no difference (to me) (if something 'makes no difference', it means it has no effect on something or someone.)

25 in spite of | being/feeling (You use a verb with -ing after 'in spite of'.)

26 haven't (got)/don't have a/have no | clue (as to) why (if you 'haven't got a clue', it means you can't understand something; it's a mystery to you.)

27 customer/customers' satisfaction | was at an ('customer satisfaction' is a common collocation; 'satisfaction' is the noun, 'satisfied' is the adjective.)

28 giving/lending me | a hand (with) lifting) (if you 'give someone a hand' with something, you help them.)

29 would/'d do whatever she could/ whatever it took (if you 'do whatever it takes', you try your very best to do something.)

30 have had | nothing to do with (if you 'have nothing to do with' something, it means you weren't involved at all.)

Part 5

31 B (Young storks fly back to Africa rather than copying their parents by staying in Spain.)

32 A (The reviewer says there's a 'profuse … cast' of birds (many species) in the book.)

33 D (The reviewer is impressed by both Rose's knowledge of birds and his use of his classical music skills to bring their calls to life.)

34 C (It's used to highlight the fact that the descriptions are complicated and that a reader may need time in order to understand it ('take that in').)

35 D (The reviewer suggests that Rose's ideas on grouse shooting are fixed and don't take important scientific evidence into account.)

36 B (It's the European politicians who can bring about change by rejecting current agricultural policy and allowing their countries to thrive as a result.)

Part 6

37 D (Morio Furukawa says that homeschooled children are almost as grown-up as their peers who go to school, whereas the other three experts say homeschooled children are more mature.)

38 B (Morio Furukawa and Virat Bhalla both think that homeschooled children have lower educational attainment than those in state schools, whereas the other two experts feel that their attainment is higher.)

39 D (Morio Furukawa thinks there should be no monitoring of homeschooled children or their parents, whereas the other experts think monitoring is necessary.)

40 C (Both Virat Bhalla and Elena Collias think that parents who are considered incapable of teaching their children properly should be prevented from homeschooling them. The other two experts think that all parents can become adequate teachers with sufficient support and training.)

Part 7

41 F (The 'treasures' mentioned at the beginning of F refer back to the masterpieces, boutiques and piazza mentioned at the end of the preceding paragraph.)

42 D ('the latter' at the beginning of D refers back to 'proliferation' at the end of the preceding paragraph. Also, 'both countries' mentioned after the gap refer back to Italy and Britain.)

43 B ('this kind of spread' refers back to the different sizes of city mentioned in the previous paragraph. Also, 'And perhaps they would be wrong' at the beginning of the paragraph after the gap refers back to the final sentence of B.)

44 G ('They' referred to at the beginning of G are the people who have talent, mentioned just before the gap.)

45 A ('it' in the first sentence of A refers back to the 'select club' at the end of the previous paragraph. Also, 'they' at the beginning of the paragraph after the gap refers back to 'government ministers' mentioned in A.)

46 C ('a megacity of this size' refers back to the city on 'a monstrous scale' at the end of the previous paragraph.)

Part 8

47 C (The final two sentences of paragraph C explain why a combination of oxygen and methane can be a possible indication of life on a planet.)

48 A (Paragraph A explains that in only 30 years, we've not only shown that there are other planets but have also found over 4000 of them.)

49 D (Paragraph D states that, 'Even with at least 40 billion other possible Earths in our galaxy, the likelihood of finding life is small.')

50 B (Paragraph B compares Earth and Venus to show how different planets' fingerprints can reveal important information about them.)

51 A (Paragraph A describes how Voyager took the first and only family portrait of our solar system, including the Sun and six planets.)

52 C (Paragraph C says that current technology can only find the largest and hottest planets in other solar systems.)

53 D (Paragraph D explains how observing a range of stars has helped identify important information about them which tells us about our Sun, and suggests we do the same with planets.)

54 B (Paragraph B explains what a fingerprint of a planet is and what scientists can learn from it.)

55 B (Paragraph B defines the 'habitable' or 'Goldilocks' zone, which is neither too cold or too hot for liquid water to exist.)

56 A (Paragraph A makes the hypothetical estimate of 200 billion planets existing in the Milky Way to support the point that our solar system is 'far from exceptional'.)

WRITING
Part 1
Essay
Example answer:
Boosting interest in the arts
Many people think that a thriving arts sector is one of the best indicators of a healthy and happy country. Having access to music, art, theatre and cinema gives people the cultural stimulation they need to be contented citizens. Boosting interest in the arts should therefore be a priority. There is much debate, however, about the best way of achieving this.

The means of boosting interest in the arts that the majority of people turn to is to increase government funding. Those in favour of doing so argue that the arts are a great investment because people are more productive workers if they access them in their leisure time. Those against raising government funding generally claim that there are far more important things to spend the money on, such as hospitals and reasonably priced housing. A second way of increasing interest in the arts is to allow students increased access to arts subjects at school. In general, these are dropped quite early in a young person's academic career. A change to the national school curriculum to ensure that drama, music and art remains in students' timetables would mean, some say, that all young people would develop a genuine interest in the arts.

In my view, the latter approach would have minimal effect. If students do not like art or drama, they cannot be forced to have lessons in them for their entire school career. Increased government funding, on the other hand, has been shown to allow the arts scene to thrive, so this would be by far the best approach.

Part 2
Report
Example answer:
Introduction
The aim of this report is to give an overview of the recent talk at the college given by the famous singer Marcela Sassoon, who was once a student here. It will also recommend other speakers who could be invited to give future talks.
Marcela Sassoon's talk
Ms Sassoon's talk was delivered to the whole school. The main part focused on the period of her career that took her from being a music student to becoming a professional singer. She explained in detail how the work she did in college enabled her to develop her knowledge of music in general and her singing skills in particular. Ms Sassoon also gave a brief account of what life is like for her now as a world-famous singing star.

Because the majority of Ms Sassoon's talk concentrated on the importance of college education for successful transition from education into a professional career, it was extremely useful for students. Some may think that what they are studying now will not really be of great use in their working lives, but Ms Sassoon clearly demonstrated this to be untrue. The enthusiastic applause at the end of her talk proved how much students had appreciated her visit.
Recommendations for future speakers
Future speakers need not be limited to former students, although this added an interesting angle to Ms Sassoon's talk. I would suggest that speakers be sought from other vocational areas, such as successful scientists, sports stars, chefs and businesspeople, in order to give a good balance of interest for students across the college.

Review
Example answer:
I've recently downloaded a music streaming app called Applause and I wanted to share my experiences of using it with you.

I'd grown a bit fed up of my old app, CreativeTune, as the bank of songs on offer in the library seemed relatively small, and I almost never liked the recommendations it came up with for me based on my listening habits.

Although it has its faults, Applause has none of the issues that motivated me to look for a new streaming app in the first place. The song library is huge! 35 million songs and counting, and your monthly fee allows you instant access to every one. You can also upload your own tracks if they don't happen to already be on there, and listen to them. Applause comes with thousands of playlists that you can stream, too. I've tried several of these based on the genres of music I'm really into, and they've generally been good apart from the odd bad song, which is kind of inevitable.

As my parents and siblings are all into music too, we got a family plan, which gives access for up to six people. It's amazing value at only $15 per month. If you're doing it individually, however, you might find it expensive compared to other streaming apps – one of the very few drawbacks I've found.

I'd recommend the app to anyone who loves music, especially if, like me, you've got broad musical tastes and want access to a wide range of music. Five stars, without a doubt!

Proposal
Example answer:

Introduction

The aim of this proposal is to suggest a usage for the piece of land next to the company buildings, and to urge senior management to retain the land for this purpose rather than selling it.

The proposed usage

The land in question is currently covered with wild plants, bushes and small trees. Staff are not allowed access to it as there is a high fence around it and the gate is permanently locked. Litter has blown into the area, making it look unattractive and potentially affecting the company's public image.

With minimal expenditure and effort, the land could be converted into a garden and outdoor rest and recreation area for staff. With the addition of seating and picnic tables, this could become an ideal location for staff to spend their breaks.

Converting the land

Much of the area already has stone pavements, which would make perfect seating areas. Most of the vegetation would need to be removed and replaced with flowers. Some of the bushes and all of the trees could remain, and the litter would need to be cleared up. Little more would be required, apart from adding outdoor furniture as described.

Benefits to staff

Currently, there is only one staff kitchen, which has a small seating area. This is usually overcrowded at breaktimes and is an unpleasant place to eat. Having external space would increase morale and foster relationships within the staff team. As all of these benefits lead to greater productivity and staff contentment, I would strongly urge management to consider this proposal.

LISTENING
Part 1

1 B (The woman says that there's the occasional advert that she finds as enjoyable as the programme, but the man says that he's yet to see one that makes him feel that way.)

2 A (The woman says that it puts toy manufacturers at a bit of disadvantage, because no other sector is prevented from showing adverts to its target market.)

3 B (The man says that many theatres have started exclusively staging pieces created by someone audiences will have heard of.)

4 A (The woman suggests the man is greatly exaggerating how many theatres are only putting on plays by well-known writers, claiming that it is nowhere near as widespread as he's claiming.)

5 A (The woman says that she's not completely sure how many more winters she can stand on the houseboat as it's so cold.)

6 B (The man tells the story to suggest that even if she decides to leave her houseboat, deciding to live there in the first place was not a mistake.)

Part 2

7 Denmark (The member of the research team who assembled the team and sorted out the financing and the boat (i.e. organised the trip) was from Denmark.)

8 filming underwater (Sandra says the organisers were keen to take people who had done lots of filming underwater, which is why she was chosen.)

9 washing machine (Sandra compares being on the boat in a storm to being in a washing machine.)

10 migration (They hoped to learn more about Greenland sharks' lifespan, but the primary aim of the project was to find out more about their migration.)

11 slow heart rate (A colleague tells Sandra this, and she shares what she already knew about the sharks' poor eyesight.)

12 polar bears (Sandra expresses surprise that the sharks target polar bears: 'I'd never have considered polar bears to be something that they would target.').

13 aggression (Sandra was expecting them to lack energy, but they didn't. They did, however, lack any sort of aggression.)

14 (certain) human illnesses (A previous research project helped with studies on climate change, but this one may help with research into human disease.)

Part 3

15 B (Karen says that she was a bit taken aback by a few of her colleagues' comments, as they appeared to suggest that her central argument was flawed.)

16 A (Ian says that it's the rapid pace of the implementation he'd question about Karen's article, and uses the example of sport to support his argument.)

17 A (Ian says that the figures in the press only actually tell us one small part of the overall picture, so the situation is actually more complex that the statistics suggest.)

18 D (Karen says that electric motors have been successfully introduced into cars and trains to help the environment, but will never be sufficiently powerful to lift something as heavy as an airliner off the ground.)

19 C (Ian says that those in power want to sustain economic growth in travel and tourism yet also promise huge cuts in emissions; Karen says it's hard to reconcile what governments say about both green issues and movement of people from place to place.)

20 A (Karen says that she uses only the carriers that offer the cheapest tickets, and Ian says that he always chooses the cheapest flights.)

Part 4

21 E (Speaker 1 says that she decided to use the gap year to develop her interest in music to see if she could become a professional musician.)

22 G (Speaker 2 says that the aim of the gap year was to decide whether to study medicine or veterinary science.)

23 B (Speaker 3 says she chose to do a gap year so that she could do some sports coaching.)

24 F (Speaker 4 says he took a gap year to get money to help pay his tuition fees and living costs.)

25 H (Speaker 5 says she took a gap year to develop her writing skills before starting a journalism degree.)

26 C (Speaker 1 says that since she realised she's not good enough to become a professional musician, she'll do everything she can to succeed in her other chosen vocation.)

27 B (Speaker 2 says his decisions are now being made from an adult perspective, rather than from that of a school student.)

28 H (Speaker 3 says that she now has more respect for the sacrifices her parents have made by working to support their family.)

29 A (Speaker 4 says that he's enjoying working for his uncle's company so much that he's wondering whether going to university is actually a good idea.)

30 G (Speaker 5 says that she's changed a lot and has become more sensible and responsible, which will serve her well at college.)

SPEAKING
Part 1
Example answers:

I'm from a small city in Poland called Opole. It's a nice place.

I'm a student at the moment. I'm studying in my final year of secondary school and I'm hoping to go to university next year. I've been studying English for about six years now.

I love learning languages anyway, but what's great about learning English is that so many people speak it. So even if I go to a country where I don't speak the language, I can be fairly sure that someone will speak English.

I'm very interested in knowing what's going on in the world, so I tend to check the news at least twice a day. I don't bother watching it on TV or getting a newspaper – I just look at a few different news websites either on my phone or on my computer.

It's essential! I have three really close friends who I spend lots of time with each week. We do loads of stuff together – playing sport, going shopping, seeing a film, that kind of thing. We've known each other for years so I can't imagine not being able to see them at least three or four times a week.

I'm not sure if it's exactly the best way, but using social media is certainly the easiest for me. It's so easy to send a quick message to someone and to make arrangements and things like that. There's nothing better than seeing each other face to face, of course, but for day-to-day keeping in touch, I think it's hard to beat.

I think I'd have to say my grandma. She's lived quite a hard life in many different ways and brought up four children while working full-time too. She's retired now but she's always there for us. I don't think I've ever seen her in a bad mood, which is amazing.

Last summer, I went to London with my parents and two brothers. My aunt, uncle and cousins live there, so we were visiting them but spent a week doing different things around the city. The first thing that hit me was how huge it was! I love the fact that it's always busy, even at night. We went to some great museums and did boat trips and that kind of thing too – it was great!

The teacher I had in my final year there. She was great – so full of energy and really enthusiastic about everything she was teaching us. She used to take us on some great little trips too, and made us think about things more deeply than the other teachers there. It was the perfect way to end my time at primary school.

If I could choose any job, I'd definitely be a marine biologist. I love anything to do with the sea, and I watch all the nature documentaries about the underwater world online and on TV. I've even learnt how to dive, so I can go and see it for myself. I'm hoping to study marine biology at university, so who knows? One day, I may even achieve my dream.

I'd like there to be more cheap or free sports facilities, especially for young people. I love playing basketball but have to travel about three kilometres from where I live to a sports centre to find somewhere indoors to play. I can play in the local park in the summer, of course, but not in the winter. It costs quite a lot to play there too, but we don't have much choice – if we don't pay, we don't play!

Part 2

Example answers:

Examiner: Candidate A, it's your turn first. Look at the pictures on page 125. They show people using communication skills in their jobs. I'd like you to compare two of the pictures, and say why communication skills might be important in these jobs, and how difficult it might be to do these jobs. All right?

Candidate A: OK, well my pictures show people doing different jobs in which communication skills are really important. I'd like to talk about two of these pictures, one of a TV reporter, probably a news reporter, and the other which shows a teacher in class with some primary school children. The reporter's out in the street and seems to be talking about a problem that's happened there, whereas the teacher's inside in a classroom talking to some young students who are sitting at desks. I think in both jobs it's really important to be able to communicate well. If the reporter can't communicate the details of the story, then the audience won't understand what's going on in the news. If the teacher's communication skills are poor, then her students won't really understand and won't learn anything. I think there's a difference in how difficult each of the jobs is, though. The TV reporter has to do her job under a lot of pressure. If she makes a mistake or doesn't explain or describe things clearly, and is reporting on live TV, then the whole country will see, so my guess is that it's a pretty stressful job, and one that it takes a certain kind of person to do well. I'm sure that teaching's stressful too in its own way, but if the students don't understand something because she hasn't explained it well, she can just try again in a different way until they learn what she's trying to teach them. Most of the time, there's no one else watching her, so she's under far less pressure day-to-day. I suppose that the teacher has to talk and communicate well over a much longer period of time, though, probably for several hours a day. The reporter's story, on the other hand, might only be a few minutes long and may well be the only one she has to report on that day.

Examiner: Thank you. Candidate B, which of these jobs do you think would be the most rewarding?

Candidate B: I think being a doctor would be the most rewarding of the three jobs. As a doctor, you have to help people. A teacher also does this of course, but not in a way that makes people feel better when they've been ill, or actually saves their lives, as a doctor does. I think it's probably more stressful, but also much more rewarding to be a doctor.

Examiner: Thank you. Now, Candidate B, look at the pictures on page 126. They show people learning how to do different things. I'd like you to compare two of the pictures, and say what the people might be enjoying about learning how to do these things, and which of these things might be most useful to learn. All right?

Candidate B: Well, I think I'll choose the pictures showing someone learning how to make a guitar and someone learning how to fix a car to talk about. Both of these are happening inside, one in a workshop where people make things with wood, and the other in a garage. The main difference between the two photos is how the people are learning. The boy making the guitar seems to be doing it from some written instructions that are on the table in front of him. In the car mechanic's workshop, they're working on the engine of a car, and the young woman who's learning how to repair the car is being taught by a teacher, who's talking her through what she needs to do and is showing her with his hands at the same time. I must say that the boy making the guitar seems to be doing a really good job because the body of the guitar that he's holding looks great. He's probably looking forward to completing the next task and to having a finished guitar that he can play that he's actually made himself. The young woman might be training to become a mechanic. She is probably enjoying learning how all the bits of an engine work and how she can repair them – it must be satisfying to learn a complicated skill like that. Unless you're thinking of becoming a professional guitar maker, I think learning how to fix a car is a lot more useful as a skill than being able to make a guitar. Not that many people actually play the guitar and they're actually quite cheap to buy. Almost every adult has a car, though, and they can be really expensive to fix, so it'd be incredibly useful to be able to do this yourself. Not only would you be able to get a job in a garage, but this skill would save you an awful lot of money over a whole lifetime!

Examiner: Thank you. Candidate A, which of these things do you think would be the most difficult to learn?

Candidate A: Making the guitar. It must be really complicated to cut out the little holes in the body of the guitar like we can see in the picture, and the neck has to be perfectly straight otherwise you won't be able to play it properly. I think he's making an electric guitar, too, which means you also need to learn all about how to put in the wires and so on, so there are a lot of different skills involved.

Examiner: Thank you.

Part 3

Example answers:

Examiner: Here are some things people do to help the environment and a question for you to discuss. First you have some time to look at the task. Now talk to each other about how useful it is for people to help the environment in these different ways.

Candidate A: OK, well I think that getting involved with a charity is definitely a good way of helping the environment.

Candidate B: Yeah, especially if you can actually do some voluntary work for them. I've seen loads of videos showing volunteers planting trees and doing things like that.

Candidate A: Yes, me too. And I suppose that if you don't have the time to do this, or can't do it for some other reason, then giving money to the charity will be almost as useful.

Candidate B: I agree. Choosing food carefully is a great way of helping too. You should choose products that are grown or made locally so that there isn't as much damage to the environment as transporting them hundreds or thousands of kilometres.

Candidate A: Yes, and I heard that eating less meat can really help too as less land's needed to grow fruit, vegetables and other crops than to raise animals for food … Almost everyone recycles these days, don't they?

Candidate B: Yes, but I think there are lots of problems caused by recycling. Quite often, the plastic or whatever's actually taken to other countries to be recycled, so loads of energy's used to transport it there.

Candidate A: Oh, I didn't realise that, so it's probably not as useful as we think then. Writing to politicians is a bit of a waste of time if you ask me. It's not that I think they don't care, it's just that they have so many letters and emails to deal with and so many other things to worry about, that it's more or less impossible.

Candidate B: I'm not convinced that's true, actually. My aunt wrote to a local politician about a factory that she thought was polluting the environment and within a month, the problem had been sorted out.

Candidate A: I don't know how often that happens, though. Anyway, using public transport instead of cars can make a massive difference and really help cut down on dangerous gases and other pollution.

Candidate B: I totally agree with you on that, and would add that cycling should be made part of any transport policy too, not just additional public transport. If far more people in cities, for example, commuted to work or school by bike, just imagine how much cleaner the air would be.

Candidate A: And how clear the roads would be too. Where I live, every day there are queues and queues of traffic, all sitting there with their engines running, going nowhere fast.

Candidate B: That's so true!

Examiner: Thank you. Now you have about a minute to decide which two ways of helping the environment are most effective.

Candidate A: Hmm, well top of my list would be the one we've just discussed – using public transport instead of cars. It'd be amazing if overnight, the majority of the population just left their cars at home and got the bus or train instead.

Candidate B: Or took their bikes … I suppose there are those who can't stop using their cars because there isn't any decent public transport where they live at the moment and it's too far to cycle, but I'm sure that if more people in general chose to use public transport it'd soon improve everywhere, so I'm with you on that one … Second for me would be the charities. I think the more people that support them financially or by volunteering, the greater the influence they can have.

Candidate A: I'm not so sure about that. I actually think that choosing food carefully might be more effective. Everyone eats, after all, so if billions of consumers switched to foods that do a minimum of harm to the environment, imagine the difference that would make.

Candidate B: Yes, I'd never thought of it like that. I think I'll change my mind and go for the option about food too.

Candidate A: Good choice!

Examiner: Thank you.

Part 4

Example answers:

Examiner: Do you think that you do enough to help the environment?

Candidate B: I do quite a lot, I think. I cycle to college every day rather than using public transport or a car, and I always try to cut down on how much electricity and water I use – just by switching lights and laptops off and things like that. It's always possible to do more, though, I guess.

Examiner: What do you think governments should do with companies that cause environmental problems?

Candidate A: I think they should be punished as harshly as possible. There's no real excuse for doing it these days. We know the environment needs our help so if a company's intentionally damaging it, something needs to be done.

Candidate B: It sends a powerful message to other companies too if they are punished – there will be consequences if you harm the world we live in.

Examiner: Some people say that air travel should be limited for environmental reasons. Do you agree?

Candidate B: This is a difficult one, because so many people fly these days and it's so cheap, relatively. Who would decide which air travel people should be allowed to do and which they shouldn't? I suppose you could limit it to one flight per person per year or something like that, but you'd have to make exceptions for certain people who need to travel by air a lot for their work.

Candidate A: The problem is, if unpopular decisions don't start being made, then nothing will really change.

Examiner: Do you think children learn enough about environmental problems at school?

Candidate A: They certainly learn a lot more than they used to but I still don't think it's enough. My parents say that they didn't really study anything related to helping the environment when they were at school, but we learnt lots about it. Things are changing so fast, though, that I think more education can only be a better thing.

Candidate B: Yes, because everyone needs to grow up knowing that it's their responsibility to deal with environmental problems – it's not just something the government or other people should sort out.

Examiner: How important do you think it is for countries to work together to solve environmental problems?

Candidate B: I think it's absolutely essential, no question about it. It's a global problem, not a national one, so we need solutions that are effective worldwide and not just in one or two countries. The only way for that to happen is for countries to cooperate with each other and work together.

Examiner: Are you optimistic that people's intelligence and creativity will find solutions to our environmental problems?

Candidate A: Yes, very much so. We can see it happening already with the massive growth in electric vehicles and renewable energy, for example. The great thing is that if people know they can make money by creating environmentally friendly solutions to things, then they'll do it. And because so many people realise how essential helping the environment is, there's a bigger and bigger market for green products and services.

Examiner: Thank you. That is the end of the test.

173

These mindfulness practices can help you to stay calm and focused as you revise for your exams.

Important

If you feel that stress and anxiety are getting on top of you, speak to someone you trust. Opening up about how you feel can really help in dealing with what can be an intense time. If you have recently experienced the loss of a loved one, a traumatic event or have been diagnosed with a mental illness, or have any ongoing physical pain, it's really important that you check in with someone (such as a parent, teacher, counsellor or doctor) before doing these practices.

What is mindfulness?

Mindfulness is essentially awareness. It is about training your attention to notice your thoughts, feelings, emotions, sensations, physical reactions, and anything around you that is happening right now, without judging them. This can help you to make better, more skilful decisions. Your brain can be 'rewired' to work in more helpful or skilful ways. In many ways it's like brain training. Just as people go to the gym and lift weights regularly to build muscle, mindfulness helps train the brain by doing the practices daily.

Preparing for exams

Neuroscientists are starting to understand more about how mindfulness practice can help. Studies indicate that it helps in two main ways, especially when it comes to exams.

1   It helps to increase the density in the front of your brain. This is the part of the brain associated with memory, your ability to solve problems and to manage distraction.

2   It helps us to manage strong or difficult emotions. Feeling some stress and anxiety around exams is natural and, indeed, can help boost performance. It's when this becomes too much that it becomes a problem.

Mindfulness helps to calm activity in the part of your brain associated with worry.

Doing and being

Very often, it is easy to want to get straight into doing a task like revision just to get it finished and out of the way. This is called **doing mode** – it helps you to get things done, but not always to consider the best way of tackling the task. Mindfulness helps by giving you a moment to pause and enter **being mode**. This allows time for you to ground yourself and be fully focused on the present moment, so you experience things more fully. Usually this will help you to take a calmer and wiser approach to a task, which will mean you're more effective.

The pressures of revision and exams may make you feel that taking 'time out' from revision to do these practices is not possible. However, regularly doing even short practices where you can drop into 'being mode' can begin to give you greater mental space or clarity.

Mindfully making a drink

- What can you **hear**? For example, when making a drink, notice the sound of pouring the drink or boiling water.
- What can you **smell**? For example, for tea, coffee or juice, notice how the smells **change** as you make the drink.
- What can you **see**? For example, notice the colours and how they **change**.
- What can you **feel**? For example, the warmth or coolness of the drink in your hands.
- What can you **taste**? For example, when taking a sip of the drink, notice how it first tastes and any **changes** in taste.
- Enjoy **being in the moment** as you consume your drink.

This simple exercise can have a big impact. Many people find they notice and taste far more.

When you take time to slow down and live in a more moment-to-moment way, you are able to experience life more fully and appreciatively.

This can then help to create a greater sense of calm.

Being kind to yourself

Exam preparation can be a stressful time, so it's important to take some time out regularly to be kind to yourself: to recharge your batteries, give your brain some breathing space and acknowledge all the good preparatory work you're putting in. Take regular breaks and enjoy some 'downtime' with your friends and family to help recharge.

Practising mindfulness

Just like learning any new skill, for example playing a sport or an instrument, mindfulness is something that has to be practised daily to have richer benefits. Doing daily practices of 10 minutes or so can really help you to move your awareness to be fully in the present moment in a non-judgemental way, helping you to avoid overthinking, which can lead to worry, anxiety and stress.

It is best to learn how to practise mindfulness through a course. There may be courses running in your area. An internet search will help you find a course local to you or one running online.

Good posture for practice

Getting your posture correct for doing mindfulness practice is really important. These practices are designed to be done in a seated position. They can also be done lying down.

Try to find a chair you can sit in that allows your feet to rest fully on the ground with your ankles, knees and hips all at right angles, with your back slightly away from the back of the chair.

The room you choose should be somewhere you won't be disturbed. Turn your phone onto silent or flight mode. Let the people you live with know that you'll be doing mindfulness practice so that they do not disturb you. Mindfulness can help you take a healthy, effective approach to your revision. But remember, you will still need to plan and revise!

Practice 1: Mindfulness of breath and body
The benefits

Very often our minds like to wander. In this practice, you focus your attention on your breathing and on different parts of your body. It's a bit like shining a torchlight so that you focus on just one thing at a time, feeling the sensations that arise. Practising this regularly helps the mind wander less, which leads to less worrying and helps with concentration. Remember – it is normal for your mind to wander while you are meditating as that is what minds do! You are just trying to train it.

The Mindfulness of breath and body practice will help you to develop your awareness and focus, which can help with revision. In addition, focusing on breath also has a calming effect (great if you are worrying about exams). Moving the focus to the body can also help to identify physical feelings caused by stress. Examples of stress in the body might be 'butterflies' or cramps in your stomach, your hands shaking, getting sweaty or your mouth going dry.

Guidance on the practice

If your mind wanders, try to bring it back with a sense of kindness. It doesn't matter how many times the mind wanders, it's bringing it back each time to focus on the breath or the body that's important, as you are increasing your concentration and training your attention each time. Don't be frustrated as it is just part of training your brain.

To access the audio file for Practice 1, please use the app.

Practice 2: The three-step breathing space
The benefits

Worrying about what has gone on in the past or what might happen in the future cannot change events and distracts you from the present – from what you are doing now. The present is something that you can change, so that is where your focus should be. For example, worrying about your exams in several months' time won't be as helpful as revising now! The three-step breathing space practice helps you to fully ground yourself in the present and gives you a few moments to rest and recharge. The practice is structured a bit like an hourglass.

The three-step breathing space is a very useful practice if ever you start to feel stressed and want a pause to help you step back and get perspective.

Guidance on the practice

The great thing about this practice is that you can do it in three minutes or less. Use it to 'recharge' yourself while revising or ground yourself just before or even during your exam.

1. Firstly, you do a 'weather check' of the mind, to see what's going on, by observing your thoughts, giving you a more objective viewpoint of how busy or calm your mind is.

2. Then you turn your attention to your breath, helping to focus you in the present moment.

3. Finally, you expand out that awareness to sensations in the rest of your body, becoming aware of where you may be holding any emotions in the body as stress or tension.

To access the audio file for Practice 2, please use the app.

The **Cambridge English Assessment: C1 Advanced**, is set at Level C1 on the CEFR (Common European Framework of Reference) scale. The exam is made up of **four papers**, each testing a different area of ability in English. If a candidate achieves an A grade, they will receive a Certificate in Advanced English stating that they demonstrated ability at Level C2. If a candidate achieves a grade B or C, they will receive the Certificate in Advanced English at Level C1. If a candidate only achieves a B2 level, they may receive a Cambridge English Certificate stating that they demonstrated ability at Level B2.

Reading and Use of English: 1 hour 30 minutes
Writing: 1 hour 30 minutes
Listening: 40 minutes (approximately)
Speaking: 15 minutes for each pair (approximately)

All the questions are task-based. Rubrics (instructions) are important and should be read carefully. They set the context and give important information about the tasks.There is a separate answer sheet for recording answers for the Reading and Use of English and Listening papers.

Paper	Format	Task focus
Reading and Use of English Eight parts 56 questions	**Part 1:** multiple-choice cloze. A text with eight gaps, and four options to choose from for each gap.	**Part 1:** use of vocabulary including idioms, fixed phrases, complementation, phrasal verbs.
	Part 2: open cloze. A text with eight gaps. Candidates write the correct word in each gap.	**Part 2:** use of grammar, vocabulary and expressions.
	Part 3: word formation. A text with eight gaps and a word at the end of the line in which the gap appears. Candidates write the correct form of this word in the gap.	**Part 3:** vocabulary, particularly prefixes and suffixes, changes in form and compound words.
	Part 4: key-word transformations. Candidates rewrite six sentences using a given word, so that they mean the same as the original sentences.	**Part 4:** use of grammatical and lexical structure.
	Part 5: multiple choice. A text with six four-option, multiple- choice questions.	**Part 5:** identify details, such as opinion, attitude, tone, purpose, main idea, text organisation and features.
	Part 6: cross-text multiple matching. Four short texts followed by four multiple-matching questions	**Part 6:** comparing and contrasting opinions and attitudes across four different texts.
	Part 7: gapped text. One long text with six paragraphs missing. Candidates replace paragraphs from a choice of seven.	**Part 7:** reading to understand cohesion, coherence, organisation and text structure.
	Part 8: multiple matching. A text or several short texts with ten multiple-matching questions.	**Part 8:** reading to locate specific information, detail, opinion and attitude.
Writing Two tasks, carrying equal marks.	**Part 1:** compulsory task. Using given information to write an essay of 220-260 words.	**Part 1:** writing an essay with a discursive focus based on two points given in the task.
	Part 2: Producing one piece of writing of 220-260 words, from a letter/email, proposal, review or report.	**Part 2:** writing for a specific target reader and context, using appropriate layout and register.
Listening Four tasks 30 questions	**Part 1:** multiple-choice questions.Three short dialogues with interacting speakers, with two multiple-choice questions (three options) per extract.	**Part 1:** understanding gist, detail, function, agreement, speaker purpose, feelings, attitude, etc.
	Part 2: sentence completion. One monologue with eight sentences to complete with a word or short phrase.	**Part 2:** locating and recording specific information and stated opinions.
	Part 3: multiple-choice questions. A conversation between two or more speakers, with six four-option multiple- choice questions.	**Part 3:** understanding attitude and opinion.
	Part 4: multiple matching. A set of five short monologues on a theme.There are two tasks. In both tasks candidates match each monologue to one of eight prompts.	**Part 4:** identifying main points, gist, attitude and opinion.
Speaking Four tasks	**Part 1:** examiner-led conversation.	**Part 1:** general social and interactional language
	Part 2: individual long turn with visual and written prompts. Candidates talk about two pictures from a choice of three.	**Part 2:** organising discourse, speculating, comparing, giving opinions.
	Part 3: two-way collaborative task. Candidates discuss a question with 5 written prompts and then answer a second question on the topic.	**Part 3:** sustaining interaction, expressing and justifying opinions, evaluating and speculating, negotiating towards a decision, etc.
	Part 4: The examiner asks questions related to the Part 3 topic.	**Part 4:** expressing and justifying ideas and opinions, agreeing and disagreeing, speculating.